The
MONTEFELTRO
CONSPIRACY

Firenze

The
MONTEFELTRO
CONSPIRACY

A RENAISSANCE MYSTERY DECODED

MARCELLO SIMONETTA

DOUBLEDAY

NEW YORK LONDON TORONTO SYDNEY AUCKLAND

DD

DOUBLEDAY

PUBLISHED BY DOUBLEDAY

Published in the United States by Doubleday, an imprint of
The Doubleday Publishing Group, a division of
Random House, Inc., New York.
www.doubleday.com

DOUBLEDAY is a registered trademark and the DD colophon
is a trademark of Random House, Inc.

BOOK DESIGN BY DEBORAH KERNER

Library of Congress Cataloging-in-Publication Data

Simonetta, Marcello, 1968–

   The Montefeltro conspiracy : a Renaissance mystery decoded / by
Marcello Simonetta. — 1st ed.

      p.   cm.

Includes bibliographical references and index.

   1. Pazzi Conspiracy, 1478. 2. Italy—History—15th century.
3. Medici, Lorenzo de', 1449–1492—Adversaries. 4. Medici, Giuliano
de', 1453–1478—Adversaries. 5. Sixtus IV, Pope, 1414–1484—
Political activity. 6. Federico, de Montefeltro, Duke of Urbino, 1422–
1482—Political activity. 7. Italy—History—15th century—Sources.
8. Cryptography. 9. Botticelli, Sandro, 1444 or 5–1510—Themes,
motives. 10. Politics in art. I. Title.
DG737.9.S56 2008
945'.05—dc22   2008009892

ISBN 978-0-385-52468-1

PRINTED IN THE UNITED STATES OF AMERICA

10 9 8 7 6 5 4 3 2 1

First Edition

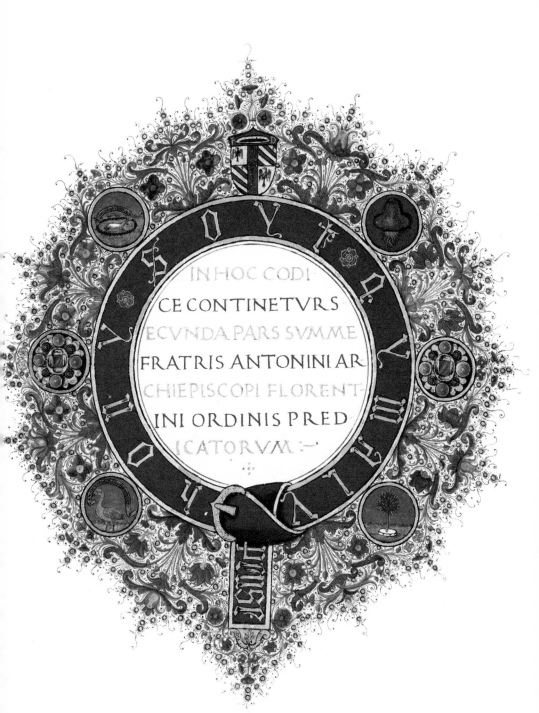

IN HOC CODI
CE CONTINETVRS
ECVNDA PARS SVMME
FRATRIS ANTONINI AR
CHIEPISCOPI FLORENT
INI ORDINIS PRED
ICATORVM :~

Contents

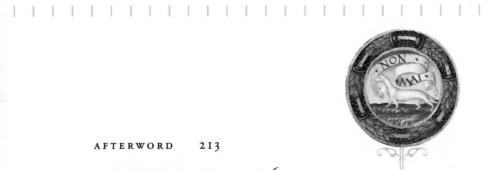

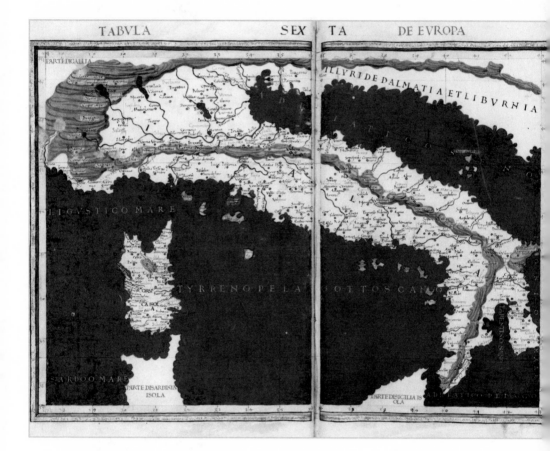

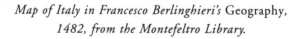

Map of Italy in Francesco Berlinghieri's Geography, *1482, from the Montefeltro Library.*

People think of history in the long term,
but history, in fact, is a very sudden thing.

—PHILIP ROTH, *American Pastoral*

Lifetimes are brief and not to be regained,
For all mankind. But by their deeds to make
Their fame last: that is labor for the brave.

—VIRGIL, *Aeneid*

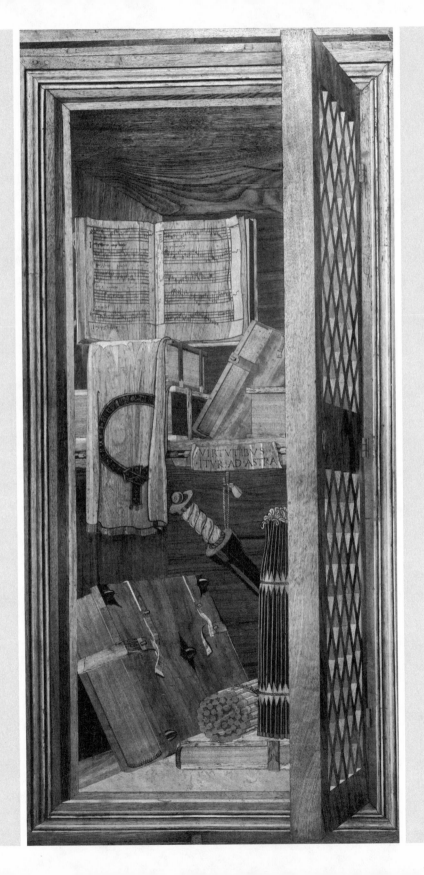

Principal Characters

GALEAZZO MARIA SFORZA (1444–1476), son of Francesco, Duke of Milan (1401–1466), inherited his father's title and estates but was unequal to the task. He was, in Machiavelli's words, "lecherous and cruel," with a list of sins longer than the Gospel. His assassination upset the balance of power in Italy and set the Montefeltro conspiracy in motion.

CICCO SIMONETTA (1410–1480) came from a humble Calabrian background, and served as secretary and advisor under the Sforzas for nearly half a century. Although Machiavelli himself admired Cicco, pronouncing him "most excellent for his prudence and political wisdom," his loyalty to the Sforza patrimony would go unrewarded.

FEDERICO DA MONTEFELTRO, Duke of Urbino (1422–1482), fought many wars in Italy and was a renowned *condottiere* (mercenary captain) and patron of the arts. The duke had a ruthless, Machiavellian side that has long been concealed.

LORENZO DE' MEDICI (1449–1492), known as "the Magnificent," was an enormously wealthy banker, humanist, and patron of the arts whose early access to power in Florence made him a target for murder.

SIXTUS IV (1414–1484), born Francesco della Rovere, was general of the Franciscan Order. Once he became pope (1471), he forgot his vow of humility and turned to greed, warmongering, nepotism, and, as this book demonstrates, conspiracy to murder.

FERRANTE OF ARAGON (1430?–1494), King of Naples from 1458 to 1494, became the most powerful man in Italy after the Duke of Milan died. Known to be ruthless with his enemies, he was rumored to have kept their embalmed corpses in the dungeon of his castle. Lorenzo relied on his intervention to force the pope to reverse the excommunication of Florence in the aftermath of the conspiracy.

GIULIANO DE' MEDICI (1453–1478), Lorenzo's handsome younger brother, was a lover of poetry. Unfortunately, his precocious death prevented him from proving himself on the political stage.

SANDRO BOTTICELLI (1445–1510), a Florentine painter, worked for the Medici over many years. In 1481–82 he was summoned by Pope Sixtus IV to decorate the Sistine Chapel along with Pietro Perugino, Domenico Ghirlandaio, and Cosimo Rosselli. His allegorical paintings still puzzle scholars, who go on searching for their hidden meanings.

SUPPORTING CHARACTERS

GALEAZZO'S MURDERERS: *Andrea Lampugnani, Girolamo Olgiati, Carlo Visconti,* and humanist *Cola Montano.*

ANTI-LORENZO CONSPIRATORS: *Count Girolamo* and *Cardinal Raffaele Riario,* Sixtus IV's nephews; *Francesco Salviati,* archbishop of Pisa; *Francesco* and *Jacopo de' Pazzi,* members of the banking family that rivaled the Medici; *Gian Battista Montesecco,* papal soldier; *Lorenzo Giustini,* captain and lord of Città di Castello; *Jacopo Bracciolini*, Florentine humanist; *Marsilio Ficino*, Neoplatonist philosopher; *Gian Francesco da Tolentino*, captain.

ANTI-CICCO PLOTTERS: *Roberto da Sanseverino*, Galeazzo Sforza's cousin and *condottiere*; *Sforza Maria Sforza* and *Ludovico Sforza*, Galeazzo's surviving brothers.

CICCO'S FAMILY MEMBERS AND ALLIES: *Giovanni Simonetta*, Cicco's brother and Sforza historian; *Gian Giacomo Simonetta*, Cicco's son and secretary of the Secret Senate; *Orfeo da Ricavo*, Cicco's military advisor.

SOURCES AND SPIES: *Bernardino Corio*, Sforza servant and Milanese historian; *Zaccaria Saggi*, Mantuan ambassador in Milan; *Giovanni Santi*, Urbino court painter; *Luigi Pulci*, Florentine poet and emissary; *Piero Felici*, Montefeltro envoy; *Baccio Ugolini*, Florentine poet and Roman agent for Lorenzo de' Medici; *Giovanni di Carlo*, Florentine friar and historian; *Luca Landucci*, Florentine diarist; *Matteo Contugi*, calligrapher from Volterra and spy in Urbino; and *Niccolò Machiavelli*, Florentine official and historian.

OTHER LEADING POLITICAL FIGURES:
Ludovico and *Federico Gonzaga,* marquises of
Mantua; *Alfonso of Aragon,* Ferrante's son and duke
of Calabria; *Ottaviano Ubaldini,* Federico's half
brother; *Ercole d'Este,* Duke of Ferrara; *Roberto
Malatesta,* lord of Rimini.

 LEADING WOMEN: *Bona of Savoy,* Galeazzo Sforza's
wife and duchess of Milan; *Lucia Marliani,* one
of Galeazzo's mistresses; *Elisabetta Visconti,* Cicco
Simonetta's wife; *Caterina Sforza,* Galeazzo's
illegitimate daughter and Girolamo Riario's wife;
Battista Sforza da Montefeltro, Federico's wife;
Ippolita Sforza Aragon, Galeazzo's sister and duchess
of Calabria; *Eleonora Aragon d'Este,* duchess of
Ferrara.

 And last but far from least, *Fioretta Gorini,* Giuliano de'
Medici's mistress and the mother of his posthumous
son, Giulio. Giulio would grow up to become Pope
Clement VII and exact an unexpected revenge on
his predecessor, Sixtus IV.

The
MONTEFELTRO
CONSPIRACY

Prologue

On April 26, 1478, during Ascension Sunday Mass, Lorenzo de' Medici and his brother, Giuliano, the young leaders of the Florentine city-state, were attacked in the Duomo. Giuliano suffered nineteen stab wounds and died instantly. Lorenzo, though injured, managed to escape. The Florentine mob, faithful to the Medici, reacted violently and slaughtered all the killers they could put their hands on.

This brazen attack, one of the most infamous and bloodiest plots of the Italian Renaissance, has come to be known as the Pazzi conspiracy. While historians have long been aware of the plot's broad outline, its far-ranging significance has not been entirely understood. And the truth behind its origins has remained elusive. As its name suggests, the plot has been considered the outgrowth of a family feud between the powerful Medici and the Pazzi, a rival merchant family aiming to replace them as the rulers of Florence and bankers to the pope.

It turns out that this is only a part of the story. One would think this period had already revealed most of its secrets, but in the summer of 2001 I had the good fortune of coming across one of its darkest ones: I found and deciphered a coded letter that exposed hitherto unknown but essential information about the Pazzi conspiracy. The discovery was that

Federico da Montefeltro, Duke of Urbino (1422–1482), portrayed for centuries as the "Light of Italy" and the humanist friend of Lorenzo de' Medici (1449–1492), was the hidden schemer behind the 1478 conspiracy to eliminate both him and his brother.

The discovery—and decoding—of this forgotten letter radically changed the perception of a turning point in Italian history. Montefeltro's letter, written two months before the attack, revealed that the complicated plot ranged far and wide, much more so than had been previously thought. This book tells the full story behind the conspiracy and its repercussions over six tumultuous years, from December 1476 to September 1482. It is a partly old, partly new story, which has never before been told in its entirety. It is one of friendship and betrayal, religious power and moral corruption, political struggle and artistic vendetta.

At the heart of the story, of course, lie the Medici, the family of patrons of arts, poets, politicians, merchant princes, and popes. Had Lorenzo not survived the 1478 attack, it is possible that Michelangelo's talent might have gone unnoticed. Nor would some of the most prized paintings, sculptures, and buildings of Western civilization have been commissioned. And two of Lorenzo's family members would never have ascended to the papacy. We tend to think of Lorenzo as the man he was at the peak of his career, forgetting how hard it was for him to achieve the reputation of "Magnificent."

The Duke of Urbino, famously painted in profile by Piero della Francesca, lends his name to the title of this book because of his pivotal role in the Pazzi conspiracy. Like the other Renaissance men readers will meet here, he is a man of many dimensions, despite the portrait's depicting only one side of his face. He was a mercenary captain, brilliant student of the classics, and a generous patron of the arts, but he also had a dark side, which has come to light to its full extent with the cracking of his coded letter.

The third man at the center of this story is the reason I was able to decode Montefeltro's letter. Born in Pavia, near Milan, almost five hundred years after the Pazzi conspiracy, I was always intrigued by the story of my distant ancestor, Cicco Simonetta (1410–1480), who served the powerful Sforza family for nearly half a century, first as a secretary, later as regent of the Milanese duchy. Cicco, also close to the Duke of Urbino, wrote the code book that allowed me to decipher the Montefeltro letter when I found it in a family archive in Urbino. (For more details on the discovery, see the Afterword.)

Of course there are a host of other characters, many of whose names will at first be unfamiliar. The story takes the reader on a tour of Renaissance Italy, a patchwork of city-states rather than a united nation. Each city-state was controlled, with varying degrees of tyranny, by one family dynasty: there were the Sforza in Milan and the surrounding Lombardy region, the Medici in Florence and a large chunk of Tuscany, the Aragon in Naples and the whole southern tip—all major states. The republic of Venice was an oligarchy ruled by rich merchant and noble families. And of course there was Rome, under the eternal and ever-changing aegis of the popes' families. Among the minor states, the ruling dynasties were the Montefeltro in Urbino, the Malatesta in Rimini, the Este in Ferrara, the Gonzaga in Mantua. Leaders of these last four, given the relatively insignificant size of their territories, were regularly employed as mercenary captains, or *condottieri,* by the richer powers. The system of *condotte,* or hiring contracts, safeguarded the political balance by preventing the ambitions harbored by these captains from becoming real threats. The Italian peninsula thus remained in a fragile peace, with the system guaranteeing that no single state could overcome the rest.

In December 1476 a sudden event occurred that tipped the balance of power. The assassination of Galeazzo Maria Sforza, Duke of Milan and strongest ally of the Medici, set the stage for years of political plotting and counterplotting. The first part of the book investigates the unfolding machinations and shifting alliances that began with Galeazzo's murder and led up to the attack against the Medici. With his death, the balance of power could be reestablished only by diplomatic compromise—or by violent means.

The Montefeltro Conspiracy also shows how majestic works of art and petty Renaissance politics are crucially intertwined. In fact, the last chapter focuses on the Sistine Chapel, the major icon of Renaissance Italy. When people walk into the chapel, they are usually overwhelmed by the powerful ceiling with the *Creation* and by the terrifying altar wall with the *Last Judgment*. These two Michelangelo masterpieces absorb most of the attention of the viewers, who only later turn their eyes to the frescoed walls, with the cycles of the Lives of Moses and Jesus, painted by earlier masters such as Sandro Botticelli.

The Sistine Chapel was built by Pope Sixtus IV, born Francesco della Rovere—one of the antiheroes of this conspiratorial tale—who had it obsessively decorated with the symbol of his family coat of arms: an oak tree on a gold and green background. This pope's portrait was eventually to be erased in an act of Medici revenge.

Any reader of this book will face one key question: What is history to us? We live in a world of constant news, made ephemeral and irrelevant by its continuous flow. Is not this information age enough to keep us busy? The plots and wars of the Renaissance pale in comparison with the ones fought today. In the twenty-first century, technology has multiplied by a thousandfold the possibility of mass murder. Back in the fifteenth century, the only way to get rid of an enemy was face to face, by knife or other blade, or by poison.

Still, the human mind works the same way now as it did then. Murdering at a distance is possible by arming someone else and pretending not to know about it. Befriending your victims, sneaking behind their backs, checking whether they are wearing body armor— these are some of the most cowardly acts of violence. The poet Dante (1265–1321) knew that very well, for he considered violent traitors to be the worst sinners, and he placed them in the pits of his Inferno (Canto XXVII). An ancestor of Federico da Montefeltro, Guido (1220–1298), was among them. A fragment of the speech Dante puts in his mouth illustrates a naked philosophy of deception and death:

Mentre ch'io forma fui d'ossa e di polpe
che la madre mi dié, l'opere mie
non furon leonine, ma di volpe.
Li accorgimenti e le coperte vie
io seppi tutte, e sì menai lor arte,
ch'al fine de la terra il suono uscie.

While I was still mere flesh and bones
My mother gave to me, the deeds I did
Were not those of a lion, but of a fox.
The machinations and the covert ways
I knew them all, and was so skilled in them
My fame rang out to the ends of earth.

Niccolò Machiavelli (1469–1527) was only nine years old in 1478. He witnessed all the violence perpetrated in the streets of Florence as a result of the Pazzi conspiracy and probably remembered it when, in *The Prince* (1513), he recommended that "since it is necessary for a prince to know well how to use the beast, from among the beasts he should choose the fox and the lion." These two animals embody fraud and force, respectively, the key ingredients for the ruthless ruler.

While working on this book, I have kept Dante's verses and Machiavelli's words well in mind. Writing the story of a centuries-old conspiracy is paradoxical since a crucial aim of the plotters was to remain covert, to destroy evidence that would link them to violent actions, in an attempt to avoid present danger and posthumous blame. Nonetheless, this story, and the history in which it finds its roots, is entirely true and astonishingly well documented. And the fame of its heroes still rings out "to the ends of earth."

Opening page of Dante's Inferno, *ca. 1478, from the Montefeltro Library. The copyist/calligrapher of the text was Matteo Contugi, a spy against Federico.*

PART I

Winter 1476 — Spring 1478

While I was still mere flesh and bones

My mother gave to me, the deeds I did

Were not those of a lion, but of a fox.

—DANTE, *Inferno*

1

MILAN

IS FOR MURDER

IN THE FIRST HALF OF THE FIFTEENTH CENTURY MILAN WAS RULED BY THE VISCONTI, AND ONLY AFTER 1450 BY THE SFORZA. The Visconti had been the most aggressive enemies of Florence. In the heated Florentine pamphlets that were circulating during the early 1400s, attacks on Florence became synonymous with attacks on freedom and on the "Florentine way of life," while the Visconti were rightly portrayed as cruel tyrants. When the *condottiere* Francesco Sforza suddenly became Duke of Milan and struck the Peace of Lodi (1454), the golden age of the Renaissance started in earnest. Francesco offered military protection to his longtime friend Cosimo de' Medici in exchange for financial support. The solid alliance between Milan and the Medici formed an axis of relative stability within the restless Italian peninsula and enhanced patronage of the arts and letters, sparking an explosion of artistic creativity and humanistic culture.

Under the founder of the Sforza dynasty Milan maintained power and gained wealth and respect. But Francesco's son, Galeazzo Maria, inherited more of the capriciousness of the Visconti from his mother than he did the wisdom of the Sforza from his father. As court poet Antonio Cornazzano eloquently wrote in his *Art of Ruling*:

Oh how many times the good Duke Francesco
Reproached a son who is no longer
For his crude and violent acts.
"The soul of Duke Giovanni has landed upon you:

It is deep within your bowels!"
He yelled, and so his prophecy came to pass.
Learn from the foul acts of Duke Giovanni
Who fed his dogs with living men
For any other sport bored him.
He met his end in San Gottardo, in the sacred temple,
Slaughtered by his most faithful servants
And such is the fate of any cruel man.

A COLD AWAKENING

MILAN, DECEMBER 26, 1476

ON THE DAY THEY WERE GOING TO KILL HIM, GALEAZZO MARIA
Sforza was due to appear at the High Mass for the feast of St. Stephen.
It was the anniversary of the death of the first Christian martyr and the
Duke of Milan wanted to celebrate the occasion with appropriate pomp.
He tried on a decorative breastplate but thought it made him look too
fat. Instead he chose a rich suit of crimson wool lined with sable. On his
left leg he wore a dark red stocking and on the right, a white one. These
were the Sforza colors. As he dressed his athletic, hairless body (he liked
to be shaved in the ancient Roman manner) in his bedroom within the
mighty walls of the Sforza castle, the flames in the large fireplace were
still turning the Christmas log, *il Ciocco,* to ashes.

Bernardino Corio, who at the time was a *cameriere di camera,* or servant of the bedchamber, an eyewitness to and chronicler of these events,
informs us that ever since a mysterious fire had burned a part of his bedroom earlier that month, the duke had become superstitious; he had had
an *instincto,* or an inkling, that it was not a good idea for him to come
to Milan (the duke spent much of his time away from the city, at one of

his many countryside villas or on hunting expeditions). His fears had
been reinforced by an incident that had occurred shortly after the fire.
One day, while riding in the fields near the village of Abbiategrasso, he
saw three crows flying slowly over his head. The duke had taken this to
be a bad omen, and shot twice at the birds with his crossbow. Putting his
hand firmly on the saddle, he had declared that he would not return to
town.

He soon had changed his mind. For Galeazzo loved his choir and,
with the feast day festivities approaching, he looked forward to the music that would be performed by his thirty northern European singers,
whom he paid handsomely for their service. But upon returning to
Milan a few days after seeing the three crows, he found himself surrounded by the resentful glares of the feudal lords and courtiers who had
come to pay their respects: they were annoyed not to have been offered
any of the usual money or gifts for Christmas.

The duke nonetheless had made his way to the castle. Under the red
ceiling of the Camera delle Colombe, the duke gave a speech to his
courtiers on the Sforza fortunes. Even if he were not a *signore,* a titled
duke, he claimed, he would have known how to live magnificently. The
thirty-two-year-old duke said he wished his father, Francesco, were still
alive to see how well he and his brothers were doing. The Sforza dynasty,
he boasted, would continue for centuries, blessed as it was with scores of
male relatives, both legitimate and otherwise. He even applauded his illegitimate daughters, two of whom were by then betrothed to powerful
lords.

Bearing plentiful offspring, in fact, was one of the ways in which
power was consolidated in the Renaissance. Galeazzo's father, Francesco
Sforza, was said to have fathered no less than thirty-five children, only
ten of whom were legitimate. The "virtuous" Francesco, as Niccolò
Machiavelli dubbed him in *The Prince,* had raised himself up from the
hard life of a *condottiere* to the heights of the richest duchy in Italy.
When Francesco died in 1466, his eldest son, Galeazzo, had inherited
the power that the "prince by virtue" had so painstakingly acquired, but
Galeazzo had not been very good at preserving either power or virtue.
The new duke was reviled by most of his subjects for a whole host of

sins. Unable to restrain his violent sexual appetites, he made the most attractive women of the duchy his prey, and occasionally even visited convents at night in order to terrorize, and possibly rape, nuns.

While celebrating the good fortunes of his family members, he did not refer specifically to his two younger brothers, Sforza Maria and Ludovico, who had been exiled to France. In June 1476, these two troublemakers had been involved in a foiled attempt to kill the duke and replace him. Indeed, Galeazzo's egomaniacal style had made many people unhappy—and not only members of his close family circle.

◦ ◦ M ◦ ◦

AFTER DELIVERING HIS SPEECH in the Camera delle Colombe, the duke had been unusually quiet and did not pursue his usual leisure activities on Christmas day, such as a tennis game in the indoor court especially built for him or a hunting expedition with falconry. He also avoided his wife, Duchess Bona of Savoy, who slept in a separate room. That morning of the twenty-sixth of December, the duchess got up very late, for, according to Corio, she had had horrible nightmares. Since their marriage eight years before she had gained a lot of weight. By now Galeazzo had lost any interest in sharing his bed with her. He had satisfied his vigorous appetites elsewhere. He had spent most of his adult life restlessly wandering throughout the Italian peninsula, hunting not only women but also animals and boys, and sometimes playing soldier and visiting his allies, especially the affluent Florentines.

Galeazzo had first visited Florence in 1459, when he was fifteen. He was then the Count of Pavia and his father, Francesco, the Duke of Milan. Francesco, a strong ally of Cosimo de' Medici, wanted to pay homage to the Florentine banker and leader who had been a staunch financial supporter of his family fortunes. "All the ink in Tuscany," as Galeazzo wrote to his father in Milan, could not describe the opulence of the crowds cheering their guest loudly on the streets, framed by the harmony of the buildings—the outstanding Duomo or the austere Palazzo della Signoria, the seat of government, with its characteristically threatening tower. "Florence is paradise on earth," he wrote in a daze of admiration.

Since then, the young Sforza had struggled to outshine his Medici allies in matters such as taste and fashion, in which they were universally considered arbiters and masters. Galeazzo, under the pretext of taking a religious vow, had returned to Florence most recently in 1471 with a retinue of two thousand people, spending two hundred thousand ducats and virtually depleting his treasury in the process. As Machiavelli later reported, Galeazzo's visit to Florence had taken place during the penitential season of Lent, in which the Church commands its faithful to refrain from eating meat. Instead, the members of Galeazzo's court fed irreverently on nothing but meat. In his portrait of a dandified Galeazzo, Florentine painter Piero Pollaiuolo captured the air of corruption that swept into town with the Milanese prince. Lorenzo de' Medici hung the work in his own bedroom, perhaps to remind himself of what he did not want to become. In this bust-length portrait, Galeazzo is shown in three-quarter view with a libidinous expression, wearing a sumptuous green robe decorated with lilies, and playing distractedly with his glove.

ON HIS LAST DAY, Galeazzo was looking forward to the singing of the ducal choir. He was delighted at the thought of those beautiful boys with enchanting voices accompanied by extraordinary musicians. They had already been dispatched to the Church of Santo Stefano, and it was too late to recall them into the castle. While he was still wondering whether to attend High Mass, Galeazzo received a visit from Cicco Simonetta, who had served Francesco in a variety of capacities for nearly half a century and had been Galeazzo's first secretary, and thus his most trusted aide, for the past decade. A dark, heavily built man in his mid-sixties, Cicco cut an entirely different figure from that of the slender, fair Galeazzo. He tried to dissuade the duke from going to Mass. Along with the duke's other advisors, he begged Galeazzo not to walk, or even ride, on such a freezing day. The duke responded that people would wonder why he had come all the way into town without making an appearance at the church. He had made up his mind: he would go to Mass.

He called in his sons, Gian Galeazzo, age seven, and Hermes, six, and placed them on either side of the window, from which he could see the

Piero Pollaiuolo, Portrait of Galeazzo Maria Sforza. *This portrait was executed in March 1471, during Galeazzo's visit to Florence. Lorenzo de' Medici kept it in his bedroom.*

white wintry landscape. He embraced and kissed the boys for a long time, seemingly unwilling to part from them. A large courtly retinue, on horse and on foot, was waiting for Galeazzo in the wide castle courtyard, under the tall watchtowers. The duke walked out arm-in-arm with his favorite ambassador, Zaccaria Saggi from Mantua. Struck by the bitter cold, he then climbed onto his horse. And so did his entourage, riding with him in the snow. In the icy streets were a few people halfheartedly cheering the duke, who was surrounded by armored soldiers. The group passed through the piazza in front of the main cathedral.

Just a few steps ahead lay their destination. The façade of the "blessed church" of Santo Stefano was small but elegantly finished in Gothic style. The gates were just being opened. It had to be warmer inside. The duke dismounted nervously. The dignitaries and the ambassadors entered the church first, with Galeazzo between them. They were followed by his slow-witted brother Filippo, his youngest brother Ottaviano, and the ducal secretary Giovanni Simonetta, who was speaking softly with his brother Cicco's military advisor, Orfeo da Ricavo. The echo of the choir from the back was becoming louder. The bodyguards, in their gleaming armor, cleared a path in the crowd with their swords for the duke and the gentlemen who accompanied him. Galeazzo stepped into the main nave and stopped in the middle of the church, looking up at the flame of a light cotton ball hanging from the ceiling. It stood for the bonfire of the vanities:

Sic transit gloria mundi!
So does earthly glory pass!

As the duke made his way toward the altar, three men suddenly approached him. They were all dressed the same way, in bright red and white: the colors of Brutus, Caesar's assassin. "Make room!" they shouted, as if to clear the duke's path. One of them came closer, apparently to ask something of Galeazzo, who waved him off impatiently. The man let a knife slide from his sleeve into his left hand and stabbed upward into Galeazzo's abdomen. When Saggi, the Mantuan ambassador, tried to brush him away, the attacker hit again, this time plunging the knife deeply into the duke's chest.

"I am dead," whispered Galeazzo as he received another stab in the stomach. Then the other two men jumped up, making a further series of swift stabs: in the throat, on the head, on the wrist, and in the back. Galeazzo shrank back and almost fell on Orfeo da Ricavo's chest. Blood was pouring out of his upper body. Orfeo tried to support him but could not hold him. The duke fell to his knees and then collapsed on the floor. He exhaled. His crimson suit, once partly white, was now soaked in dark red blood.

The assassins tried to take flight. A tall Moor, Galeazzo's loyal servant, ran after one of them, who had rushed up the stairs into the women's section. The fugitive tripped on the women's voluminous dresses and fell. The Moor grabbed him and slew him, amid the gasps and cries of the terrified ladies. Other bodyguards caught and killed the second assassin on the spot, but the third one vanished into the fleeing crowd.

◦　◦　M　◦　◦

SUCH WAS THE MURDER OF Galeazzo Maria Sforza, Duke of Milan. Galeazzo's brief life and sudden death raise fascinating questions. Was he truly the gruesomely corrupt tyrant and sexual predator described by numerous witnesses and historians? And if he was, how did Cicco, who worked for him for a decade after Francesco's death in 1466, put up with him? Was he corrupt as well? Or would he have been able to steer the young prince, whom he had known since birth, toward better behavior and more effective rule? It is certain that both father and son attracted violent resentment, particularly from members of the old Milanese nobility, who perceived them as foreign usurpers.

Cicco was of humble origins. He was born in 1410 in Caccuri, a small fiefdom in southern Italy that came under the control of Francesco Sforza at the time of his first marriage, to Polissena Ruffo of Calabria. As a young man, Cicco studied civil and canon law in the nearby monastery of Rossano, a lively center of Catholic and Christian Orthodox culture, where he quickly mastered Latin and Greek. Around 1430, through his uncle, the Sforza agent Angelo Simonetta, the twenty-year-old Cicco entered the service of Francesco Sforza, then *condottiere,* or mercenary captain, as a member of his traveling chancellery.

A military career during the Renaissance was harsh, but potentially full of rewards for ambitious and skilled captains. Once they had demonstrated their strategic ability on the field, the *condottieri* could advertise their abilities to the highest bidders. Most of the major political powers in Italy had no drafted armies. These mercenaries were paid to fight, but also to keep out of trouble and to refrain from such misdemeanors as unleashing their troops against defenseless towns and villages. The most famous *condottieri* were in a good position to improve their lots considerably—as did Francesco Sforza—by becoming self-employed. When in March 1450, after months of besieging the city and starving the people of Milan, he was finally hailed duke, he chose Cicco Simonetta, his loyal aide for twenty years, as his chancellor.

In the service of Duke Francesco Sforza, Cicco became a man of the sword as well as of the word. As soon as the duke's son Galeazzo was orphaned, Cicco and his brother Giovanni, who later became the biographer of Francesco, provided a kind of statesman's education to the young heir. Cicco's paternal, albeit respectful, relationship with Galeazzo emerges from his diaries, in which he dutifully recorded all courtly activity (diplomatic secrets excepted). But the archives reveal a somewhat more complex story than that given by this partial and self-serving memoir. The Mantuan ambassador Zaccaria Saggi, who happened to be next to Galeazzo when he entered Santo Stefano and tried to push away his killer, wrote, during the period when Galeazzo was duke, that Cicco was a "very good shield" against his impetuous nature. The chancellor resisted his lord's fits of anger and procrastinated rather than acting immediately on the duke's rushed decisions, so that "all good political action taken in Milan" happened thanks to him. For instance, to the ducal agent in Bologna, who wished to falsely denounce the Jews in order to confiscate their properties, Cicco replied that "these were rotten things to do, things that left a bad taste in the mouth." If this response was perhaps prompted by the duke, the language was certainly that of the chancellor. It is also true, on the other hand, that under Galeazzo's rule some wealthy citizens and talkative poets were thrown into jail on questionable charges with the aim of either draining their pockets or simply shutting their mouths.

At the time of Galeazzo's death, Cicco gained absolute control of the

Francesco Sforza enters Milan unarmed, to be hailed duke, while his soldiers distribute bread baskets to the people, in March 1450. A twentieth-century etching.

police forces in the duchy. It did not take long before they caught the third and only surviving killer, Girolamo Olgiati, the twenty-three-year-old scion of a good Milanese family. Girolamo's father, horrified by the son's deed, had denied him help, but his mother had sent him in disguise to the house of a priest friend. Two Olgiati family servants tried to defend the young man; they were caught, and then drawn and quartered.

By all contemporary accounts, Girolamo Olgiati was "very literate and erudite." He claimed that he and his friends wanted to emulate the ancient Romans and set the country free by killing the tyrant in the hope of provoking a popular uprising. The reconstruction of the plot against Galeazzo relies heavily on Girolamo's full confession. This document, written in an excited though not inelegant Latin, allows us to look into the mind of a "terrorist" of sorts. Imbued with the love of ancient anti-tyrannical writers, Girolamo had run away from home ten years before, as a mere thirteen-year-old, to follow his teacher, Cola Montano. Montano was a humanist—that is, a follower of the Renaissance movement that revived the study of the ancient Greek and Roman classics and emphasized secular over religious concerns—who, charged with rape, had been publicly whipped on Galeazzo's orders. As a result of this humiliation he had been exiled to Bologna more than a year before Galeazzo's assassination. It is unclear whether he was the one who masterminded the plot against Galeazzo. What is certain is that Cola was responsible for having turned a young and impressionable mind into a very peculiar version of a bookish one. In his confession, Girolamo proudly mentioned two epigrams he had composed, one for Galeazzo ("What a thousand armed phalanxes could not do . . .") and the other for Giovanni Andrea Lampugnani, the ringleader of the trio of assassins, who had been killed in the church and whose corpse had been dragged through the streets by the Milanese populace shortly after the duke's murder.

It is interesting that Girolamo was more afraid of being forgotten by history than of undergoing the same physical fate that befell Lampugnani. Like many fanatics, he was a one-book man. He had studied ad nauseam *The Conspiracy of Catiline,* the work of the ancient Roman writer Sallust and the all-time handbook of plotters, a text that exudes both a fascination with and a revulsion for tyrannicide. Girolamo was, in fact, so obsessed with Catiline's legacy that he is reported to have said to himself before the executioner started to cut his naked body into pieces: "Pull yourself together, Girolamo! The memory of this deed will long endure. Death is bitter, but fame is perpetual."

These lofty words would feed the romantic myth of the rebel for centuries to come. What exactly motivated the killers? Girolamo seems to have been the only one who was involved in it for genuine ideological reasons. The other two plotters had personal and political grudges against the duke. Both Giovanni Andrea Lampugnani and Carlo Visconti, the other conspirators (the verb *conspirare* in Latin literally means "to breathe together"), were disgruntled courtiers. Visconti's sister, it was said, had been raped by Galeazzo, who then had passed her on to a youth in his close entourage. Apparently, Lampugnani's wife had also fallen prey to Galeazzo's appetites.

Lampugnani may also have had an additional grudge against Galeazzo. Lampugnani had claimed a few days before the murder that he wanted to insist on the duke's intervention to settle a petty dispute over some possessions and was ready to do anything to this end. Nonetheless, Lampugnani's terrible rage against Galeazzo seems to have somewhat exceeded the offenses he allegedly received at the duke's hand. "Everything was done," added Orfeo da Ricavo, Cicco's military advisor, "by instigation of the treacherous Giovanni Andrea, who was evil, malicious, proud, choleric, vengeful, ruthless and of the worst nature ever born." Even if these moral charges can be discounted as fabricated after the fact, Girolamo's vivid description of Lampugnani rehearsing the murder provides some insight into the extent of his anger: he attacked with knives a wooden dummy of the duke dressed in gold brocade, charging it with the fury of a bull. If this anecdote seems real enough, so do other details of the bloody pact that were recorded in the confession: the three plotters went to a consecrated altar where they allowed their own fresh blood to fall on the holy bread of Christ, before cutting it into three pieces and persuading the priest to administer it to them.

So the killers were not merely motivated by sheer homicidal passion. In fact, like most self-righteous avengers, they each believed that they had in some way been chosen for a highly important, if not sacred, mission. They swore to slaughter Galeazzo in front of the statue of Ambrose, the patron saint of Milan, asking that he "be favorable to our enterprise, and show by favoring justice that injustice displeases you." Choosing the church of Santo Stefano as the setting for the murder was also an idea born of necessity. The duke was surrounded by bodyguards wherever he went and it would have been almost impossible to approach him in the street or anywhere in the open.

Galeazzo's exiled brothers, Sforza Maria and Ludovico, left France in early January 1477 as soon as they heard the news of the duke's death, but did not actually come back to Milan until later that month. There was little time to settle things before the return of the renegade brothers. If anyone had more information about the secret ramifications of the Milanese murder, it was Cicco Simonetta, but he prudently kept whatever he may have known to himself. Pragmatic as he was, Cicco's main concern at this point was to keep order in the duchy. In this he undoubtedly succeeded. And he calmly led the panicky Duchess Bona through the first chaotic moments after her husband's death.

Giovanni Andrea Lampugnani's body had been dragged around the streets for days and was finally fed to the pigs. His right hand was nailed to the top of a column, where it was burned. The heads of the two other assassins were hanged on the Broletto Market Tower, while their body parts were left dangling from the city gates. Such warning signs against rebellion were eloquent enough. The public execution and the display of the dismembered bodies of the conspirators served to subdue the restless populace, as did some well-timed tax cuts devised by Cicco.

Galeazzo's corpse was left overnight on the cold pavement of Santo Stefano, since nobody dared to go back into the streets after dark. A hasty burial was then arranged, with the Mass this time celebrated in the city's Duomo. The sudden death of the duke raised a tricky theological problem, however, since he had not had the chance to confess his sins. Duchess Bona showed some belated devotion in order to save Galeazzo's soul, directing a desperate appeal to the pope, Sixtus IV. She asked him to grant a posthumous absolution to her husband. The list of the deceased's sins, which she included in her appeal for forgiveness, certainly explains its urgency: acting like a tyrant, making war justly and unjustly, sacking cities without mercy, robbery, extortion of subjects, negligence of justice, injustice actively committed, illegal enforcement of taxes even from clerics, adultery, rape of virgins and of other people's wives, whoring, scandalous simonies, as well as other transgressions too numerous to cite. Bona promised on her part to pray for Galeazzo Maria until his unhappy soul should emerge from purgatory cleansed for its entrance into heaven. She would also fund monasteries and hospitals and provide dowries for poor young virgins. Apparently, the pope complied.

The widow was not the only woman concerned about Galeazzo's afterlife. Bernardino Corio, the servant turned historian, tells us, among many other juicy details, that some of Galeazzo's mistresses (whose names he was at least discreet enough not to disclose) had also been summoned to the funeral Mass for the duke at the Duomo. Despite Corio's reticence, it is more than likely that among them was Lucia Marliani, Galeazzo's passionate lover during the preceding couple of years, who also happened to be pregnant by him. A macabre mystery surrounds her role in the burial. As recently as 2001, a team of forensic scientists examined a skull unearthed in the Church of St. Andrea di Melzo, Lucia's own chapel just outside Milan. Its age and features (among others, holes in the upper lobe of the cranium and evidence of dental disease) would seem to match those of Galeazzo. It is possible that, at a later date, Lucia may have managed to sneak her lover's skull out of his provisional tomb and place it in the chapel that belonged to her.

BONA WAS WELL AWARE of her incompetence in state matters. Now that her unfaithful husband was not around anymore, she spent most of her time in bed with Antonio Tassino, a Ferrarese servant, who, as Machiavelli dryly observed later, must have had a "secret virtue." She therefore relied on the advice of the Secret Council, a cabinet of courtiers usually composed exclusively of Milanese noblemen. Under Galeazzo, government business had been effectively run by the chancellery staffed by Cicco and his close associates. After the duke's death, Cicco prompted an immediate reform of the Secret Council, making himself, his brother Giovanni, and his military advisor Orfeo da Ricavo its most influential members. His eldest son, Gian Giacomo, became its secretary. Gian Giacomo was the scribe of the founding document, dated December 30, 1476, which gave full governing powers to the council. But it was written in the name of the duchess, addressing the members of the Secret Council, now elevated to Secret Senate, in a solemn self-celebration of the council's prerogatives. The goal of the acting government was to "preserve the style of our late lord and husband, since calling up everybody [all the members of the Milanese nobility] would be too much," thus establishing de facto a strictly oligarchic regime. The Senate granted a general amnesty for pending trials and showed clemency for petty criminals (except political rebels). It also set down strict preventive measures against potential plotters: gatherings in private homes were to be prohibited in the name of order, public peace, and respect for the duchess's period of mourning. Cicco thereby had become the effective regent of the Duchy of Milan.

The Milanese citizens were in fact very quiet at this stage, apparently enjoying their new, seemingly benevolent government. But threats to the freshly shaped status quo were about to come from within the ruling dynasty. Galeazzo's first cousin Roberto da Sanseverino had been for years another major player on the Sforza scene. A fearless and able captain, and a rather bombastic character, he had fought many wars as a mercenary. He had also made a pilgrimage to Jerusalem to cleanse his soul. Because of personal disagreements with the duke, he had moved his base of operations to Bologna, the city where Cola Montano, the "teacher of evil" who had inspired Girolamo Olgiati and his gang, lived unharmed. As soon as the news of the events at Santo Stefano reached him, Roberto rode back to Milan. He was especially outraged at the fact that a chancellor of humble background such as Cicco lived inside the castle and had actually moved into Galeazzo's private apartments for "security reasons." More murder was to be expected in Milan.

2

OVERLY CAUTIOUS

THE SFORZA CASTLE HAD BEEN BUILT ON THE RUINS OF THE VISCONTI CASTLE, WHICH WAS DESTROYED BY THE MILANESE PEOPLE AFTER THE DEATH OF THE TYRANNICAL DUKE FILIPPO MARIA VISCONTI IN 1447. When Francesco Sforza had become duke in 1450, he had at first promised he would not resurrect that old symbol of oppression, but soon realized that he needed to create a fortress to defend his family—more than the city—from external dangers. He hired Florentine architect Antonio Averlino, known as Filarete (Greek for "lover of virtue"). While constructing the castle, Filarete also wrote his groundbreaking *Treatise on Architecture* (c. 1464) in which he describes the utopian city of Sforzinda, a place that would be full of buildings designed to strike the fancy of King Zogalia (an obvious anagram of Galiazo, that is, Galeazzo). The castle would be erected at the center of Sforzinda, surrounded by watchtowers, moats, and a labyrinthine system of walls. Many of Filarete's intricate and visionary ideas were actually executed in the invisible structure of tunnels and dungeons beneath the Sforza castle. The construction of the castle was completed under Cicco Simonetta's watchful eye.

Filarete and Cicco also collaborated on improving Milan's civic structures. The architect and the chancellor joined forces to build the Ospedale Maggiore, a huge and elegant hospital complex—much needed in a densely populated and often plague-stricken area. What's more, these two brilliant brains shared a passion for complicated mind games, and especially for designing virtually unbreakable codes.

This portrait shows Cicco Simonetta holding chancellery papers to the right of Duke Galeazzo Maria Sforza on his throne, ca. 1475.

A CHANCELLOR'S CHANCE

FOR ALMOST THIRTY YEARS, CICCO SIMONETTA HAD BEEN RISING at dawn and going to his chancellery office to check that the previous day's correspondence had been placed in the appropriate files. Not all letters were treated the same: some were securely locked in his personal desk and some were copied in cipher before being sent out. In an age when all news had to travel by horse and on the insecure roads of Europe, everyone involved in politics knew very well that messages had to be encrypted with sophisticated systems. Cicco had devised a highly complex system to encode his messages to his associates and allies. Each Milanese ambassador was given a different set of symbols. Altogether there were about 250 random symbols, which stood for single, double, and triple characters. Some fifty others designated people or powers. Every few months, the sets were completely changed.

As chancellor of the mightiest city-state in Italy, Cicco had always been aware of the huge responsibility that rested on his shoulders. Francesco Sforza was an expert soldier and a skilled politician, but he had never run an organized state. The humble man from Calabria, on the other hand, had been studying the ways of diplomatic communication ever since the beginning of his career. Under Francesco, and as soon as he had a centralized office in Milan, Cicco had selected the best agents and instituted the first resident ambassadors in Italy and the rest of Europe. He corresponded with each of them and created the widest network available during the fifteenth century. When Galeazzo became duke after his father's death, keeping control over this web of information was key to preserving the power of the newly established *signore*.

Galeazzo, like his father, entrusted Cicco with reading all the incoming dispatches and with drafting many of the responses. During

Galeazzo's reign, Cicco would visit the duke in his chambers and brief him on any given situation. Galeazzo was not a morning person. Sometimes he received the secretary in the nude after rudely pushing his nightly prey out of bed. Cicco, accustomed to this scene, would wait until no one was in earshot, and then provide the important news of the day, often cutting out many details and focusing the maverick mind of his master on the most urgent matters at hand. Cicco's own elaborate signature, which marked the many thousands of outgoing dispatches of the Sforza, represented the entire Milanese state.

Now, eleven days after Galeazzo's death, the day of Epiphany—January 6, 1477—Cicco awoke in the duke's room. For the first time in many years, he had no one to report to, except for the ineffectual duchess, who had ceded any power she may have had to Cicco. It was both a relief and a burden. New challenges awaited him. In a timely fashion, Cicco was informed that Roberto da Sanseverino had arrived the night before from Bologna, and had entered the city gates.

Cicco had called the first meeting of the Secret Senate for that day. Roberto strode into the meeting room and had the gall to demand to be hired with a stipend (*condotta*) as high as that of Federico da Montefeltro, Duke of Urbino, the best-remunerated *condottiere* in Italy. If his request were not granted, he said, he would not waste time "disputing with doctors" (that is, arguing about legal matters) and threatened to obtain what he wanted "the military way" (*more militari*).

Even before that meeting, the chancellor knew he had immediately to begin securing the duchy's existing ties to the neighboring political powers. And so, that very day, he wrote a letter, in cipher, to his ally Federico da Montefeltro. Bypassing the niceties of diplomatic jargon, he went straight to the point: now he needed his old friend of many wars and peace treaties to come to Milan and calm things down. Federico had already rushed to Milan's succor once, in 1466, right after the death—of natural causes—of Francesco Sforza, to help Cicco prevent upheavals in the duchy before Galeazzo was able to take power. Ten years later Cicco was calling on Federico again. The Duke of Urbino, with his exalted military reputation, was needed to help crush the absurd pretenses of Roberto da Sanseverino.

Cicco had known Roberto since the latter was a child. As Francesco

Sforza's nephew, Roberto had always enjoyed special treatment at court. His athletic and martial prowess had been evident very early on. Unlike Galeazzo, who loved elegance and refinement, his cousin was more interested in jousting and riding. Not that Galeazzo had been weak or unmanly. On the contrary, his father, Francesco, administered a good beating every now and then to prevent him from turning vicious later on. (Francesco's methods clearly had failed.) Roberto, on the other hand, had always been Francesco's favorite. He was a natural soldier who liked to command as well as to take risks.

Cicco fully expected that Roberto, who had grown weary of Galeazzo's despotism, would behave with the strongest sense of entitlement at the now dukeless Sforza court. Although Cicco had been very helpful to Roberto in difficult times, he was also aware that the hot-tempered *condottiere* would threaten anybody who stood in his way, especially a sixty-seven-year-old man for whom he had never had much sympathy. Nor did the impulsive Roberto, who was about to turn fifty, have any respect for the patient work of politics. He did not understand the ways of persuasion and compromise. Yet, to fulfill his ambitions, he required the assistance of unscrupulous accomplices.

THE STATE MUST GO ON

AFTER TRAVELING THROUGH FRANCE, GALEAZZO'S EXILED brothers, Sforza Maria and Ludovico, finally returned to Milan in late January. When they arrived, separately, at the castle gates, they discovered that the access system had been radically changed. Now, under the rule of Bona and Cicco, everyone needed a written and chancellery-sealed permit to enter and could do so only "as private courtiers." In other words, the brothers were not treated as Sforza heirs: they were forced to dismount from their horses before the bridges, leave their entourage outside, and walk alone and unarmed into the court. Their presence at the meetings of the Secret Senate (of which they were members by default) was "more shadow than fact," as Sforza Maria, the older of the two, would later put it. The brothers immediately teamed up with the resentful Roberto and swiftly managed to have Cicco move out of Galeazzo's rooms and into the chancellery offices.

This was only an apparent victory for them, however, since the chancellor had already taken precautions to protect himself. Over the years, Cicco had familiarized himself with all the secret passageways and hidden staircases constructed in the cavities of the walls by Galeazzo so that he could move through the crowded castle without being seen. The old chancellor, having overseen the castle's construction, was the only one who had access to every room.

Galeazzo's brothers and cousin openly claimed that they did not want to leave the government of such a wealthy and powerful state in the hands of a widow and a child heir. But there was one main obstacle to the political, if not physical, annihilation of Bona and the firstborn son, Gian Galeazzo: old Cicco. In early February, the three accomplices hired a man named Ettore Vimercati to sneak into the chancellor's rooms in the castle. It was not a friendly visit: Vimercati's mission was to "cut him into pieces." He would have succeeded, "had Cicco not been alerted" by one of his many spies. In the plan of the plotters, revealed by Vimercati's confession, Sforza Maria would immediately have been given the strategic castle of Sartirana Lomellina, the large estate of the Simonetta clan that provided the fresh greens and fat capons brought to Milan to be cooked by Cicco's personal chef. His creations had to be tasted before being served to any family member: this was the period in which poison started being used systematically to settle political scores. Vimercati was later reported to have called Cicco "calf's head," because of his tendency to eat a lot of meat and to gain weight. That unhealthy diet was probably the cause of the gout that troubled him more and more as he aged.

Nonetheless, in matters of security Cicco was highly disciplined. He had always insisted his employees unfailingly apply the strict rules that he had drawn up for his own household, under threat of expulsion: no one was to mention anything about the duke's business that was not already said on the street or in the piazza. If an employee were ever to divulge secrets acquired during contact with the chancellor, this would count against Cicco's hard-earned reputation of loyalty and discretion. Most crucially, when he went to work in his *studiolo,* a guard was to watch the doorway and nobody was allowed inside. When the chancellor was absent, his room had to be locked at all times and nobody must enter. At night, the gates of his Milanese palace, not far from the Sforza castle, were shut and only after visitors had clearly identified themselves might they be allowed inside. The servants were not supposed to accept any gifts or bribes from anybody, and if they were promised something, they were to immediately report it to their master. They should be grateful for leading a lavish life, for receiving good salaries, and also for enjoying banquet leftovers. If some food remained untouched, it was to be given to the poor for the love of God. Cicco further strengthened this set of rigid rules when, leaving his wife to guard the family palace, he himself moved back into the Sforza castle. Now, from his sealed chancellery, Cicco was able to control the unfolding diplomatic game.

His obsession with secrecy, which bordered on paranoia, had proven to be especially useful in this attempt on his life. While Cicco secured his status for the moment by preventing attacks on his person, his close collaborators and extended family (he had married a noble Milanese lady, Elisabetta Visconti, who bore seven profitably betrothed children), he also transmitted coded messages to his allies. He had already dictated a letter on behalf of the duchess, copied by his son and signed by Bona's hand (*manu propria*), thanking Lorenzo and Giuliano de' Medici for their heartfelt condolences on Duke Galeazzo's death and stressing the fact that "our welfare and yours are attached to an identical thread," recalling their "old friendship" since the time of Francesco Sforza and Cosimo de' Medici. The letter also included this ominous warning: "Please use the maximum prudence and watchfulness to preserve our state, and keep in mind that, when necessary, you should change your daily plans—which we will hold very dear, since what you will do for us, you will in fact be doing for yourself."

In January 1477 Cicco had also sent as gifts to Lorenzo de' Medici, formally on behalf of Duchess Bona, four falcons. The meaning of this gift was not lost on its clever recipient: Milan was requesting protection from Florence. Cicco had good reason to do this: he knew that Italy's

Terra-cotta bust of Lorenzo de' Medici, by Andrea Verrocchio, ca. 1470.

four major military powers—Pope Sixtus IV in Rome, King Ferrante of Aragon in Naples, the Republic of Venice, and even Federico da Montefeltro in Urbino—would be more interested in controlling the duchy than in supporting it at this difficult juncture.

o   o   ◯   o   o

FLORENTINE FALCONS
(AND FLEAS)

EVERY MORNING, WHEN HE GOT OUT OF BED, LORENZO DE' Medici faced the portrait of Galeazzo painted by Piero Pollaiuolo. Despite their very different temperaments and ruling methods, Galeazzo had been Lorenzo's main ally since he had taken over the Medici reign in Florence in 1469. Lorenzo, only five years younger than Galeazzo, now sorely missed him. The portrait, and especially the detail of the duke holding the left glove in his gloved right hand, seemed to bear a coded meaning. It was the gesture of a hunter who prided himself on the fact that his falcon returned freely to his master's bare hand. One of the last favors offered by Galeazzo to his friend Lorenzo had been to give him his best falcon-trainer, a man named Pilato. Now it was the turn of the Medici heir to try to become the chief predator in Italy.

The Medici were bankers who had done extremely well in Florence over the last three or four generations. Cosimo the Elder, Lorenzo's grandfather, had managed to establish himself as the *Pater Patriae,* father of the fatherland. Returning from exile in 1434, he had inaugurated the family's leadership, which at first had run parallel to the formal republic, an elected body of representatives over which the Medici gradually gained control. Cosimo had effectively designated the main candidates in the government elections, while enhancing enormously his own family's wealth. He also had supported Francesco Sforza in his rise to power in Milan and filled the empty pockets of the new duke. Sforza, in turn, was to always lend a strong arm to enforce the Medici policies, in exchange for hefty "loans" that often were not returned. At the time Cosimo died in 1464, he was widely considered the unofficial prince of Florence.

Cosimo's son, Piero "the Gouty"—father of Lorenzo—had kept the family fortunes intact, shielding himself with the help of Sforza troops from an attempted coup organized by a group of wealthy Florentine citizens. Piero had died in December 1469, leaving his firstborn son, Lorenzo, barely twenty, with a financial empire to administer and political capital to invest. Lorenzo had accepted, albeit reluctantly, claiming that his true calling was poetry.

MONDAY, FEBRUARY 17, 1477, was the day before Mardi Gras. Already thinking of the upcoming Lent, Lorenzo had probably had Galeazzo's portrait covered with a thick black cloth, as a sign of respect for the dead. But Lorenzo loved and celebrated life. These famous lines, which he would write for a Carnevale years later, capture his philosophy of carpe diem:

Quant'è bella giovinezza
Che si fugge tuttavia.
Chi vuol esser lieto, sia:
di doman non c'è certezza.

How beautiful youth is
Though it flees away.
Let him who wishes to be happy:
Nothing's certain tomorrow.

In his effort to become the perfect Epicurean, Lorenzo had honed both his agile mind and his athletic body. He had triumphed in the city's joust of 1469 (his younger brother Giuliano would go on to win the joust of 1475). Lorenzo was known for his love of luxury and his taste for elegance. It is said that he had his charms, but they were hardly evident in his physical appearance. As the result of a childhood injury, his face was dominated by a large flattened nose, which gave his voice a peculiar nasal sound. Unfortunately, he had also inherited his great-grandfather Giovanni's strongly protruding chin and large mouth.

However, his unattractive looks were of no hindrance to him. He had married Roman noblewoman Clarice Orsini, who had so far produced two sons, Piero and Giovanni. At this point, Lorenzo was a bold twenty-eight-year-old who controlled his family's fortunes as well as the country's politics from his headquarters in the Medici palace.

On that Monday morning, Lorenzo had to respond to the pressing requests for advice that had arrived from Milan with the four falcons. Lorenzo instructed the Florentine ambassadors to speak freely and convey "the content of the republic's letters as much as everything else to Cicco, with whose judgment one cannot go wrong." Lorenzo was establishing a confidential channel of communication with the chancellor, excluding not only the Florentine Signoria (the elected republican government), but also other parties like the Sforza brothers in Milan. Under the young Medici, more than ever before, the supposed republic of Florence had turned into an effective oligarchy, one that the Milanese regency now very much resembled.

Cicco had first met Lorenzo in the spring of 1465, when the then sixteen-year-old Medici heir, on an official visit to Milan, had come to pay homage to Francesco's daughter Ippolita Sforza. She was on her way to Naples to be betrothed to King Ferrante's son, Alfonso of Aragon. Lorenzo had stayed a few days in Milan and then visited the famous Visconti-Sforza library in nearby Pavia, which was under Cicco's personal supervision. The learned chancellor certainly took pride in showing the young, promising humanist and future head of state the most precious item in the collection, the illuminated and annotated copy of Virgil's works that had been owned by the great Italian poet Petrarch. After leaving Lombardy, Lorenzo requested a magnificent painted armor with the Sforza arms and devices and vowed an enduring loyalty to the dukes of Milan: "As long as I live and whatever becomes of me, I will not carry your emblems on my shoulders, but I will sculpt them in my heart."

Since the time of this emphatic declaration, throughout some of the happiest and the darkest moments of Italian history, Milan and Florence—the Sforza and the Medici families—had retained the closest ties. Now that Galeazzo was gone, Lorenzo knew it was better for him to deal with the old chancellor than with the restless brothers. After expressing his amazement at Cicco's ability to escape "clean" from the attempted coup, Lorenzo also touched on one of the most delicate diplomatic subjects at hand, Federico da Montefeltro's *condotta,* or hiring contract. In the last few years, the once friendly relationship between Medici and Montefeltro had become increasingly tense. Lorenzo, in fact, had refused to pay Federico some of his back wages as a Florentine commander, forcing the proud *condottiere* to beg for what was owed to him: "This is a very little thing, very easy for Your Magnificence . . . it is only reasonable and fair for my own honor!" It was not the first time that Federico had been at odds with Lorenzo. Just a few years before, the famous mercenary had politely refused a Florentine business proposal, on the grounds that he was already employed by the pope and by the King of Naples, two very strong and tight allies.

As soon as the news of Galeazzo's death reached Rome, Pope Sixtus IV is reported to have declared: "Today, peace in Italy is dead." Rather than prophesying, however, it seems the pope was promising trouble. For, in the midst of these secular struggles, the papacy played a crucial role. Ironically, the Signoria of Florence had written to Sixtus that the pope could provide the only real foundation for Italian peace. The Florentine Republic, at Lorenzo's prompting, had sent concerned messages to the four "falcons"—the pope, the King of Naples, the Doge of Venice, and Federico, Duke of Urbino: "We urge you to do all you can, and what you can do is much, to favor peace in Italy."

This flattering language was not enough to quiet the ambitious potentates, or even to win over the experienced *condottiere.* Federico replied that, after the "untimely and most atrocious" death of Galeazzo, he would do his best to contribute to preserving the Italian peace that Galeazzo's presence had guaranteed, but he did not commit himself to doing anything specific. He did believe, though, that the job of peacemaker might be the most rewarding of all. According to Giovanni Santi—author of *The Deeds of Federico da Montefeltro, Duke of Urbino,* a celebratory biography in verse composed in the late 1480s—Federico was sorry about Duke Galeazzo's "cruel death" because the assassination had killed his *pensiero bello,* that is, his beautiful vision for a general truce. Federico claimed he had deflected the ongoing hatred between

Milan and Naples. As a result, the other major powers, including Venice and Rome, along with the Florentines, were deterred from waging wars and ready to make a lasting peace.

The assassination of Galeazzo created a momentous imbalance that urgently needed to be addressed. This is why the question of who would be the guardian of young Gian Galeazzo Sforza was a matter of acute concern outside Milan. Cicco wanted Federico to come to Milan and help him secure the ducal power. But Lorenzo had a slightly different agenda. On February 1, he had informed the Medici agent in Rome: "I will write to Nomio" (as Federico was confidentially nicknamed, for his ambition to govern and regulate—*nomos* is the Greek word for law—all Italian business) "in my own hand that he should not go to Milan. I am surprised that the King of Naples would insist on it, since in my opinion this is not a thing for him. I believe that the Pope agrees only because of Nomio's insistence, and that Nomio understands the situation much better than his patron." In other words, Lorenzo, unlike Cicco, did not want Federico to become the military and political guarantor of stability on the Milanese scene, because the Duke of Urbino would have replaced the Medici influence there.

Thus Lorenzo prevented Federico from going to Milan. Things might have turned out very differently if he had not. Instead, he put forth Federico's competitor, the old and less ambitious Ludovico Gonzaga, Marquis of Mantua. It was under Gonzaga's scrutiny that finally, on February 24, detailed agreements were sealed in the Sforza castle between Duchess Bona and Galeazzo's brothers. In exchange for their obedience, Bona granted them an annual stipend of twelve thousand ducats each—a generous sum on which to live in a style befitting the sons of dukes—the command of one hundred elite troops, and the keys to one minor fortress. But despite these formal concessions, the control of government in the duchess's name stayed firmly in Cicco's hands. Roberto da Sanseverino acted as a witness in the sealing of the agreements, probably repressing his desire to jump at the chancellor's throat in the process.

o   o   ◯   o   o

LORENZO GUESSED CORRECTLY both that Roberto was up to something since his powerful cousin the duke had died, and that Galeazzo's brothers were eager to fill the vacant position at the top. Lorenzo, as it happens, was a good friend of Roberto's. The Florentine leader admired the mercenary captain's courage, but he was also very critical of his impulsive and reckless nature. He thought he should keep an eye on Roberto and make sure that he would not do anything too rash against Cicco's regency. He knew one man who would be particularly well suited to the task: an old acquaintance of his, the poet Luigi Pulci.

Pulci is known for his mock-heroic poem *Morgante,* a fantastic and humorous epic that inspired Rabelais and Cervantes. Something of a ne'er-do-well, Pulci had been a friend of Lorenzo's when the latter was still a child prodigy. They wrote satirical poetry in imitation of each other, and Pulci sent wildly funny letters to his younger but wiser friend. Later summoned to run the state, Lorenzo began to distance himself from the companion of his youth. Unwilling to go so far as to actually hire such a feckless character as Pulci, Lorenzo nonetheless introduced him to the bombastic Roberto in the early 1470s. Pulci immediately took a liking to Roberto: in many ways the soldier resembled the Christian knights whose adventures he would so irreverently recount in his *Morgante.*

The poet's affection was to be amply repaid: Pulci claimed to have "much familiarity with Roberto" and to "have found him very grateful and humane with everyone and especially with those who loved him." Implicitly, he was lamenting that Lorenzo was not as generous a patron. Pulci had accompanied Sanseverino to his native Milan in September of 1473, a journey that he recorded in two satirical sonnets parodying the dialect of the northerners. But his services as a diplomat were clearly less appreciated than his verse. In 1476 Pulci was described by a Florentine ambassador as a most bizarre envoy: "Despite the fact that he is an insipid sauce with little meat whose flavor is quickly grasped, he seems to understand and know a lot: he comes from a race of bloodsuckers that latch on quickly." Pulci (which means "fleas" in Italian) would soon live up to the bloodsucking reputation implied by his name.

In early 1477, Pulci wrote to Lorenzo: "I heard about the duke's death. It pains me to think that it pains you . . . and if you need me to go to our lord Roberto for any reason, or indeed anywhere else, I am ready to ride. It seems useful to me that Roberto is there for several reasons. I am grateful, especially under the circumstances, that he is now completely devoted to you and your interests, and only you may reach out to him [i.e., through me] as you please, here or there, however you want." Pulci had the ear of Sanseverino in a way that no one else did.

In mid-February 1477 dilettante spy Pulci therefore left for Milan, where he himself was spied on by the professional government officials. In fact, when he tried to send confidential messages to Lorenzo in March, his letters were intercepted by the Florentine ambassador there, at the request of the all-controlling Cicco Simonetta. Cicco did not approve of "the hellish picture" that Pulci painted in witty words. Both Lorenzo and Cicco agreed that Florence must contribute to Roberto's new *condotta*, though they would not meet his demand that his salary be as high as Federico's. The competition between the two mercenaries for money and fame would eventually turn ruthless and deadly.

"FORTUNE IS ALWAYS LURKING"

WHILE THE DIPLOMATIC DEBATE WAS STILL UNFOLDING, A FURther crisis arose in the duchy. The uncertainty over the succession in Milan had left the door open for a sudden uprising in Genoa. Once a powerful maritime republic, over the last decades Genoa had succumbed to the greater military might of Milan. As soon as the Milanese grip on the city appeared to be loosening, Genoese factions rose up and declared themselves independent from the Sforza. Galeazzo's brothers and Roberto da Sanseverino could not imagine a better opportunity for a display of youthful energy and ambition. In late March 1477 they launched a punitive expedition—and in this venture they had Cicco's full administrative support. The Milanese army marched to Genoa and put down the uprising. By mid-April, Federico da Montefeltro had already sent a congratulatory letter to the duchess for having crushed the state's enemies and restored peace.

Emboldened by their easy victory, the Sforza brothers and Roberto began making plans for a military coup against Cicco. But the seasoned chancellor was fully alert to this possibility. Cicco followed every step made by the plotters and their acolytes. He targeted one captain, Donato del Conte, who had loyally served under the Sforzas for many years and was a longtime friend of Roberto's. In one swift, falcon-like move, Cicco jailed Donato, who knew every detail of the ongoing plot. With the assistance of some "rope"—the name given to the most popular and painful method of Renaissance torture, involving the twisting of the victim's shoulders under his own weight while he hangs from a rope—Donato readily revealed the plan. According to his confession, when Sforza Maria, Ludovico, and their younger brothers Ascanio and Ottaviano had promised to renew their agreements with the duchess in mid-May, they were really just trying to buy some time. In fact, they had planned to kill Cicco and seize the Sforza castle while Roberto rabble-roused in the streets.

On the night of May 25, 1477, news of Donato's detention reached his coconspirators while they were all dining together. Nobody touched the food as silence filled the room. The shrewd Cicco had struck them before they could strike him. The next morning they appeared before the duchess, requesting that Donato be released immediately. They apologized for having shown up armed in her presence, against their signed agreements. Cicco himself was nowhere to be seen, as he was busy organizing a full counterattack. To prevent a coup, he simply arranged for the ducal guards to parade en masse around the Sforza castle and the city of Milan.

Roberto was forced to flee at once. On May 28, on his way to Piedmont, he wrote a characteristically unapologetic letter: "I was bored with the Council's meetings in the castle; my job is to serve in armor, and I am much happier with my soldiers." Roberto's claim of separating his military and political duties came a bit late. Despite his defeat, he swore to himself he would get revenge on Cicco. On the next day, Lorenzo warned Roberto directly not to try "some stratagem that goes against any good." On June 5, Lorenzo explained to the Florentine envoy in Milan, who was close to Cicco's ear, that the incarceration of the "rebel" would not have been wise, as it would have pushed his violent temper to despair. The letter to the envoy is the purest expression of the Medici modus operandi: on the one hand, he scolded Roberto for his reckless behavior; on the other, he tried to send a message to the all-powerful Cicco that "human things are subject to change and everything is ruled by fortune." Pulci, back in Florence since April, must have smiled at Lorenzo's echoing of *Morgante*'s cautionary verse:

Ma la fortuna attenta sta nascosa
per guastare sempre ciascun nostro effetto.

But fortune is always lurking
waiting to ruin our every scheme.

The duchess pardoned the brothers but exiled them to three distant locations: Sforza Maria to Bari, Ludovico to Pisa, and Ascanio to Perugia. Ottaviano, the youngest, feared the punishment so much that he fled in the direction of Venice and drowned trying to cross a river at night. Upon receiving the news about the events in Milan, Federico da Montefeltro wrote: "I am sorry for anyone's misfortune and especially for Ottaviano's death: he was so young that if he had become obedient he could have made a good *signore* out of himself. I believe that from the disorder of others will ensue a perpetual stability of the state." He went on to compliment Cicco for having been so prudent and clairvoyant.

Fortune seemed to be on Cicco's side at that point. The external and internal rebellions had been repressed and there was a moment of stability for the regency. On June 30, according to the Florentine ambassador in Milan, there were a "select few who govern and they suffer from the envy of many, but conditions are more stable every day and will continue to become more so, and day by day, the government will continue to gain in strength." For his part, Lorenzo was satisfied with the new stability and looked forward to maintaining the alliance between Florence and Milan, the centerpiece of the Italian "balance of power." He did not know that someone was secretly plotting to destroy this precarious balance.

3

NOTHING UNSAID

GUBBIO IS A BEAUTIFUL MEDIEVAL TOWN, STRATE-
GICALLY LOCATED ON THE SLOPE OF A STEEP
HILL, ABOUT FIFTY MILES SOUTH OF URBINO,
THEN THE CAPITAL OF THE MONTEFELTRO TERRITORY.
Federico da Montefeltro was born in Gubbio in 1422, a bastard son of
the local lord, Guidantonio. Federico's son Guidobaldo was also born
here in January 1472, when his father had just turned fifty. Before then,
Federico's wife, Battista Sforza (distantly related to the Sforza of Milan),
had given birth to four daughters, who—because of their sex—were in-
eligible as heirs. Six months after delivering the eagerly expected male
heir, upon her husband's return from the war against Volterra, Battista
suddenly died (probably weakened by too many pregnancies), leaving
Federico a widower and Guidobaldo an orphan.

In their native town, Federico built a stunning ducal palace in which
he commissioned a *studiolo* (its gorgeous inlaid wood panels are now preserved in the Metropolitan Museum of Art in New York). The Gubbio
studiolo mirrored Federico's refined taste in art and culture. As a
teenager, Federico went to one of the best schools, the Cà Zoiosa, or
Joyous House, an elite institution just outside Mantua. (Other students
included Ludovico Gonzaga, Marquis of Mantua, and Mantuan ambassador Zaccaria Saggi.) Classical authors from Greek and Latin antiquity
were taught by the famous humanist Vittorino da Feltre. There was also
serious martial and athletic training. It is no surprise that Federico took
seriously the education of his son, who embodied the living hope of sur-

vival for his long-term plans. He hired the best teachers and bought the best books. And in the Gubbio *studiolo* Guidobaldo's name was to be inscribed next to an open page of Virgil's *Aeneid*:

> *Every man's last day is fixed.*
> *Lifetimes are brief and not to be regained,*
> *For all mankind. But by their deeds to make*
> *Their fame last: that is labor for the brave.*

"DANGEROUS DANGERS"

ON JULY 2, 1477, IT MUST HAVE BEEN HOT IN THE GUBBIO *studiolo*; only the slight summer breeze coming through the window would have made the inside temperature more bearable. Here Federico da Montefeltro could gaze upon the surrounding walls' trompe-l'oeil images, in the most elaborate inlaid wood, of objects that looked so real one could have reached out and touched them: shelves, books on lecterns, musical and scientific instruments, weapons and pieces of armor, all arranged in a disorderly fashion. These were the objects that befitted the humanist soldier Federico when he needed solitude or contemplation.

The gold lettering (possibly dictated in Latin by Federico himself) that ran along the top of the *studiolo*'s paneling read as follows:

> *You see how the eternal students of the Venerable Mother*
> *Men exalted in learning and in genius*
> *Fall forward in supplication with bared head and bended knee*

Paintings representing the seven liberal arts encircled the upper walls in an encyclopedic homage to the duke's erudition. Each of the arts, em-

The original panels of the *Gubbio* studiolo *are now preserved at*
the Metropolitan Museum of Art in New York.

X OMNIBVS AI
XANDRI RER\
scriptoribus quæ pthol
us Lagi et Aristobolus A
boli de rege ipso consent
memorie prodiderunt u
te uerissima Litteris mai
ui · In quibus uero eos
screpare animaduerti e
delegi quæ probabilio

Portraits of Ferrante of Aragon (left) and of Federico da Montefeltro (right), decorating the top border of a manuscript about the life of Alexander the Great.

bodied by an allegorical female figure, handed her precious gifts to a powerful, bareheaded male figure. From the corner of his left eye, Federico could catch a glimpse of his own portrait, in which he was shown kneeling, his red-felt hat resting on the elegantly carpeted steps. Just above him in the picture, a shield with the Montefeltro coat of arms held by the imperious Montefeltro eagle surmounted a metal sconce. To the right of the figure, a painted window frame opened onto a room with an open door, the traditional symbol of the gateway to knowledge.

Federico is seen being offered a thick volume by a woman, the allegorical figure of Dialectic, one of the liberal arts. Dialectic, or logic, is the queen of the *trivium*, which lays the foundation of language and thought, along with grammar and rhetoric, the two sister liberal arts as codified in antiquity. The book Federico receives has a golden clasp and is decorated with an image of the nude Hercules. The depiction emphasizes the strength of his logical reasoning, the stringency of his mental acuity as much as of his military action.

That morning, preparing for dictation, Federico undoubtedly summoned his secretary, who would have bowed respectfully and taken a seat at a little desk next to him. The duke's letter to Cicco Simonetta, his old friend and now the all-powerful regent of the Milanese duchy, begins this way:

> *Through letters sent from Milan I have been informed how trustingly and lovingly Magnificent Messer Cicco and his son Messer Gian Giacomo have conveyed the news of the events occurring up north, and most importantly all the reasons why they do not want to come to any agreement or intelligence with His Majesty the King of Naples. I am pleased and satisfied that Their Magnificences behave towards me with the faith and sincerity that I deserve for my* devotion *and fidelity to Duchess Bona and Duke Gian Galeazzo and the* affection *I have for Their Magnificences, whom I confess to revere as much as I am obliged to the welfare and honor of His Majesty the King of Naples. However, if I thought I was speaking against conscience and truth and the need of the Milanese state or Their welfare, I would rather be silent and would not talk at such length as I have, without any regard to my special interest. Nevertheless, I am only judging what is good and honorable for both parties, and mostly for the one that is* in the most dire need . . .

Since January 1477 Cicco and Federico had been corresponding in cipher. The Milanese chancellor had first called Federico to Milan to help him stabilize the duchy. Federico had responded enthusiastically, but Lorenzo's intervention had prevented him from coming. Now that Cicco Simonetta (addressed as "Magnificent," as was customary in Renaissance diplomatic jargon) had assumed the role of guardian to the fatherless Gian Galeazzo, the Milanese state was indeed "in the most dire need" of external support, as Federico pointed out in his letter.

By now, halfway into 1477 and six months after the Duke of Milan's assassination, Italian politics were at a delicate juncture. With the general league, or alliance, among Venice, Milan, and Florence becoming weaker in the face of the united front formed by the King of Naples and Pope Sixtus IV, the Duke of Urbino, serving as a mercenary captain to both of the latter powers, wished to be at the center of any decisive intelligence in Italy. If only he could persuade the Milanese regent to switch sides, the ensuing isolation of Florence would allow him and his patrons to put enormous pressure on the Medici brothers, Lorenzo and Giuliano. They would be able to kick those two rich and influential youngsters out of Florence—violently or otherwise—and replace them with a more complacent set of rulers. The Duke of Urbino was laying the groundwork for what would become the Pazzi conspiracy, well ahead of its actual execution.

Perhaps Federico took a deep breath and paused before resuming his dictation. He may have looked at the painted panel on his left: it depicted an older woman holding an armillary sphere, which she was handing to a middle-aged man kneeling before her. His jeweled crown shone on the steps. The man thus represented here as Ptolemy was Federico's close ally and protector Ferrante of Aragon, King of Naples, who was known to have a great passion for astronomy, which in this era was almost identical to astrology. The Ptolemaic king embodied the higher powers, the heavenly realm above Italy. But on the panel, he was placed next to the matching portrait of the Herculean captain Federico, who partook of the earthly realm.

Astrology and politics were closely linked during the Renaissance. Even the fate of these proud self-made men was seen as being tied to the inescapable influence of the stars. An emerging sense of the significance of the individual did not prevent the most learned and active figures of the fifteenth century from relying on astrology or holding superstitious beliefs. Federico's attribution of the heavenly realm to the King of Naples was both a philosophical and a political statement.

Nonetheless, mythologizing was only one aspect of Renaissance politics. Federico had gained a lot of power over many years of relentless soldiering. He was the only hired captain of his generation who was truly successful. With Francesco Sforza, another *condottiere* who had managed to become head of a major state, he shared an early understanding of the centrality of propaganda in wars. Reporting a victory was always more important than winning an actual battle or than killing a large number of enemy soldiers and suffering fewer casualties. Discrediting the honor or reputation of the competitor, the general of the opposing army, was at least as important as actual deeds of heroism on the battlefield. Machiavelli later defined the virtue of the *condottiere* as a deadly combination of force and fraud. He thus evoked Federico's ancestor Guido da Montefeltro; left to burn in Dante's Inferno, Guido says:

le mie opere
non furon leonine, ma di volpe

the deeds I did
Were not those of a lion, but of a fox

A land of many foxes and few lions, Italy was the theater of silent war and constant betrayal. Hence the importance of friendship, sincere or simulated. Federico remembered that during a visit to Milan, Duke Galeazzo Sforza—who did not get on particularly well with his father's friends—was so angry with him that he secretly had threatened to chop off his head. Fortunately for Federico, Cicco Simonetta had warned him in advance to flee.

The affection between Cicco and Federico evoked in the July 1477 letter had begun much earlier: the two had met during the hard-fought campaigns of the 1440s in the Montefeltro region. Cicco was then a young man from Calabria, serving the future Duke Francesco Sforza, himself only a freelance *condottiere* at that point. In 1444 Federico, at the age of twenty-two, became Count of Urbino overnight, immediately succeeding his stepbrother Oddantonio after the latter had been killed by disgruntled citizens. Rather conveniently, Federico had been waiting outside the city walls with his soldiers and later claimed he had had no knowledge of the plot, but he gladly accepted the title of count to rule the Urbinati.

Back then, Federico was the only loyal ally of Francesco Sforza. To celebrate the new dukedom acquired by Francesco in 1450, Federico arranged a joust that would demonstrate his "devotion" to the Sforza. But an accident happened: as a result of a mischievous move by his opponent, Federico lost his right eye. And so the lord of Urbino subsequently preferred to be portrayed in profile. Later, malicious rumors began to circulate according to which the duke also had his nose surgically carved after the accident to allow him to see an approaching killer from his blind side. At any rate, Federico took to wearing an eye patch.

Before his faithful scribe on that hot July day in 1477, however, Federico probably did not bother to cover up the long-scarred wound. The little hole of blackened skin would not have distracted the secretary when the duke, summoning his rigorous powers of concentration in the rising heat of the *studiolo,* resumed dictation of the letter to his old friend Cicco:

> *While all the reasons for which the dukes of Milan cannot make their foundations on the Signoria [government] of Venice are worth considering most prudently, and we might accept them as most true and without any contradiction, I cannot bring myself to like in the least the fact that the state of Milan is relying only on itself or on the alliance with Lorenzo, who is himself not secure, and is in fact extremely dangerous, as Messer Cicco knows better than me. He and his son Gian Giacomo cannot find any foundation in Lorenzo's friendship and benevolence, since it can be seen in the past and in the present that Lorenzo does not care at all for the peace and progress of the Milanese state.*

Dialectic is the art of refining the strength of an argument in a heated debate. Words can cut more than swords, even if they come from a professional soldier. Federico was attacking Lorenzo's lack of steadfastness subtly and incisively. But why was he so angry with the young Medici?

o   o   N   o   o

FEDERICO'S FRIENDSHIP with Lorenzo seems to have peaked in 1472 when the Florentines hired the mercenary to wage a punitive campaign against Volterra. This Tuscan hill town was rich in alum mines, a major source of income for a Florentine consortium backed by the Medici bank. When the Volterrans refused to share the alum profits with

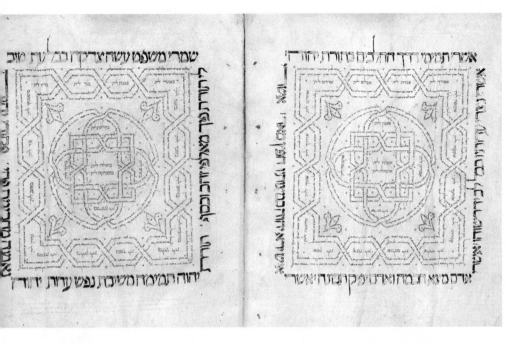

A Hebrew manuscript pillaged by Federico during his merciless sack of Volterra and added to his growing library.

Florence, Lorenzo had called Federico to wipe out the rebellion. Volterra is set in a nearly impregnable position, and the insurgents were holding out. After besieging and bombarding them for weeks, Federico finally obtained their unconditional surrender before unleashing his troops, who sacked the city, raped most of the women, and killed many of the men. One of the victims was a Jewish merchant named Menahem ben Aharon: his large collection of Hebrew manuscripts was seized by Federico, who proudly created a whole new section in his library.

Lorenzo ordered lavish celebrations in Florence to honor Federico's deed. The *condottiere* was welcomed triumphantly to the city in the manner of an ancient Roman hero; he received banners embroidered with his coat of arms, along with splendid textiles wrought with gold. He was granted Florentine citizenship and was promised a glorious silver-gilt helmet embellished with enamel and a figure of Hercules subduing a griffin, the symbol of Volterra.

Federico da Montefeltro holding a copy of Cristoforo Landino's Disputationes Camaldulenses, *from the Montefeltro Library.*

A few months later, along with the helmet, Federico received a highly precious, beautifully illuminated codex. The Florentine humanist Cristoforo Landino had dedicated to the prince of Urbino his *Disputationes Camaldulenses*. In the preface of this work, Federico was celebrated as the supreme champion of both the contemplative and the active life, the master of war who aimed for peace, the philosopher and commander who remained in spiritual touch with divine ideas and yet had a solid grip on reality.

Upon receiving the magnificent manuscript, Federico wrote a letter politely thanking both Landino and, in somewhat patronizing and condescending terms, Lorenzo, that most skilled "young man" whom he embraced "as a son with particular benevolence, and as a brother with honor." Lorenzo himself appeared as one of the speakers in Landino's dialogue championing action over contemplation and chose none other than Federico as a model. These are the laudatory words on statesmanship uttered by the fictional Florentine friend Lorenzo:

> *In our times we have Federico da Montefeltro, prince of Urbino, whom I doubtlessly consider worth comparing to the best captains of the ancient era. Many and most admirable are the virtues of such an excellent man: his penetrating wit is passionate about everything. He gives himself the leisure and the company of the most erudite and cultivated men, while reading many books, listening to many disputes, participating in many debates, as well as being a man of letters in his own right. However, if he had allowed his speculations to replace the vigilant hold on his state and the strong hand on his soldiers, he would have been reduced to nothing.*

Such a balancing act between contemplation and action was undoubtedly easier described than performed. Lorenzo—Landino implied—had yet to learn how to juggle between the two from his proclaimed master. Landino was resorting to a highly contrived rhetoric, rather than using dialectic, the subtle art of investigating and conveying the truth. This was quite typical of Florentine culture: instead of sticking to hard factual logic, Florentines tended to create a soft fictional

A Montefeltro family emblem with an ermine.

A Montefeltro family emblem with an ostrich.

grammar. In his proudly presented *Disputationes,* Landino avoided any reference to the sack of Volterra, for instance. More poignantly, he wrote a commentary on Canto XXVII of Dante's *Inferno* in which, when referring to Federico's ancestor Guido, he described a politician's *ingegno,* or wit, as the ability to be cunning and to discover covert ways to deceive without being caught. Covertness was precisely what one of the Montefeltro emblems represented: Federico had adopted from the House of Aragon the depiction of an ermine, with the motto NON MAI (never).

The ermine hides in dry, dark spots, and in order to find it, hunters surround its hideout with mud, since the furry animal does not ever want to dirty its gorgeous white fur. But prudence must be matched by toughness. Another emblem that had been in the Montefeltro family for a century showed an ostrich with an arrowhead in its beak; below, ran the ancient German motto HIC AN VORDAIT EN GROSSEN ISEN (I can swallow a big iron).

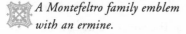

FEDERICO REMAINED FAITHFUL to these family mottoes as he wrote his letter to Cicco on July 2, 1477. Each smooth turn of phrase was an iron fist cloaked within a velvet glove. If Lorenzo really cared about Milan, Montefeltro argued in his highly factual, deceivingly precise prose, "he would not, from the beginning of Cicco's regency, have opposed twice with such passion my coming to Milan, since I [Duke of Urbino] would not have desired anything but the good and honor of the duchy." More to the point, Lorenzo "would not have kept up his contacts with the exiled Sforza brothers and Signor Roberto da Sanseverino, after having received information about their machinations" against Cicco, Duchess Bona, and the all-too-young Duke Gian Galeazzo.

Indeed Cicco had asked Federico to come to Milan twice before— first right after Galeazzo's assassination and again after Cicco had expelled the Sforza brothers and Roberto da Sanseverino for plotting against him and the dukes. Roberto was clearly a hothead, although at least he had inherited his uncle's Machiavellian virtue, or skill, as a *condottiere*. Thus, Federico wrote on: "in Florence they are trying to excuse Roberto while charging Cicco, showing with covert words that everything [the supposed Sforza plot revealed by Donato del Conte in May 1477] had sprung from Cicco and not from Roberto; they are also trying to contract the captain."

Lorenzo's leniency toward the rebel soldier Roberto was bad enough, implied Federico, but to actually maintain a friendship with the treacherous heirs of the murdered Galeazzo, as Lorenzo was doing, especially with Ludovico Sforza in Pisa, was even more damnable. The young Sforza brothers were weak and cowardly, and therefore very dangerous— as Cicco well knew. And so the old chancellor, fully in charge of the government, had to protect the young Duke Gian Galeazzo, the weak widow Duchess Bona, and himself from attack. Acutely aware of this, Federico continued to dictate:

> *Gian Giacomo says he wonders whether Lorenzo is sinning against the Holy Spirit. Well, I say he is, since he's desperate for the grace of God, having offended the King of Naples and me—just a poor private gentleman . . .*

The Montefeltro fox was packing several layered elements into this passage. Federico was the godfather of Cicco's firstborn son, Gian

Giacomo, and he had always been very protective of him. Hinting at Gian Giacomo's doubts with regard to Lorenzo's lacking "the grace of God" was a way for Federico to say something rather hostile while hiding behind his godchild's qualms. And with "sinning against the Holy Spirit" he was referring, metaphorically and not so subtly, to the tense relationship between the Medici and the pope, Sixtus IV. Furthermore, Federico's casting of himself as "a poor private gentleman" was also a message that Cicco could understand: Federico had been on bad terms with the "lowly merchant and citizen" Lorenzo for some time, and Cicco knew about it. The warnings that followed in the letter could hardly come as a surprise:

> *I cannot concur with the opinion of the Magnificent Messer Cicco according to which it is good to be so careful not to displease Lorenzo just to go after Lorenzo's dangerous dangers and passions . . . He could not hate Cicco more, as he has always hated him, at all times. And I do have true notice of it. And if it were otherwise, I would not speak like this. Although Lorenzo is, for no reason, so ill-disposed towards me, I would never put my special interest before the truthful and dutiful reason in such important matters, since I know all too well that in case I need any help, I can be helped by your State only if it stays strong, and that I would not be able to help the State, if it is not quiet and secure. This is so clear, that in my view it makes itself understood.*

This passage is replete with innuendos and reads almost like a tract on political behavior—Machiavelli *avant la lettre*. Federico touches here on a very delicate subject: the Simonettas, like the Sforzas, were upstarts in Milan and had gained all their power on the basis of their merits and abilities despite, rather than because of, their blood. By pointing out the Medici family's hatred, a word that meant something more like disdain, for the lowly Simonetta chancellor, the Duke of Urbino was forcing Cicco to reconsider his friendship and excessive kindness to Lorenzo merely as a hopeless attempt to become part of a class to which he did not belong.

Federico warned Cicco that "he better not want to follow Lorenzo into the abyss: he should rather be pulling him in his direction." The consequences of such a perilous choice were unspoken, but nonetheless clear. The Duke of Urbino outlined the "dangerous dangers" threatening the Duchy of Milan, and he emphasized them to scare Cicco. He then smoothly moved on to the strategic perspective of Naples. This was the most sensitive point in Federico's scheme against Lorenzo: he had to persuade Cicco to trust the King of Naples as much as Federico himself had trust in the seasoned chancellor. He introduced the topic in the most flattering language:

> *I want you to be sure that the King has always thought that in the Milanese state there could never have been a person more suited to the requirements of the task than his Magnificence, as the one who, with his long experience, prudence, and exceptional faith, has surpassed anybody else, and if there had not been one like him, we would have had to create one of wax!*

Francesco Sforza had once famously responded to an envious Milanese courtier who had suggested that Cicco's immense power be reduced, that Francesco as a duke could not do without his trusted chancellor, and that he would have to make a "clone" out of wax if he ever lost the original. Federico was familiar with this saying about Cicco, a proverb of sorts in Milan by then. By quoting it, Federico was at his most ingratiating, and therefore it was safe for him to move on to the next most delicate topic.

Federico informed Cicco that he was sending his trusted chancellor Piero Felici to the King of Naples "with such instructions that everything will be all right, avoiding any fabricated charge against Cicco or Gian Giacomo"—as if any charge should be made against them in the first place. In other words, if Cicco did not side with the king, he would find himself under attack. The affectionate assurances at the end of the long letter hardly made the overall message less threatening:

> *Cicco's and our common sons' interests are in my heart, especially that of my Gian Giacomo, no less than those of my own state and life.*

> —*Given in Gubbio, Second Day of July 1477, Federicus dux etc.*

Federico must have paused for a minute, while his secretary wiped small beads of sweat from his forehead. One can imagine that the secretary's hand was hurting from scribbling away. The duke might have looked at him with a hint of irony while the scribe was preparing to leave. Then Federico's face would have turned stony and serious again. He decided to add a short, unambiguous postscript:

P.S. The "general league" [of Milan, Florence and Venice] cannot succeed unless Lorenzo is made aware that he won't be allowed to govern the state of Florence, and that nobody will be above the King of Naples (the King will be under nobody's will).

Finally the secretary wrapped up the letter and was ready to go to his office to transcribe it into cipher. Federico instructed him to use as many varied and void characters as possible, so that the letter would be practically impossible to decipher if it should fall into enemy hands. The code would be more complex than the usual one between Federico and Cicco.

Cicco would certainly have appreciated the cipher. Indeed, if Montefeltro was credited with the composition of a little treatise on code-writing, *De furtivis litteris,* Cicco was the master in code-breaking and the inventor of the most complex ciphers to date. For the enemy to break an intercepted dispatch from Milan might take months, if not years. By the time the solution to the code was found, the information would be obsolete.

But the most important part of communication was still left to the old art of dialectic, to its subtle powers of persuasion. Federico had used his most convoluted prose to convey a very simple message: that Cicco better cut the old ties between Milan and Florence and side with Naples, if he wanted to survive. But the Duke of Urbino had been extremely careful not to mention the pope in his cunning letter. He counted on the fact that Cicco was well aware of Lorenzo's extremely tense relationship with Rome. There was no need to speak about it openly, or even in code.

4

THE INVISIBLE
HANDS

ROME IN THE LATE FIFTEENTH CENTURY WAS NOT YET THE GRAND CAPITAL FILLED WITH THE GREAT CATHOLIC MONUMENTS THAT ONE ADMIRES TODAY. The ancient ruins were covered with dirt and grass; sheep and goats strolled undisturbed among them. The city was inhabited by hordes of parasites and whores who lived at the expense of the corrupt papal court. It had been no better in the fourteenth century, when Peter's heirs were exiled to Avignon: then foxes, wolves, and beggars had roamed the streets. The popes were able to govern Rome only when they made deals with the local barons, such as the Colonna and the Orsini families. The Roman populace had in fact welcomed the new pope, Sixtus IV, on the day of his election by stoning him. Reportedly, the papal miter had fallen from his head, a very bad omen. However, in a few months he had learned the ways of Rome and got a solid grip on the city.

Under Sixtus IV, Rome underwent many architectural renovations. It once again became habitable, and the pope did much to improve the sanitary conditions of the city. He brought down water from the Quirinal Hill to the Trevi Fountain. The Sistine bridge connecting the city center to Trastevere was built in 1475, the same year in which the Vatican Library was inaugurated. And the Sistine Chapel was created and painted between 1477 and 1482. Michelangelo, then only a Florentine boy learning the rudiments of sculpture, had not yet set foot in Rome. The early Christian basilica was yet to be replaced with the grandiose St. Peter's

Basilica. The first stone of the new cathedral would not be laid for another thirty years by Sixtus IV's nephew Pope Julius II. At the Vatican, family ties were extremely helpful.

A FAMILY PORTRAIT

LORENZO DE' MEDICI'S AGENT IN ROME, BACCIO UGOLINI, had written after the murder of Galeazzo Sforza that "all the people who understand something about state matters think that Italy will be at peace." Lorenzo replied cuttingly to this optimistic assessment, adding that corruption in the Roman curia was so rampant that nobody could be trusted there: "if it wouldn't create a scandal, we would rather have three or four popes!" This rather heretical thought was rooted in a recent history of mistrust between the Church and the Medici family, which was feeding into the sourest of political feelings.

In hindsight, the relationship between Lorenzo and Pope Sixtus IV had begun in the most promising way. In August 1471 Francesco della Rovere, general of the Franciscan Order, ascended to St. Peter's throne choosing the name of Sixtus, the first Church reformer. The Florentines sent a congratulatory delegation headed by the twenty-two-year-old Lorenzo, who returned home bearing expensive antique objects purchased from the papal treasure. The banking heir and the new pontiff got along very well. Lorenzo understood that the pope, despite having come from the ranks of the Order of Poverty and Humility, was very greedy and ambitious, and herein lay potential conflict. The pope's close family members suddenly found a very convenient vocation for the ecclesiastical career. His nephews, in fact, formed a small army of young, go-getting relatives, all eager to jump at anybody's (and at one another's) throat to grab as much money and power as they could. It is no coincidence that the word *nepotism* (from the Italian *nipote,* nephew) was coined around this time.

The picture that best captures life at the court of Sixtus IV was painted by the great Melozzo da Forlì around 1475. It portrays the pontiff, sitting at the right, surrounded by four of his nephews and by the kneeling figure of humanist Bartolomeo Platina, the newly appointed Vatican librarian. They are all framed within a perspective of sumptuous marble columns and a decorated ceiling, with a black pillar in the middle.

Sixtus IV is shown in profile, enthroned like a Roman emperor. He enjoys his superb position of power and exhibits his supreme patronage of art and culture, which made him a direct competitor of Lorenzo de' Medici. The theological godfather thrived in protecting his close family members. Towering in front of the pope, in a red robe, is Cardinal Giuliano della Rovere, tall and strong. Another nephew, probably cardinal-to-be Raffaele Riario, is lurking behind his powerful uncle. Behind Platina's shoulders are Girolamo Riario, Count of Imola, and Giovanni della Rovere, Prefect of the City of Rome. The two nephews on the right half of the painting were clergymen, while the ones on the left were given secular jobs.

Two figures dominate the scene: Cardinal Giuliano and Count Girolamo. They are facing opposite directions, and indeed, in life they competed to lord over the pope's divided soul. While the cardinal is reverently watching Sixtus, the count is staring intensely at a blank point outside the boundaries of the painting. He is dressed in an elegant blue robe and wears a thick gold chain, hiding his hands inside the large sleeves.

At first, Sixtus had favored neither of them, preferring instead Pietro Riario, Girolamo's brother. Pietro, shortly after his elevation, became the most decadent cardinal of the time and was secretly nicknamed after the infamous Roman emperor Caligula by courtiers wary of his majestic manners and expensive tastes. He was rumored to furnish his guest rooms with golden chamber pots and to cover the fingers of his many mistresses, who danced naked for him, with diamond rings. The only people Pietro cared about were his loving uncle and his younger brother.

Melozzo da Forlì, Sixtus IV with his nephews and Vatican librarian Bartolomeo Platina, *1475.*

When in August 1472 Girolamo returned from his first official visit to Florence, Pietro thanked Lorenzo and Giuliano for their "incredible goodness and true love," which he claimed "would never fall out of his mind and heart." But Pietro's heart and mind collapsed under the excesses of a wildly sinful, unregulated life. As poet Santi put it, after describing the lavish visit he paid to Federico:

> *The locust well might typify his life:*
> *In youth a friar, but no longer bent*
> *On things of such high import, now he deemed*
> *Himself all but supreme. Yet of his deeds*
> *No record lives in prose or lofty song . . .*
> *Just as a locust by the sun struck down,*
> *So perished in their prime his fancies vain,*
> *Despite the projects hatched beneath the shade*
> *Of his red hat . . .*

Pietro's no less ambitious but much more aggressive younger brother took over his role as the pope's favorite nephew. In 1473 Girolamo acquired the title of Count of Imola, a small city in Romagna southeast of Bologna. In order to achieve this, however, the papacy had to purchase Imola from the Duke of Milan, Galeazzo Sforza. Lorenzo, worried by the papal aspiration to extend control over central Italy, had denied the loan Girolamo required for the purchase. But this had not stopped the pope, who had managed to obtain most of the funds he needed from the Medicis' rival banking family in Florence, the Pazzi. Federico da Montefeltro, for his part, eagerly promised the final five thousand ducats needed, to make sure he would be on the good side of the deal. As a result, Girolamo's "invisible hands" grabbed the city of Imola. He also married Caterina Sforza, Galeazzo's legitimized daughter, to strengthen his ties with the duke. Cicco Simonetta presided over the ceremony in Milan, hoping that this marriage between the Sforza and the papal heir would bring some peace to Italy.

It was wishful thinking. The Church had always been riven with conflicts. With the election of Sixtus IV to the papacy, the turmoil that had beset the papal state during the last decades was growing. The ambitions of the pope and of his aggressive family infuriated local potentates. The Church was unpopular with the people, too: the inhabitants of the cities and villages under the Church's control in central Italy feared that they would be squeezed by new taxes. Some of the more ruthless warlords exploited these worries in order to claim freedom and independence from the Church.

In 1474, Città di Castello, a prosperous Umbrian town, was one of the first to rebel against ecclesiastical rule. This time Sixtus sent Giuliano della Rovere to punish the insurgents. Although energetic and courageous (he would become known as the Warrior Pope, Julius II, by the end of his life), the cardinal did not have much experience in besieging a city. For months he camped outside the city walls, as the fortified *città* seemed to be endlessly supplied with ammunition and food. As it turned out, the leader of the antipapal rebellion was secretly being helped by Lorenzo, ever more wary of Sixtus's intentions to occupy land bordering Tuscany. While Lorenzo perceived the pope's initiative as an aggressive interference in the control of central Italy, the pope regarded Lorenzo's actions as an offensive betrayal. Both felt wronged and their alliance was over.

THE HOLY SWORD

WHO WAS CALLED TO SORT OUT THIS MILITARY MESS? Sure enough, the best soldier in Italy, Federico da Montefeltro, Count of Urbino. At the end of July 1474, while in Naples—where he had received the prestigious Collar of the Ermine from King Ferrante as a sign of favor—Federico wrote to Lorenzo that if he wanted to be as pure and innocent as the "candle of the Virgin Mary," he had better be sincere and find a settlement about Città di Castello, in the name of their friendship and brotherhood. This had been perhaps their last moment of confidence before the upcoming struggles. Federico was still awaiting his late payments from Florence. He had been preparing for some time to leave Lorenzo to his fate of unholy enemy of the Church. The Florentine leader would have to light many candles to the Virgin Mary in the next few years.

Federico signed his letter to Lorenzo as Count of Urbino. But already on August 13, according to a Mantuan ambassador in Rome, he was "awaited like a Messiah." On August 21, 1474, exactly thirty years after he had become lord of Urbino, Federico was elevated to the title of duke by the pope. That was a truly glorious day for Federico, a lifetime's achievement. The ancient St. Peter's Basilica was adorned in imperial style, with triumphal festoons and burning incense. A huge crowd cheered Federico, and a large retinue of Roman barons, ambassadors, and dignitaries welcomed him at court. After entering the cathedral, the Count of Urbino was brought into the pope's chambers, and surrounded by the College of Cardinals. Sixtus laid the ducal sword on Federico's shoulders and handed it to him while solemnly stating that he should wield it to fight and crush the Church's enemies. The "secular nephews," Girolamo Riario and Giovanni della Rovere, put golden spurs on his feet. Federico grabbed the sword and, extending his arm forward, brandished it three times with great swiftness. Girolamo took back the sword, while Giovanni untied the spurs. Then they gave him a ducal robe of golden brocade and a ducal cap. The pope blessed the kneeling duke. Federico swore eternal loyalty to the Church and finally stood up and kissed the pope's hands. Sixtus embraced him tenderly, and the new duke was then allowed to sit among the cardinals.

This elaborate ceremony was heavily symbolic, evoking the power of the Church to bestow the weapon of righteousness into the ruthless hands of secular power. The air reverberated eloquently with the clang of trumpets, the drone of bagpipes, and the crash of artillery from Castel St. Angelo, Emperor Hadrian's mausoleum, which had been turned into a papal fortress and prison. But an accident occurred that spoiled the perfect day. As Federico's retinue crossed the bridge in front of the castle, a sudden gust of wind broke the two staffs holding up the ducal standards, which plummeted to the ground. This was interpreted as a bad omen, just as had been the papal miter falling from Sixtus's head on the day of his own election. The next day, however, Giovanni della Rovere's engagement to Giovanna da Montefeltro, one of Federico's legitimate daughters, was formalized. Blood sealed what God had determined. On August 31, Federico marched to Città di Castello, where Giuliano della Rovere was still struggling to kick out the rebels. By appearing with his fearsome troops and field guns, the duke provoked the immediate surrender of the city. It is likely that the still fresh memory of the gruesome sack of Volterra persuaded the inhabitants to submit.

But the situation in Città di Castello was very different. In Volterra Federico had fought on Lorenzo's side and with the pope's approval. Now that Sixtus was on bad terms with Lorenzo, the duke just "christened" by the pope perceived Lorenzo as a potential enemy he should destroy with his Holy Sword. Lorenzo, for his part, was said to be nurturing a "deadly hatred" for Federico, noticeable through his resentful silence after the ducal promotion, widely considered illegitimate in Florence, and after the shameful demise of Città di Castello. Blowing on the burning coals, Federico sent to Florence Piero Felici, one of his most reliable ambassadors, who had been his envoy to Florence for many years. Sharp-tongued Florentines had nicknamed him after his feline insincerity, coining a saying about the "she-cat who licks you in front, and claws you from behind."

This renowned agent provocateur, "young in age but old in wits," asked Lorenzo for a contribution to his duke's recent campaigns. It was an astute, shameless insolence. Even Giuliano de' Medici, usually the quiet brother, confided cockily to the Milanese ambassador that the "Count of Urbino" would be repaid in kind. The Florentine Republic firmly refused to make any payment, and Federico promptly recalled his sly diplomat before he could be expelled. Another saying about Federico himself started circulating in the streets of Florence: "Too much humility is really great haughtiness." Rage and fear among the populace ensued: what if the man who had defended them so effectively in the past now turned against them and attacked?

The Felici incident happened in October 1474. Federico was then back in Rome, pampered by the pope and the cardinals. He was seen rid-

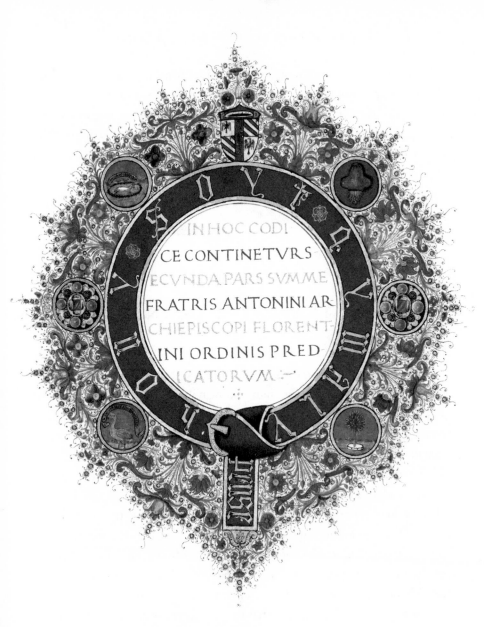

The Order of the Garter.

ing in the streets wearing the incredibly elegant outfit with the Collar of the Ermine. Later the same month, in Urbino, Federico solemnly received from Edward IV, King of England, the chivalric Order of the Garter. This exclusive order's motto, HONY SOYT QUY MAL Y PENSE

(Shame on him who thinks maliciously), ironically fit his situation. While being honored by one of the highest powers in Europe, he was being slighted by a city of lowly merchants. It should have come as a warning sign that on December 30, 1474, when Lorenzo asked Federico if he could borrow a horse for Florence's joust, the Duke of Urbino replied that he had already lent it to a member of the Pazzi family.

THE PAZZI CLAN

THE PAZZI FAMILY OWNED A BANK IN FLORENCE AND WERE perhaps even more affluent than the heavily indebted Medici. In the 1470s, the family leader was Jacopo Pazzi, famous for his gambling talents no less than for his money-making ability. His nephew Francesco, "small in body but great in spirit," ran the Roman branch of the bank. They were both extremely ambitious and wanted to replace the Medici as city leaders and as papal bankers.

One man represented the perfect link between all of the Medici enemies. This was Francesco Salviati, related by blood to the Pazzi and by politics to the Riario, the nephews of the pontiff. Salviati came from one of the noblest Florentine families (theirs was older money than that of the Medici). After wasting his patrimony in disastrous investments and dubious activities, he had resorted to a clergyman's career to pay off his debts. In 1471 he was among the first to latch himself onto the family of the new pope, Sixtus IV. He quickly became part of Cardinal Pietro Riario's entourage of debauched courtiers, and he was the one who had personally brought to Milan the money lent by the Pazzi to Girolamo Riario for the key purchase of Imola in 1473. In exchange for his services, in October 1474 Salviati was elected archbishop of Pisa. But the pope made this appointment without Florentine approval, which it was customary to obtain. Sixtus had done this deliberately to embarrass Lorenzo, the putative leader of the Republic. If the all-powerful Medici accepted the appointment of Salviati, he would look weak. If he rejected it, he would appear arrogant. Since in politics there is nothing worse than looking weak, Lorenzo chose the latter course, after close consultation with his allies in Milan.

After some frantic diplomatic exchanges in early 1475, Lorenzo sent on a mission to Rome his faithful agent and friend Franceschino Nori along with his brother Giuliano, who needed to be taught the rudiments of Roman politics. Nori reported to Lorenzo that Count Riario could be bought with money and friends, if only Jacopo Pazzi (whose name was encoded in Nori's letter) "would mind his own business—which was very unlikely." By this he meant that the rival Pazzi bank was going to fill the pockets of the pope's nephew with money, in effect making the Medici bank appear useless. Nori and Riario managed to reach a truce about the archbishopric of Pisa, but the threats kept coming at Lorenzo, from inside and outside Florence.

In February 1475, Cicco had issued an alarm, warning Lorenzo to watch out for his personal safety. The Milanese chancellor did so after receiving a confidential dispatch from the Sforza agent in Naples, according to whom Federico had complained about the tax exemption that the Medici bank had been unexpectedly awarded in the whole Kingdom of Naples. The dispatch reported that Federico was not praising the ever ambivalent king, but that he was "supremely sorry" for him, since he thought that his majesty "not only did not have to bow in front of a lowly merchant and citizen like Lorenzo de' Medici, who was the worst and most dangerous enemy he had there," but he "better kick him out of Florence or have him cut to pieces." Federico had added that this would be easy to do since Lorenzo was hated in Florence, considered a tyrant by the largest and best part of the citizens, who did not dare to speak out of fear. But with Lorenzo out of the picture—Federico continued—"they would join their hands to God thanking His Majesty for having liberated them from such a tyranny, and would make them eternally obliged and well-disposed to him."

When Cicco read these words, he suddenly realized that Federico was

serious in his menace. The Duke of Urbino had put his heavy-duty political clout at stake, in an effort to embarrass the "lowly merchant."

At the same time, Sixtus made a provocative double move: he suddenly replaced the Medici with the Pazzi as the official Church bank,
while requesting an official audit for the Medici branch in Rome. This
amounted to an open declaration of financial and political war. It was a
very big blow for Lorenzo, who complained in a letter to Galeazzo Sforza
dated September 7, 1475: "all my troubles derive from the same source,
these Pazzi relatives of mine [Lorenzo's sister had married Guglielmo
Pazzi], who are seeking to hurt me as much as they can, both through
their own ambition and with the support of the King of Naples and the
Duke of Urbino . . . I will make sure that they do not harm me and I
will keep my eyes wide open."

In the end, Lorenzo had to yield on the ecclesiastical front, and
Salviati became archbishop of Pisa in October 1475, a year after his uni-
lateral papal nomination. As he now earned four thousand ducats a year
from the richest church of Tuscany outside Florence, Salviati stopped
watching his tongue and played a nasty practical joke on Lorenzo. As
part of his personal dues to him, in June 1476 he sent along one hundred pounds of rotten fish, accompanied with a mocking note: "If the
fish is not worthy of you, nor of my desire and debt, I apologize to you,
since fishing is a game of Fortune, and She often does not satisfy our
great longings."

THE CONSPIRACY AND
THE CONFESSION

THE GAME OF FORTUNE THAT WAS PLAYED OUT ON DECEMBER
26, 1476, had removed Galeazzo Sforza from the Italian scene. The

bloody murder in Milan had set the stage for a new, even more daring plot. Without Galeazzo—Lorenzo's most reliable ally—Riario, Salviati, and his Pazzi friends quickly realized that this was the time to escalate violence and eliminate their enemy. They believed Lorenzo could not count on Milanese troops as readily as before, assuming that Cicco had a weaker grip on the ducal army. And they had full military support from the Duke of Urbino.

Sometime in the spring of 1477, the archbishop and Francesco Pazzi approached Gian Battista, Count of Montesecco, a town just a few miles south of Urbino. Possibly trained by Montefeltro, Montesecco was a military veteran who had become a loyal soldier to the pope. Imprisoned after the Pazzi conspiracy, he was to be the only plotter to make a full confession. The following account of the events leading up to the conspiracy is taken from a confession written by him, on the morning of May 4, 1478, before he was beheaded in Florence. It has been argued that he had been promised freedom to induce him to be forthcoming, but it is just as likely that, good Catholic that he was, he simply wanted to discharge his conscience before it was too late.

Montesecco recalled having met Salviati in the archbishop's apartments in the Vatican around May or June 1477. Salviati and Francesco Pazzi had introduced their proposition obliquely. They said they wanted to reveal to him a secret scheme, which they had been thinking about for a long time. First, they had him solemnly swear to keep absolutely silent about it. Then they hinted that a regime change (*mutatione de lo stato*) was needed in Florence. Montesecco answered that he would do anything they asked, but as he was in the pay of the pope and Count Riario, he could not be part of their plans. They replied that it was unthinkable that they would act without Count Riario's consent. In fact, they wanted to make the count bigger and stronger, a foil against Lorenzo's passionate hatred. Montesecco then asked why Lorenzo was so hostile to Count Riario. They gave him a long-winded and vague explanation and left the matter to be settled later.

After a couple of weeks, a second meeting was set, this time in Girolamo Riario's palace. Montesecco recounted the chilling conversation word for word in his confession:

RIARIO: We have a business at hand. What do you think of it?

MONTESECCO: I have no opinion of it, since I have not yet heard enough about it.

SALVIATI: Did we not tell you that we want a regime change in Florence?

MONTESECCO: Yes, you have told me that, but not how. Without knowing the way, I don't know what to say.

RIARIO: Lorenzo is full of ill-will and hatred towards us. If the Pope were to die, my state would be seriously endangered by Lorenzo. Changing regime in Florence would secure Imola, which he has coveted since the beginning. We need a preventive strike: for this we want to act.

MONTESECCO: And how? With what support?

SALVIATI: The houses of Pazzi and Salviati make up half of the city.

MONTESECCO: All right. But how do you plan to proceed?

SALVIATI: There is no other way than to cut Lorenzo and Giuliano into pieces. First we have to hire the troops and gather them without raising any suspicion. That would be a job well done.

MONTESECCO: My lord, do you realize what you are saying? This is a major undertaking, nor do I know how you can do it, since Florence is a big city and the Magnificence of Lorenzo enjoys a lot of benevolence there, as far as I know.

RIARIO: These people [Pazzi and Salviati] say the opposite! That he has little favor and he is ill-regarded and if the two brothers are dead, everybody will join their hands in thanking God!

SALVIATI: Gian Battista, you have never been to Florence. We know these things better than you—we know what benevolence or malevolence the Florentine people have. Don't doubt that this business will succeed—true as the fact that we are in this room now. We just have to decide how to do it.

MONTESECCO: Sure. So how can we do it?

SALVIATI: We have to warm up Jacopo Pazzi to the whole thing. Right now he's as cold as ice. If we have him on board, the deed is just as done.

MONTESECCO: All right. How will the Pope like all of this?

SALVIATI: We will have Our Lord do all we want Him to do. Also, He despises Lorenzo: He desires this more than anything else.

MONTESECCO: Have you spoken with Him?

RIARIO: Yes, for Madonna's sake! And we will have Him speak to you so you will know His intentions. We just have to figure out how to put together the troops without raising any suspicion, and the rest will work out just fine.

Montesecco, though, was still perplexed. Or at least that is how he portrays himself in a later conversation with the pope, Count Riario, and the archbishop, also recorded in his confession:

MONTESECCO: Holy Father, these things will hardly be feasible without killing Lorenzo and Giuliano, and perhaps some others.

SIXTUS IV: I don't want the death of anybody at all. It is not part of my office to consent to somebody's death. Although Lorenzo is a villain and is behaving badly with us, I would not want his death, but a regime change.

RIARIO: We'll do what we can so that death does not happen. If it were to happen, Your Holiness will forgive the ones who will have done it.

SIXTUS IV: You are a beast! I'm telling you: I don't want anybody dead, but just a regime change. And I say to you, Gian Battista, that I am longing for a regime change in Florence, and for Lorenzo to get out of the way, because he's a villain and an evil man, and he does not respect us at all. And once he is out of Florence, we can do whatever we like with that Republic, and it would indeed be a good thing for us.

RIARIO AND SALVIATI: Your Holiness says the truth, as when you have Florence under Your control and command—and ours—Your Holiness will control half of Italy and everybody will kill to be your friend. So then, be content to see that all that is needed for this purpose will be done.

SIXTUS IV: I'm telling you: do whatever you want as long as nobody gets killed. I will provide any support and military help, or anything that could be necessary.

SALVIATI: Holy Father, are you content that we steer this boat? We will guide it well.

SIXTUS IV: I am content, but preserve the honor of the Holy See and of the count.

Immediately after the pope's vocal request that no one be killed, Montesecco, Riario, and Salviati discussed the matter in the count's chambers. They concluded that it could not be settled without killing Lorenzo and his brother. When Montesecco objected that the plan was ill-conceived and evil, they replied that great things could not be achieved otherwise. In those same days, Salviati replied to a friend who asked him if he could intervene in some legal tangle of his: "Such proceedings of justice are limited in a way that you cannot pervert their style; in these *little* legal affairs it does not seem appropriate to make an *extraordinary* effort." In other words, law is for the slow and powerless, but one can rise above morality if one has a "higher end." This is a perfect justification for the hubris that Salviati and Riario needed to rely on in order to devise their murderous plot.

And indeed the good God was being challenged: the pope's concern with the honor of the Church (and of the count) went to hell. Could Sixtus really be so naïve as to think that the regime change in Florence might occur without killing the Medici brothers? Was the pontiff a puppet in his nephew's "invisible hands"? Or did he just want to achieve his "higher end" (Lorenzo "out of the way") without naming the unholy and unjustifiable means? Here is a mystery worthy of the devilish Machiavelli, the first to describe in depth the necessity to ruthlessly "enter into evil" in *The Prince,* where he called Sixtus "a gutsy pope." Cosimo de' Medici's maxim—"Men cannot govern states with paternosters"—acquires a new, perverse meaning in this context.

With or without Sixtus's approval, Riario decided to dispatch Montesecco to Florence, so that he could familiarize himself with the city and his target. Sometime in midsummer—while Federico wrote to Cicco trying to alienate him from Lorenzo—Montesecco arrived in Florence. He went to the Medici palace and was received informally by Lorenzo. Lorenzo spoke very affectionately and warmly about Count Riario, who had been "like a father and a brother" to him. (These are the rather improbable words conveyed by Montesecco while being held after the Pazzi coup by the Florentine authorities, when he knew full well that his life depended on Lorenzo's clemency.) Lorenzo then recommended that Montesecco travel to Imola, to reassure Riario that everything was in order in his city-state.

After the meeting, Montesecco went to the Osteria della Campana, a dingy inn where he would not be recognized. From there he sent a message to Jacopo, the richest member of the Pazzi clan, letting him know that they needed to talk. Jacopo appeared at the inn after dark. They met secretly in a bedroom. Montesecco offered him the greetings of the pope, the count, and the archbishop, showing all of their letters of credentials. At first Jacopo showed some reluctance, but it was easily overcome.

— What do we have to say to each other, Gian Battista? Do we have to speak about the Florentine State?
— Yes, in fact.
— I don't want to hear you at all. These people are racking my brains, and want to become lords of Florence. I know better than them about these matters. Don't you speak to me at all, I don't want to listen.
— I want to impress on you that the Pope, with whom I spoke before leaving Rome, exhorted me to take care of this business of Florence, because He does not know when the next opportunity will happen that can allow Him to keep so many soldiers on the ground; and since waiting around is dangerous, He urges you to do this. His Holiness said he wanted a regime change, not the death of anybody.

There is a bit of a contradiction in Montesecco's confession at this point. He claims to have reported verbatim the exchange he had with Sixtus IV, Riario, and Salviati. If indeed he had truly been skeptical about the feasibility of the plot, as he later recounted, he could hardly have persuaded the hesitant banker. At any rate, that evening he did not reach any conclusive agreement with Jacopo Pazzi, since Jacopo's nephew Francesco, without whom nothing could be done, was not in town. Montesecco then went on to Imola, to complete his official mission as Lorenzo had encouraged him to do. He stayed there a few days and on his way back stopped in Cafaggiuolo, the favorite Medici countryside villa, where he met with Lorenzo and Giuliano, under the pretext of reporting about his successful trip to Imola. Montesecco then accompanied the Medici brothers back to Florence—while Lorenzo continued to show off his so-called love for Riario.

Montesecco seemed to be in awe of Lorenzo's grace and personality. Lorenzo had treated him in a familiar, friendly manner and had seduced him into believing that he would be generous with and helpful to him. One can easily picture the reactions of Count Riario and Archbishop Salviati to Montesecco, who returned hastily to Rome on August 27 and reported his encounter to them fully, unable to hide his sympathies. Riario was not too impressed with Lorenzo's courtesy. On the spur of the moment, he wrote a letter where love seemed implied, but the exact opposite was meant:

> *Magnificent Lorenzo.*
> *Gian Battista [Montesecco] came back and conveyed to me what is un-*
> *doubtedly thought by Your Magnificence. In fact, I am supremely grate-*
> *ful for it. I do not want to thank you through this letter, because I*
> *cannot give you anything but words. I have determined that you will*
> *see some effects of my actions, through which you will be able to judge*
> *how I love you from the goodness of my heart, as your uncle Giovanni*
> *[Tornabuoni] will hear day by day. I recommend myself to Your*
> *Magnificence. Rome, September 1st, 1477.*
>
>   *Of Your Magnificence*   *Girolamo Viscount*
>   *of Riario in his own hand*

Riario liked to remain in the shade, but his "invisible hands," as depicted by Melozzo in his portrait of Sixtus IV's family, were all the while twisting words and passing deadly, ciphered messages. He certainly showed this little masterpiece of double-talk to Archbishop Salviati, the man who had authored the sardonic letter to Lorenzo accompanying the rotten fish. Now it was fishing time for real: Lorenzo was to become the fish of Fortune.

Before leaving Florence in late August, Montesecco, as he recounted, finally met Francesco Pazzi, and they decided that he would not depart before having reconvened with Jacopo Pazzi. That night Francesco came to pick him up and brought him to Jacopo's palace. They made a list of things that they needed in order to expedite their business. First, Archbishop Salviati would come to Florence with a good excuse, to avoid raising suspicions. After Salviati's arrival, they were to determine along with the Pazzi the best way to take action. Second, they created new ciphers, through which they could communicate safely with one another. They had no doubt that with the support of the papal troops and with Federico as a commander-in-chief, their plan would be successful.

THE MONTONE AFFAIR

IN HIS LOVING LETTER TO LORENZO OF SEPTEMBER 1, 1477, Count Girolamo Riario had written that Giovanni Tornabuoni—Lorenzo's uncle and agent for the Medici Bank in Rome—would report "the effects" of Riario's own good heart "day by day." He kept his promise faithfully. The first truly loving effect emerged on September 3, when Giovanni informed Lorenzo that he had officially become an absent defendant in the trial against the citizens of Perugia, who had themselves been charged by a papal official with aiding Carlo of Montone, an anti-Church rebel and Lorenzo's ally. Carlo offered an excellent pretext for the operation: the plotters decided to lay siege to his citadel Montone—a small Umbrian stronghold only one day's march from Florence—and to keep the siege going until the business was expedited. The idea was simple: by moving the troops around from camp to camp, one could avoid their being detected by Lorenzo or by the Sforza spies.

Federico da Montefeltro left Urbino in early August 1477 as the captain of this enterprise. He started besieging Carlo's hometown, but the protracted resistance put up by Montone was somewhat unexpected. Federico was using his famous field guns with painstaking and devastating precision, striking the thick walls of the citadel, to no avail. He was impatient to end the siege—he certainly had more pressing matters to attend to—but he would not leave any unfinished business behind. He had never done so in his long and virtually flawless military career.

Why was Federico in such haste? The best informed person about everything was, not surprisingly, Cicco Simonetta. The Milanese chancellor had been receiving worrisome reports from his Roman agent, Sacramoro da Rimini, who wrote on September 14 a lengthy letter that contains some extraordinary revelations about the ongoing plot. He introduced the information with extreme care, knowing he could not just drop such a diplomatic bomb without corroborating it with considerable evidence: "Your Lordships of Milan seem not to disbelieve what I have expressed about the hostile attitude against Lorenzo de' Medici etc. Once again, I want you to be certain that every day I become more convinced of such an opinion, and with arguments and evidence which are more than an opinion. Let us leave words aside, since too often the ambassador of the Duke of Urbino keeps just talking and talking." Sacramoro added that the Urbino ambassador, Agostino Staccoli, was just too excited about the news he was receiving to keep it to himself. That was a serious breach of confidence.

That same night "in great secret" Sacramoro spoke to a Filippo da Montegridolfo, envoy to the pope on behalf of the Lord of Rimini. Sacramoro, who was himself a native of Rimini, had befriended this fellow countryman and colleague. Filippo was in constant contact with the Urbino envoy, Staccoli, and they spent much time talking together. Staccoli had apparently said that "this thing has gone so far already, that if the Duke of Urbino would end his siege of Montone soon enough, he may venture to give a big scare to Lorenzo." The informant was talking so positively that Sacramoro felt compelled to report this warning to

Milan. Filippo da Montegridolfo claimed to have spotted on Staccoli's desk deciphered letters from Naples to the Duke of Urbino, in which the king was asking Federico to send news about how quickly he could deal with Montone, so that "if he gets it done soon, he can think of trying out the other business. Such business is not specified, unless Filippo interprets it on the basis of these and other circumstances." Therefore Sacramoro had "immediately communicated to Lorenzo to stay alert and watch himself, and to keep an eye also on the members of his inner circle."

Although the roundabout spying revelation was hardly understated, the expert envoy Sacramoro customarily deferred to Cicco's prudence, casting some doubts on his own ability to grasp the situation. Then he went on: "Today I spoke with Count Girolamo and His Holiness, persuading the one and pleading with the other not to trust passionate people." The Italian word *appassionati* (whose etymology is rooted in the Latin verb *pati*, from which the Italian *passione* and *pazzia*, madness, come) was in fact a clear, coded reference to the Pazzi clan.

Sacramoro reported having tried to utter in the Roman court the proverb "It is good to show a good face in order not to make other people suspicious, and not to threaten." To which "Our Lord the Pope replied: 'very well!' and so did Count Girolamo. They jointly had me write a very reassuring letter to Lorenzo on this matter. However, I fear that a pretty incident might occur to someone, and even without the Pope's consent they would go for it, since I believe the goodness and faith of His Holiness and I judge it very well, since He is good and peaceful. But I'm afraid that others (thanks to His goodness) may take advantage of Him and become too bold. Let us keep our eyes wide open!"

An ambassador could barely be more explicit about the threatening tone of the conversation he had just witnessed. In the final page of his dispatch, which was written by a secretary, Sacramoro also attached one postscript in his own hasty handwriting: "Your Lordships have to believe that the attitude of King Ferrante towards Lorenzo is not good, that of the Duke of Urbino is not any better. They do not think of anything else but giving him a severe beating, if only they could." Nearly frantic with concern, Sacramoro added another telling detail: in Montone "the Duke of Urbino was spending money and more money, up to thousands of ducats," because he needed to deliver a speedy, convincing victory. In fact, Federico later received a papal reimbursement for some "secret expenses" made at the time of this siege, perhaps money used to bribe somebody inside the citadel into betrayal.

On September 16, when Sacramoro reported that the gathering of so many troops in Montone had raised some alarm in nearby Tuscany, the pope sarcastically replied that Lorenzo should not worry, since his intention was to do nothing different from what had been done in the rebellious Città di Castello in 1474. Indeed, that unfortunate enterprise had been precisely the beginning of their open friction. As Sacramoro wrote in his letter, the pope was still angry about Lorenzo's betrayal there. Clearly this papal reassurance—which was really a warning—should have made Lorenzo very nervous. The peace of Italy did not appear particularly high on the list of Sixtus's priorities.

The pope, Sacramoro continued, sought to use all of his clout to punish Carlo of Montone and, "in his own words, to exterminate him!" So much for the Sistine peaceful nature and "His goodness" Sacramoro had prudently mentioned when he was referring to the pope's Pazzi connections. In the end, Sacramoro went on, ever more ironic, he himself did "not disbelieve that there were some agitators who proposed plots to His Holiness," but he was probably moving in the only right "direction." The underlying meaning of these ambiguous phrases was, quite simply, that the pope was claiming to work for peace while acting violently and preparing to wage war.

The cat was out of the bag. In Florence, thanks to the timely revelations of the Sforza spies, Lorenzo was ready to defend himself. Archbishop Salviati, who left Rome on September 11, arrived in Florence via Pisa on the seventeenth, carrying a formal protest against Lorenzo: he should not have been involved in the Montone affair. (The Italian verb *impacciarsi* [to involve oneself] might be another coded reference to the Pazzi clan.) In their official response of September 18, Lorenzo and some Florentine officials wrote, not without a hint of mockery, that they by no means would ever oppose "any deliberation or enterprise worthy of the Vicar of Christ and of the Christian Shepherd." The pope, surely, could not be involved in any violent enterprise.

Bypassing Archbishop Salviati, the papal nuncio, Lorenzo for now had managed to corner Sixtus: to preserve his religious authority and theological integrity in the face of this smart insolence, the pope could only absolve Lorenzo of his alleged friendship with Montone, enemy of the Church. He wrote him an official pardon to that effect.

Federico's attack on Montone, after eight weeks of heavy bombardment—and possibly some bribery—was finally bearing fruit. His five-year-old son, Guidobaldo da Montefeltro, arrived at the camp just in time to see his father's triumph, which was meant to be a good lesson and a promising omen for the young heir. (Antonio, Federico's illegitimate son, was a successful mercenary captain, but could not inherit his father's title.) In those same days, Federico received counsel from an astrologer of Gubbio, who prophesied not only that he had a "very hard job at hand, besieging a well-defended town amply provided by nature or art," but that even greater challenges awaited him in the near future. Superstitious as he was, Federico understood that the time was not ripe to attack Florence. In fact, Carlo of Montone had left his town just before Federico's troops stormed it and quickly rode with his soldiers to Florence. There, he lodged in the Casa de' Martelli, a few steps from the Medici palace. Carlo and his men in effect became Lorenzo's unwitting bodyguards. Ironically, all the maneuvering designed to weaken the Medici had made them stronger.

As Montesecco would later put it in his confession, the plotters had "decided to let the Medici brothers be until the next occasion." This holdup did not please Girolamo Riario, the pope's nephew, who was the invisible architect of the plot. Baccio Ugolini, the Florentine poet, actor, and spy based in Rome, reported to Lorenzo in a confidential letter of October 6 that "Riario had said there was no news." This, for Count Girolamo, meant bad news. He must try to revive his plan. And he knew he could count on the eager help of the Duke of Urbino. Ugolini added in code that this was the time to "move the pawn" and try to turn the pope against Federico by persuading Sixtus that in the affair of Città di Castello the Duke of Urbino had not been blameless: "that affair has been the origin of all the subsequent conflicts, and in such a way we would kill two birds with one stone by taking a huge weight off our shoulders and putting it on the other's." Ugolini closed his letter with an enigmatic, semi-ciphered postscript: "Your Magnificence will hear from Messer Rodolfo [Gonzaga, a mercenary soldier loyal to Lorenzo] some words that the *Pope* said . . . about *King Ferrante* and the *Duke of Urbino* that I did not want to write down."

Ugolini had some understanding of the Montone affair, but he was unable to elaborate a viable defense plan. In a letter of October 25 he went on to suggest that, since the time of Galeazzo Maria Sforza, Count Riario had been asked to do all he could to compete with Federico da Montefeltro in matters of military *condotte* and that a private rupture had occurred between the two, who were in fact "forced to be friends." The strategy to follow in Rome, suggested Ugolini, was to pitch Riario against the Duke of Urbino. This could not hurt, because if the Count fell for it, they would gain "a good help," and if he did not, at least they would know on which side he actually stood. But even as Lorenzo's man knew enough to blame Federico for past and present dangers, the Duke of Urbino, too, kept his experienced eyes wide open.

5

ELIMINATE THEM!

RBINO TODAY REMAINS A JEWEL OF A CITY, AS FAMOUS FOR ITS FAIRY-TALE PALAZZO, ONE OF THE MOST BEAUTIFUL IN ITALY, AS IT HAS BEEN SINCE THE RENAISSANCE. Baldassarre Castiglione, the author of the best-selling *Book of the Courtier* (1528), set the leisurely conversations of his courtiers in its rooms, famously dubbing it "more a city in itself than a palazzo." Federico da Montefeltro had this structure built by the greatest architects over a period of about twenty years beginning in the 1450s. In Castiglione's words, Montefeltro "furnished it not only with what is customary, such as silver vases, wall hangings of the richest cloth of gold, silk, and other like things, but for ornament he added countless ancient statues of marble and bronze, rare paintings, and musical instruments of every sort; nor did he wish to have anything there that was not most rare and excellent."

Federico's library, housed in a large room that opened on an elegant courtyard, was the repository of the most important collection of illuminated manuscripts in late-fifteenth-century Italy; it was even larger and richer than the holdings of the Medici Library. Federico was not only a busy politician and mercenary captain. He was also a man of taste endowed with artistic passion. He loved painting, music, and literature. He also hired humanists to read the classics to him during meals.

The famous Urbino *studiolo*, even more lavish than the one in Gubbio, is concealed in the heart of the palazzo. A secret wooden panel in the room slides open onto the private balcony, itself set between the two tall,

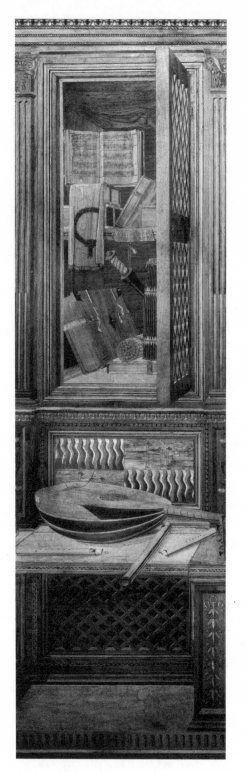

✠ ABOVE, LEFT & RIGHT, AND RIGHT PAGE:
Details of trompe l'oeil bookshelves from the Urbino studiolo.

Portrait of Federico da Montefeltro on in-laid wood panel from the Urbino studiolo.

slender towers overlooking the hilly landscape of the Montefeltro region. Federico used to gaze at this very scenery when he went out to take a breath of air after dictating his most devious dispatches.

THE MONTEFELTRO CODE

IN EARLY OCTOBER 1477 FEDERICO SUMMONED FIVE SQUADRONS of Neapolitan troops to the Maremma marshes in southern Tuscany. At first, his plan was probably to use them in a few weeks' time against Florence. However, with the cold season approaching, Federico had to dismiss the army. After returning to Urbino, he wrote several ciphered, flattering letters to Cicco, promoting himself as the best candidate to become the commander in chief responsible for all the troops in the entire Italian peninsula. But an unexpected event would hinder Federico's ambitions. In late November, under mysterious circumstances, he seriously injured his left leg and ankle. It is unclear whether this was a real accident or a "pretty incident" of the kind that Sacramoro feared might happen to Lorenzo.

The Urbino courtier and painter Giovanni Santi, who was most likely with his lord at the time of the accident, gave a full account of events. While the sun was setting on the hills of the Marche, Federico climbed up the loggia of the small Montefeltro palazzo in San Marino to look at the beautiful view. He soon started boasting to his courtiers about his youthful battles and victories against his late archenemy, the lord of Rimini, Sigismondo Malatesta. Inflamed by his own rhetoric, and "burdened with glory," he trod on some rotten wood in the dark and fell one flight down through the floor of the loggia. According to the only other account of the mishap, Federico, on his way to bed after dining at a local *signore*'s palazzo, fell through the cracks of the wooden stairs. This sounds a little more suspicious, but we have no evidence of a plot to kill the Duke of Urbino.

Despite Santi's emphasis in his report on Federico's resistance to physical pain—the doctors carved at least five holes in his flesh to bleed him and let the bad humors out—an inevitable sense of doom emerges from his depiction of the injured *condottiere,* who now risked being permanently "deprived not of one eye but of his own body!" It was a big blow to the reputation of a great fighter, the winner of countless battles, to cripple himself in a mere domestic accident. Federico's recovery was slow and uncertain, and it was unclear whether he would ever be able to ride again, an essential prerequisite for a soldier of the time.

Qualms about Federico's health notwithstanding, the bargaining about his *condotta* still raged in Rome. A great deal of ciphered correspondence began flowing from Urbino to Naples. In November Count Riario dispatched his favorite henchman, Lorenzo Giustini of Città di Castello, to Naples. There he was briefed at length by King Ferrante, Federico's oldest employer. Giustini then returned to Rome "with a mouthful of news," as the Milanese ambassadors at the Vatican readily informed Cicco.

Giustini was the key link between the Roman plotters and Federico. Indeed, this shady character had known Federico since at least 1474, when the then newly designated Duke of Urbino marched on Città di Castello to repress the antipapal revolt with the intention of replacing the local warlord with Giustini himself. A self-proclaimed knight and doctor of law, Giustini was, in fact, neither. Born to an ambitious but plebeian family, Giustini was a typical Renaissance social climber. In 1464 he walked into Perugia with a papal recommendation for the prestigious post of captain of the people's army. The city's College of Law, however, challenged his claims and ruled not only that he lacked blue blood but also that his doctorate had been unlawfully granted. He was not appointed.

Later on, Giustini managed to obtain recommendations from several cardinals for the position of *podestà,* or city's judge, in Florence. Lorenzo de' Medici did not trust him, however, and opposed his candidacy for more than a year. When Giustini was finally nominated, he refused the appointment on the grounds that he was busy with other tasks. By then, he had become one of the most trusted agents of the Riario family. In 1473 he was sent to Milan to witness the wedding of Caterina Sforza to Count Girolamo Riario and to receive the keys of Imola, the city that the pope's nephew had just purchased from Galeazzo Sforza. Most recently, in September 1477, Giustini had personally made the case against Lorenzo in the trial of the Perugia rebels, after which he had ridden straight to the siege of Montone. From the very beginning, he had a place in the inner circle of the plotters.

It should have come as no surprise that Giustini was the person Count Riario chose to go to Urbino at the most delicate point in the machinations. With Federico incapacitated by his injury and unable to lead his troops, the Roman clan needed at least a military contribution from the duke, if not his precious strategic presence. The meeting between Montefeltro and Giustini occurred on February 14, 1478, in the *studiolo,* the most secret room of the ducal palace. This meeting remained undetected until the coded letter that Federico wrote that day came back to light in 2001.

o   o   E   o   o

SHUFFLING ABOUT ON HIS INJURED LEG, Federico had only to cross a short distance from his bedroom to the *studiolo.* On the door facing the bedroom he would have read the motto he had had inscribed there: MELIUS TE VINCI VERA DICENTEM QUAM VINCERE MENTIENTEM (It is better to lose by telling the truth than to win by lying). In light of what was about to happen, this motto is quite ironic, especially when considered in relation to another on the northern *studiolo* wall: VIRTUTIBUS ITUR AD ASTRA (Through virtues you will reach heaven).

The Urbino *studiolo* is structurally much more complex than the one in Gubbio. Instead of the allegorical paintings of the seven liberal arts, there were twenty-eight portraits of poets and philosophers, prophets and popes above panels of intricately inlaid wood. The only living contemporary figure depicted here was Pope Sixtus IV—besides Federico himself, whose portrait was set in one of the wood panels: dressed in a white Roman tunic, he is shown holding a spear upside down, recalling

Portrait of Pope Sixtus IV in the Urbino studiolo.

the image of Mars, the god of war, in the guise of the peace-seeker, as often portrayed on ancient Roman coins.

In the privacy of the enclosed space of his *studiolo,* Federico could freely discuss the current state of affairs. Giustini's visit became the occasion for the most crucial planning before the execution of the plot. The two men had to assess the risks involved. If the scheme should fail, the powers of the general league (Milan, Florence, and Venice) would come after the pope in anger: this was the point of no return.

Immediately after the meeting, Federico called his secretary and began to dictate a letter to his envoys in Rome, chatty Agostino Staccoli and sly Piero Felici. Of course, the contents of the letter were intended to reach the pope himself. Felici, always present at the key points in Federico's covert activities, had been summoned to the curia by Riario in January, joining resident ambassador Staccoli. Even though the letter's contents would be coded, Federico thought he should refer only elusively to the "main business," that is, the elimination of the Medici brothers. If the letter were to be intercepted and deciphered by Florentine or Milanese spies, Federico would be in a good position to deny his involvement in any compromising activity.

But he had little to worry about: apart from Federico's legible signature at the bottom of the letter, the rest is a tangle of garbled symbols.

When the letter emerged out of a private archive in Urbino (for a detailed account of how I came across the letter, see the Afterword), it seemed at first that the code would have to remain impenetrable. But Cicco Simonetta himself provided a way out with his *Rules for Extracting Ciphered Letters Without a Sample,* a little tract about the art of codebreaking. The *Rules* are based on a simple mathematical model that allows the code-breaker to calculate the statistical occurrence of letters in Latin and in Italian. Vowels, for example, are very common in Italian, especially *e* and *a.* The words in Federico's coded letter were not separated, making the text all the harder to break down. After much trial and error, I identified the repetition of a string of symbols:

$$1\ 2\ 3\ 4\ 2\ 3\ 2\ 5\ 6\ 7\ 6\ 2$$

Assuming that it contained the vowel *a,* I calculated that it could correspond to:

1A suA sAntitA,

First page of the coded letter from Federico da Montefeltro to his envoys in Rome.

Third page of the coded letter.

Detail of the coded letter with the repeated string of symbols.

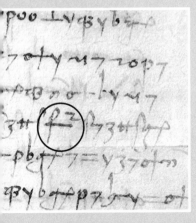

*Detail of F2 in
the coded letter.*

0   00   000   0
og. ll. man. nn. pp. rr. ll. tt
24. 24. 26. 27. 28. 29. 30. 31.

c23	Fiorenza	f1
c24	fiorentini	f2
c25	fameglie de	f3
c26	fantaria	f4
c27	fanti	f5
c28	ferma	f6
c29	florini	f7
c30	fossombrone	f8
c31	fano	f9
d1	facto	f10
d2	feri	f11
d3	faro	f12
d4		
d5	s. Gismondo	g1
d6	Gennes	g2
d7	Genua	g3

Page from the Montefeltro Codebook.

*Detail of R2 in
the coded letter.*

m1	quello	o2	treugua
m2	quale	o3	torto
m3	quanto	o4	tanto
m4	quanto	o5	tale
m5	cintineg	o6	tu
m6	quatro	o7	tre
m7	Re de cicilia	r1	Venexia
m8	Re de francia	r2	Venetian
m9	Re de ragona	r3	vececan
m10	Ruina	r4	Vrbino
m11	Referma	r5	Vgolino
m12	Recoman ala s	vr6	oonua
m13	Reame	r7	Valesse
m14	Receuo	r8	Valere
m15	Rexeruito	r9	vole
m16	Receuere	r10	onde
	Receuero	r11	nostro
n1	Respondo	r12	vita
n2	Respost	r13	
n3	Respondere	r14	
n4	Respondero	r15	

Page from the Montefeltro Codebook.

which in Italian means "His Holiness." Ironically, what allowed me to crack the code was the sacred title of Pope Sixtus IV, the ultimate recipient of the letter.

All the other symbols, based on the statistical occurrences inferred from Cicco's *Rules,* were easy to decipher. Yet some of the names of the other people involved were encrypted with single symbols. One could only hypothesize about the people to whom those symbols referred, but without being absolutely certain, as each one was used no more than once throughout the letter. Fortunately, these same symbols happened to be recorded in a codex of ciphers at the Vatican Library, where all the manuscripts once owned by Federico are now preserved. This discovery further helped confirm the earlier hypotheses. The symbols *F2* and *R1* stood for the Florentines and the King of Sicily (King Ferrante of Naples), respectively.

In other instances, specific figures were only vaguely referred to, as in the case of the Pazzi family, simply described in the letter as friends. But the conspiratorial language was clear enough. From the decoded letter emerges the cold, calculating voice of Federico, as well as some insight into the workings of the commander's mind. He was used to making quick decisions under the pressure of time and events, assessing the advantages and the dangers of action, and swiftly disposing of enemies. Federico urged the pope to take the king's rather than Count Riario's "road" in this instance: in other words, to lean more on Neapolitan military strength than on his family's political ties. The plot was "so far ahead," the duke argued, that it was well worth trying to pursue it with some vigor. This was an approach that represented the triumph of Machiavellianism before Machiavelli: and in fact *The Prince* could not have existed without the inspiration and example of Federico da Montefeltro and his kind.

Decoded, the letter to Staccoli and Felici begins:

My dearest sirs. *Messer Lorenzo Giustini has been here and having understood what he has said and examining between ourselves which is the best road to take for the King* [R1] *and for the Count, we have come to this conclusion, that it would be more expedient for His Holiness to take the King's road rather than the Count's for many rea-*

sons and mostly with regard to the main business [the plot against the Medici], *which is so far ahead that it is worth seeing whether it will succeed or not. If it succeeds and goes according to our intention and aim, it is necessary that it* [Florence] *should come under His Holiness and the King given that those friends* [the Pazzi] *will not be able to trust those powers with which they are now allied* [i.e., Milan and Venice, which were tied with Florence in the general league] *and for this and any other viewpoint and reason there is, it is necessary they take the opposite road to the one they have taken so far because these other powers with which they have been allied will take this fact very badly. If the business does not succeed or is discovered, there is no doubt that there will be great enmity toward our pope not only from the Florentines* [F2] *but also from all those powers that are allied with them and in this case His Holiness is absolutely compelled to have the King's support and for this reason I believe that it would be good, and so you can say to the pope on my behalf, that the sooner the better to execute anything there is to do along with the King, so that it would not look like the pope and the King are compelled by necessity to take the King's road. In any event it seems that it is best for the pope, and also for the aforementioned count, to take the King's road, for which reason it seems to me* [a good idea] *to do all we can in favor of the friends* [the Pazzi] *so that we prevail and things go well without any hesitation or reservation whatsoever, since perhaps I would think differently if the business were not so far ahead. I will inform Messer Lorenzo* [Giustini] *how many of my infantry and cavalrymen I can give him from here, both in words and in effect to act more quickly and how many I could give him with a little more time and after these I will send a trusted person to Siena and without saying or doing anything he will stay there until the thing happens and as soon as it happens I will request the troops of that Signoria* [Siena] *since I am sure that they will not deny them being so close and almost on the spot. The magnificent messer Lorenzo* [Giustini] *will also be able to go that way with his soldiers securely on those borders, as from his magnificence himself will be better and more fully explained to the Count, whose* [Giustini's] *writing I rely upon, since he is very well informed of my intention and of my opinion.*

Concerned with the tactical aspects of the attack, Federico here painted a picture of a swift and ruthless move to seize Florence, with subsidiary troops coming from Siena, under the command of his illegitimate son Antonio. The duke's military contribution was not yet quantified at this stage, though it would be as large as six hundred of his famously well-trained soldiers (in wartime, Federico was paid to keep a total of eight hundred). Acting "without any hesitation or reservation" was the key to success. A significant section of unciphered text followed the coded main portion of the letter:

> *You will thank as much as possible His Holiness and the Count for the rich and beautiful jewel that His Holiness has been so gracious to send as a gift to Guido. This gift has been the greatest pleasure and favor that His Holiness has done for me since giving it to Guido was as if he had given every gratifying thing to myself and certainly it could have been said that Guido participated in those things at Montone since he came to the camp and right after his arrival we conquered that city, so that you will thank His Holiness greatly and the Count as we said a thousand times.*

The gift to Federico's son Guidobaldo was a thick gold chain. The young *duchetto* showed it proudly around town.

Shortly after Guidobaldo had received the gift, Federico commissioned from painter Bartolomeo della Gatta a portrait showing his son wearing the chain with a red robe and a red ducal hat. The subject is seen in profile, just as in Piero della Francesca's famous portraits of Federico. The gold chain had sealed the deal to kill the Medici brothers. It also carried a significant political meaning: Sixtus IV, after granting Federico the title of duke, recognized the legitimacy of the Montefeltro dynasty, which thus received the ecclesiastical investiture for generations to come. This was characteristic of Sixtus's devilish role on the Italian stage: he behaved in a corrupt way himself while pretending to be corrupted by violent people.

In a final section of the letter addressed to the pope, Federico complained that His Holiness was giving him his due with less punctuality than he was the king. The delay, he argued threateningly, might have an

Bartolomeo della Gatta, Portrait of Guidobaldo da Montefeltro. *This portrait was executed around March 1478, to celebrate the golden gift that Pope Sixtus IV had sent to Federico's son.*

impact on his military efficiency and steadfastness. He needed to be compensated "both for the past and for the future," since he was facing so many expenses already.

The letter is currently preserved in Urbino in the Ubaldini family archive, which owes its name to Ottaviano Ubaldini, Federico's half brother. Ottaviano himself was interested in alchemy and astrology more than in politics, even though he occasionally acted as a counselor to Federico (and became Guidobaldo's guardian after Federico's death, running the affairs of state for him). He was also a close friend of the Florentine Neoplatonist philosopher Marsilio Ficino, who was deeply involved in the Pazzi plot despite his reputation as a loyal follower of the Medici. In the Ubaldini archive's file containing the coded dispatch, there is also a letter from Ottaviano to Piero Felici, the same ambassador addressed by Federico in his ciphered letter. On February 15, the pious astrologer wrote to Felici, an old acquaintance of his:

> Piero. I received your letter and as for the lord's decisions you will see what you have to do. Sir Lorenzo Giustini was with him. I did not take part in the meeting because I was busy that morning, which was yesterday; I did it also on purpose so that he could speak more freely about the main business, although I am certain that he would have not watched his tongue in front of me. You will see what has been decided. You know how much hope I have in this thing, and my only little consolation is that so far it has been conducted without any scandal, as if God was guiding it.

The language used by Ottaviano betrays his full knowledge of the plot. His apparent relief that no scandal had (yet) arisen from the "main business" is quite revealing of his pessimism about the whole enterprise. It shows that Federico was perfectly aware that his reputation was at stake, no less than the much-desired monetary reward. Federico had always been the active brother, whereas Ottaviano had comfortably taken the role of the contemplative one, in an almost caricatured division of labor. Another passage in the letter evokes very vividly the scene in Urbino at this time:

The aforementioned Sir Lorenzo brought to Count Guido the present
on behalf of His Holiness. You cannot believe how cheerful he is about
it, and he shows it around to the people. This morning he wore it dur-
ing Mass, and you cannot imagine how well it suits him. I think that
upon receiving these letters you will feel as if our world is undergoing a
huge metamorphosis.

Once again, Ottaviano's astrological-alchemical language ("huge
metamorphosis") conveys his mixed feelings about the situation. Apparently, at Sunday Mass Guidobaldo had shown off the gift he had received
from the pope, "during Mass," in fact. There is no doubt that a six-year-
old child would enjoy such a fancy gift and that the people in Urbino
would have rejoiced at the apparent show of benevolence from the pope,
unaware of the hidden motives behind such generosity. In the rest of the
letter Ottaviano described Federico's recovering health with a slightly
forced optimism that revealed his fatalistic anxiety about the future.

THE HOLY BAIT

HAVING SET THE MILITARY MACHINE IN MOTION, THE PLOT-
ters required a good excuse to arrive in Florence fully armed. In
December 1477, Sixtus IV had appointed yet another relative to the position of cardinal. Raffaele Riario was Girolamo's nephew and had received the red cardinal's hat when he was not even seventeen. He was the
youngest cardinal to be picked by a pope during the closing years of the
fifteenth century. Indeed, every other cardinal elevated at this time was
old enough to be Riario's father. Raffaele was still in college at this point,
studying in Pisa, and living in Archbishop Salviati's palace. His private
tutor was the Florentine humanist Jacopo Bracciolini, son of the greater

and more famous chancellor Poggio. Jacopo had himself been a student of Ficino's and was also close to the Duke of Urbino, to whom he had offered some lavishly illuminated manuscripts. In his dedication of his father's *Florentine History* to Federico, Jacopo had written that "facts must come before words" and that "history is a mirror." But the mirror of history often tends to be a bit dark. Jacopo pretended to respect Lorenzo's authority as well, and dedicated to him a widely circulated commentary on Petrarch. The author in fact hated the Medici leader and wanted him out of Florence to restore the old Republic.

A few months prior to the execution of the plot, the officially pro-Medici philosopher Marsilio Ficino gave Jacopo Bracciolini a treatise on *Truth* to be presented to Cardinal Raffaele Riario. On that occasion, Ficino warned the young cardinal against any "ill-intentioned interpreter" who might well have guessed its hidden, subversive meaning. The letter of recommendation sent in mid-January by Girolamo Riario to Lorenzo de' Medici in Bracciolini's favor was supremely hypocritical: "Knowing Sir Jacopo, son of Poggio, man of letters, honest, virtuous and gentlemanly, I had the idea of enrolling him in the service of his Excellency the Cardinal in order to instruct him on the moral life." In the same letter, the count entrusted Jacopo "to say certain things to your magnificence." The treacherous Jacopo was to invite Lorenzo to Rome on the pope's behalf, in order to take care of the "public business of the Florentine Republic and the Medici's private ones." This invitation had the sole purpose of drawing Lorenzo away from Florence in order that he might be murdered.

An excerpt from Montesecco's confession sheds light on the action from the plotters' perspective. They kept debating the right moment to strike:

MONTESECCO: So, how are you going to do this?

RIARIO: Lorenzo has to come here this Easter. As soon as we learn of his departure, Francesco Pazzi will also leave [from Rome] and will take care of Giuliano and will settle things so that before Lorenzo leaves [from Rome] everything will be set up.

MONTESECCO: Will you kill him?

Equestrian portrait of Federico da Montefeltro in Poggio Bracciolini's
Florentine History, *with the city of Volterra in the background.*

RIARIO: No, I don't want something bad to happen to him here. But before he leaves, things will be fixed in good form.

MONTESECCO: Does the Holy Father know about this?

RIARIO: Yes.

MONTESECCO: For the devil, it's no small matter that He gave His consent!

RIARIO: Don't you know that He does whatever we want? As long as things go well.

But things were not going that well. In fact, Montesecco also reported a slur uttered by the pope in private about Archbishop Salviati and Francesco Pazzi: "They don't know how to poach three eggs in one pot," declared Sixtus. "They are no good at anything except boasting. Whoever gets involved [again, the verb *impacciarsi*] with them will be sorry!" Whether the pope actually said this or not, the statement turned out to be true. Many days of waiting passed in these painstaking preparations: would Lorenzo accept the invitation or not? That year, Easter fell on March 22, 1478, but Lorenzo did not make his way to Rome. At this point, the plotters discussed their plan over and over again in Count Riario's palace across the Tiber from Castel St. Angelo, knowing full well that they could not wait any longer. Too many people knew about the "main business." They had to act quickly.

The studious Cardinal Riario cut short his university term. Raffaele had arrived at the Pazzi Villa La Loggia in Montughi, just a couple of miles outside of town, in March. He stayed in the environs of Florence for more than a month; given his high ecclesiastical rank, he could not enter the city without a proper official welcome. And so it was arranged that the Medici brothers would be killed at a banquet organized in the cardinal's honor in the hills of Fiesole outside Florence.

On March 27, a secret meeting was held in the Apostolic Palace in the Vatican. Girolamo Riario, Lorenzo Giustini, the Aragon ambassador Anello Arcamone, and the Urbino envoys Agostino Staccoli and Piero Felici were in attendance. Federico's alter ego, Felici, personally drew up an agreement to proceed that was signed by all the parties and was sent to Naples to be sealed by the king. While Montesecco and Gian Francesco da Tolentino, Riario's military factotum, were dispatched to

Imola, Giustini rushed all the way back to Urbino to take command of the six hundred soldiers supplied by Federico and bring them to Città di Castello. Meanwhile, the military supplies being brought in drew the attention of the local Florentine spies, but they took no initiative to monitor the troops. Federico even wrote to Milan to fetch one of his favorite weapon-makers. He was still corresponding with Cicco through the usual confidential channel, perhaps to maintain the impression of normality.

It is worth asking whether the conspiracy was not aided by a failure of intelligence on the part of Lorenzo or of Cicco. Since early September 1477, and then again in January 1478, warnings had been pouring into Florence from Rome, Venice, and Milan. The reports outlined that "the Duke of Urbino and some others have an evil plan against the very person of Lorenzo, and the plot involves people inside Florence." The Milanese chancellery duly passed on the alarming information to Lorenzo. But we do not know whether Lorenzo did anything about it. On the basis of the collected evidence, it is clear that the plot could have been averted. But the cautionary "Watch yourself!" became a sort of game of cry wolf that hardly served to increase Lorenzo's alertness to the very real danger. What is more, Lorenzo had a striking sense of his own invulnerability. He was convinced that no one would dare touch him or his brother—the two towering figures in town—on their home turf.

On April 2, 1478, the Milanese ambassadors in Rome once again reported to Cicco a delay in the bargaining to finalize the Duke of Urbino's hiring salary, in which his men were heavily involved. Count Girolamo Riario was quoted as saying emphatically: "I won't let this thing die down!" The ambassadors thought he referred to the sealing of Federico's *condotta*, but he was actually referring to Lorenzo's assassination.

The comedy of diplomatic errors continued until April 24. During these months Sixtus IV played his role with considerable mastery, as even the well-seasoned Sforza ambassador in Rome, Sacramoro da Rimini, reported: "The words, the countenance, the most recent acts of the pope are worthy of a Vicar of Christ on Earth, whom it is reasonable to trust . . . He proceeds sincerely and not deceivingly." If Cicco had been as watchful as usual, his instinct would certainly have been one of caution. On that day, however, this comment from Rome was probably received with little attention in Milan. The regency was busy with the huge April 24 celebrations of the festival of St. George, an occasion for the confirmation of the ducal title for Gian Galeazzo Sforza, Galeazzo's son, now eight years old. Hundreds of well-armed soldiers solemnly paraded in the streets of Milan. But despite the show of force and pomp, Milanese military strength had declined in recent years. The soldiers were growing old, perhaps too old to fight. And, more alarming, there was no longer a strong military leader capable of commanding them.

The high point of Cicco's government can be seen in an official oration given by one of its members, Agostino de' Rossi, in the Duomo on St. George's day. De' Rossi had delivered the speech celebrating Francesco Sforza's triumphal entry into Milan exactly twenty-eight years earlier. Now he provided a manifesto of the magnificent, progressive agenda of the Milanese regency. The continuity between the origins of Sforza power and its latest incarnation was made less cheerful by the presence of some of the same aging men in the pageant. But only two days after Cicco's ecumenical dream, peace in Italy would be shattered: the plotters in Florence finally swung into action. The Pazzi conspiracy would definitively crush the shaky stability Cicco had attempted to restore in Milan. Exactly sixteen months had passed since the murder of Galeazzo Sforza.

PART II

Spring 1478 — Summer 1482

For when the power of thought

is coupled with ill will and naked force

there is no refuge from it for mankind.

—DANTE, *Inferno*

6

FLORENCE IS FOR FEAR

FLORENCE HAS NOT CHANGED DRAMATICALLY SINCE THE DAY OF THE PAZZI CONSPIRACY. IN FACT, MOST OF ITS CHIEF MONUMENTS WERE ALREADY IN PLACE. Filippo Brunelleschi's dome on the cathedral dedicated to Santa Maria del Fiore had been completed in the 1430s, and the Palazzo Medici in the 1440s. Palazzo Vecchio, as its name suggests, was even older. In the 1560s it was linked with a tall bridge to the Uffizi Palace (today a museum), and with Vasari's corridor to the Palazzo Pitti on the other side of the river Arno, across the Ponte Vecchio. The corridor was intended as a safe passageway, an escape route for the members of the ruling Medici in case of an attempted coup. By then, history had taught a valuable lesson to the family, whose dynastic power would not be extinguished until the eighteenth century, when its last member, Anna Maria Ludovica, died peacefully, willing all her possessions to the Tuscan grand duchy.

Florence is now one of the top tourist destinations in the world. Most people visit the Duomo or the Medici tombs at the back of the Basilica of San Lorenzo, once the Medici family's church. In both places they may hear the famous and shocking story of the assault on Lorenzo and Giuliano de' Medici. But they are rarely told all of the horrific details of that gruesome day.

There are a few published Renaissance reports and literary adaptations of these events, but one in particular was overlooked for many years. It is a manuscript, today housed at the Vatican Library, written by Giovanni di Carlo, a Dominican friar who was at the time the prior of Santa Maria Novella, the second most important church in Florence. Between 1480 and 1482 he composed a *History of His Times* in three books, each based on the struggles of a leading member of the Medici family to rise to power or to maintain it: Cosimo returning from exile (1434), Piero resisting the early Pitti conspiracy (1466), and Lorenzo surviving the Pazzi conspiracy (1478). I have drawn many firsthand details from Giovanni di Carlo's account. Niccolò Machiavelli ransacked much of it in his *Florentine Histories* (1525), commissioned by the Medici pope, Clement VII, son of the murdered Giuliano. Giovanni had witnessed the events in person but since he was not a Medici client he had a slightly less biased take on them than would Machiavelli.

BLOODY SUNDAY

FLORENCE, APRIL 26, 1478

ON THE DAY THEY WERE GOING TO KILL HIM, GIULIANO de' Medici woke up with a stomachache. This unpleasant indisposition had, in fact, saved his life only a few days earlier, when it had prevented him from attending a banquet in Fiesole to which the plotters had invited him along with his brother Lorenzo. Francesco Pazzi had left behind his Roman bank business to join Cardinal Riario, Archbishop Salviati, and the others in the Pazzi's Villa La Loggia, two miles outside Florence. They had asked Lorenzo to organize a banquet at his own beautiful villa on the hills of Fiesole (he enjoyed large dinner parties) and then to visit the Badia, a monastery built by Cosimo. They knew of a secret room there, accessible through a spiral staircase, where it would have been easy to trap and quietly murder the Medici brothers. The Pazzi had also asked both of them to come to Fiesole with only a small entourage,

Map of Florence in Poggio Bracciolini's Florentine History. *Poggio's son Jacopo dedicated this copy to Federico himself. Jacopo, one of the plotters against Lorenzo, ended up hanged from the upper windows of the Palazzo Vecchio, at the center of the map.*

since they wanted all of them to *starsi alla dimesticha,* to feel at home, and to be attended only by their servants. But that day Giuliano had an *anghio,* a biting stomachache, and could not come. When Lorenzo showed up on his own, the plotters tried to convince him to call for his brother, but to no avail. Since they wanted to kill them both, they refrained from taking action on that occasion.

Over the next few days, Giuliano ignored many warning signs and bad omens. He had horrible dreams, though these might very well have arisen from his stomach problem. He was very slender and ate little. He was only twenty-five years old, with an open face, and a modest and benign countenance. He was easygoing, handsome, and gracious, and thus endeared himself to everyone. He was very different, in other words, from Lorenzo, who was obsessed with his own success and oblivious to the possibility of a turn in his fortunes, and who never hesitated to favor his acolytes, even non-Florentines, over the interests of the local citizens. Giuliano, revolted by Lorenzo's ambition (Giovanni di Carlo used the Latin word *stomacans*: literally, nauseated to the stomach), had once said to his brother: "Watch out, O brother: by wanting too many things, all of us might lose everything." Perhaps his stomachache was a political premonition.

On the day Giuliano was going to be killed, the Medici brothers were planning to throw another lavish banquet in their palace in Florence for Cardinal Riario, who had never been there and claimed he wanted to see the Medici's famous collection of artworks, medals, and coins for himself. The plotters had arranged for the cardinal to celebrate High Mass that Ascension Sunday in Florence's Santa Maria del Fiore, the Duomo. The banquet was planned as the after-Mass reception, which would have to be worthy of a princely household.

Scores of waiters were ready to serve an elaborate meal at the elegantly laid tables, lavishly decorated with a profusion of tableware and linen. Tapestries adorned the walls and carpets covered the floors throughout the house. Festive garlands hung everywhere. Ephemeral contraptions of all sorts, exotic Eastern cloths, and stuffed animals, both wild and domesticated, were on show, gifts once supplied to the hosts' ancestor Cosimo the Elder, in whose age "a cargo of Indian spices and

Greek books were often imported in the same vessel." In another section of the palace, gold and silver vases, ancient and new, were displayed alongside precious statues, stones, gems, and jewels, some of them intended as gifts for the cardinal. Amid this show of material wealth and magnificence, the brothers went about their tasks in a state of fevered anticipation. Giovanni di Carlo later quoted a line of Virgil's from the *Aeneid*: "This was the last day in which we, miserable creatures, were to decorate our city with festoons, while our destruction was imminent." Cardinal Riario's expedition was a Trojan horse. The new plan was to kill the brothers inside their own palace and sack all their property.

⚬ ⚬ F ⚬ ⚬

ON SUNDAY MORNING, after arranging the military details outside the city, the plotters left the Villa La Loggia and rode on horseback to Florence. The company included Cardinal Riario, Archbishop Salviati, Gian Battista Montesecco, and Jacopo Bracciolini, who was acting as a secretary to the cardinal. Meanwhile, a group of Florentine citizens converged on foot in the direction of the Duomo. It was led by Pazzi family members, among them the unwitting Guglielmo, Francesco's brother and Lorenzo's brother-in-law. The members of this substantial *brigata* concealed weapons under their elegant clothing.

The riders dismounted at the Palazzo Medici, where no one welcomed them since they were expected to go directly to Santa Maria del Fiore. Only after Mass were they supposed to walk to the banquet. This misunderstanding created a bit of mayhem. When the Medici brothers heard about the cardinal's arrival, they left the Duomo to fetch him at their palace. Cardinal Riario had changed from his riding dress into his ecclesiastical garb. They all met in the courtyard, under the thin shadow of Donatello's bronze David. Lorenzo politely kissed the ring on the young cardinal's hand, as did Giuliano. They walked back on via de' Martelli toward the church. Giuliano was walking between Francesco Pazzi and Bernardo Bandini (another student of the philosopher Marsilio Ficino), who embraced him fulsomely in order to check whether or not he was wearing a breastplate under his red robe. As

Machiavelli would later remark, hiding so much hatred behind dissembling hearts was a "thing truly worthy of memory."

Cardinal Riario, barely seventeen, admired the baptistry with its golden door, and the unfinished marble façade, for which Lorenzo himself had submitted a design. Once inside the cathedral, he marveled at its outstanding dome. Lorenzo and Giuliano let the cardinal take his seat under the cupola, where he would celebrate the Mass. They then circled the choir on opposite sides, at a good distance from one another—a precaution the brothers customarily took in public.

The cathedral was filled with the chatter of well-dressed citizens. In the hubbub, Giovanni Tornabuoni, the brothers' loving uncle, said aloud that Giuliano was not well and that he might not attend the banquet later. Somebody else spread the rumor that a number of unidentified crossbowmen had been spotted outside the city gates (they were in fact Federico's men). Francesco Pazzi and Bernardo Bandini overheard this too. They had to hurry. That morning they had revealed their intentions to too many accomplices and the longer they delayed, the greater the danger of their being caught before the act. They eagerly waited for the moment to strike and, abandoning their plans to kill him later at the palace, started moving toward Giuliano.

Giuliano was blissfully listening to the *"Agnus Dei"*—*Agnus Dei, qui tollis peccata mundi* (Lamb of God, who takes away the sins of the world)—while, next to Cardinal Riario, a Florentine priest raised the Holy Bread of Christ. Francesco and Bernardo, in their hooded cloaks, silently approached their target along with some servants. Using a short dagger, Bernardo struck Giuliano in the side, murmuring, "Take this, traitor!" Then Francesco plunged another blade into Giuliano's chest. Giuliano shrank back a few steps, holding his abdomen, then fell to the ground. The murderers kept raging over him, cracking his skull with a heavy weapon. The assault was so violent that Francesco wounded himself in the thigh.

On the other side of the altar, killers appointed at the last minute—two disgruntled priests—proceeded haphazardly with their given task. Unlike Montesecco, who backed out at the last minute in a sudden crisis of conscience, Jacopo Pazzi's chaplain and chancellor (one Stefano da

Bagnone) and the apostolic secretary Antonio Maffei of Volterra evidently had no scruples about perpetrating a killing in a church. But they approached Lorenzo too slowly and were unable to hit him effectively. He instinctively turned, avoiding the full force of the first knife blow and suffering only a light wound on his neck. Lorenzo's friend Franceschino Nori, who threw himself in the way of the attackers, was wounded in the stomach and struck down.

Lorenzo was quick to wrap his mantle around his left arm and to draw a dagger in his right hand. He deflected another couple of swipes, and while his brother's killers were coming after him, he ran into the Old Sacristy, to the left of the main altar, helped by a young man from a wealthy family Lorenzo happened to have graced and liberated from jail just days before. Lorenzo and a few loyal friends shut the heavy bronze doors behind them and looked at each other anxiously. One Antonio Ridolfi, a longtime Medici client, thought that the offending blades might have been poisoned. Bravely, he sucked Lorenzo's wound.

Panic and confusion took hold in the cathedral. The crowd of fashionable citizens started running out, according to one witness, with their hearts in their throats. Some women screamed hysterically. General pandemonium broke out.

Just before the attack on the two brothers, Archbishop Salviati, who was sitting next to the cardinal, had left suddenly, claiming that he had to visit his ailing mother whom he had not seen in a very long time (hardly an impressive excuse for such a bold schemer). He was actually headed for the Signoria in the Palazzo Vecchio with his servants and Jacopo Bracciolini, intending to take over the government seat, the ultimate symbol of Florentine freedom. It was almost noon (the Mass had been delayed by the cardinal's late arrival) and the city officials were ready for lunch. In Italy it is rarely a good idea to interrupt someone's lunch. When Archbishop Salviati appeared unannounced, they became suspicious. The most inquisitive among them, Cesare Petrucci, a veteran militiaman, quickly saw through Salviati's garbled claims. He drew his sword and with the help of the servants kicked the archbishop and his men out of the room. In the meantime, Jacopo Bracciolini and some others had sneaked into the chancellery of the Signoria. The security door locked behind them, though, and it could not be opened without a secret key. They had set themselves up.

The Sonare di Palagio, a set of bells that was used as the government's emergency call to arms, was rung. Jacopo Pazzi reached the piazza on horseback at the head of a small army of hired soldiers and desperately tried to act as a ringleader, shouting "Hail to the People!" and "Freedom!" But the people took up their weapons and cried *"Palle, palle!"* (Balls, balls!, a reference to the Medici coat of arms) and *"Arme, arme!"* (To arms! To arms!). The staircases of the Signoria soon became a battleground. By the end of the fight, the steps were covered in blood and amputated human limbs. Scattered around were severed hands still holding swords and other blades.

◌ ◌ F ◌ ◌

ACCORDING TO GIOVANNI DI CARLO'S *History,* the sudden change of plan in the Pazzi plot was reminiscent of Gian Andrea Lampugnani's attack on the Duke of Milan in Santo Stefano sixteen months earlier. But the anti-Medici plotters either applied excessive force or lacked energy and precision. In any event, they did not achieve the same level of success as the Milanese killers, who had been practicing on a wooden dummy for weeks before the actual attack.

The military action throughout the conspiracy had been ineffectively executed. Preventing the Sonare di Palagio from ringing was key to allowing external troops into Florence. Once the bells had rung, all the city gates were sealed. Federico da Montefeltro must have been very disappointed with the feebleness of the conspirators. The only experienced soldier among them was Montesecco, who had refused to take the initiative on moral or religious grounds. The rest of the bunch were dilettantes of violence—mere big mouths, as Sixtus himself had reportedly described them to Montesecco.

Gian Battista Montesecco claimed that he had wanted to tell Lorenzo everything about the plot, but that he had not managed to do so. Giovanni di Carlo says that Gian Battista was a "naive soul" and found the murder of a gifted young man repugnant on principle. Gian Battista

The Pazzi conspiracy: in the mayhem Giuliano de' Medici lies dead on the
floor of the Duomo in Florence. A twentieth-century etching.

had not dared to kill in a holy church. He had refused to commit sacrilege, betrayal, and homicide.

About an hour after the attack in the church, Lorenzo managed to come out of the Old Sacristy. Armed followers and trustworthy friends came knocking on the bronze doors and explained that the uprising was being put down by the enraged Florentines. The very people the Pazzi had counted on to topple the Medici regime had turned against the conspirators and crushed them. Lorenzo walked out of the cathedral and was hurriedly escorted back to his palace, where the elaborate banquet lay untouched. He was probably not given the chance to see his brother's corpse lying on the floor in a pool of his own blood. Giuliano had been stabbed nineteen times. Franceschino Nori had died of his stomach wound.

PAYBACK TIME

As soon as the news of Lorenzo's survival spread in the streets, people rejoiced. His nearly miraculous escape reinforced their leader's power. His vendetta was carried out swiftly and without pity. The immediate, chaotic aftermath of the conspiracy was vividly described to Cicco Simonetta by Filippo Sacramoro, the Sforza ambassador in Florence, in a letter dated April 27. In the hours after his brother's assassination, Lorenzo, already recovering from the wound to his neck, walked around the Medici palace dressed in mourning clothes. He occasionally waved from the window to the crowds gathered in the streets or in the courtyard to express their sympathy and allegiance. The popular rage had not been prompted by Lorenzo, insisted Sacramoro.

The Florentine militia seized Francesco Pazzi, stark naked, from his private room in the family palazzo, where he was contemplating suicide. But he preferred to face certain death for the "ferocity of his soul," as

Giovanni di Carlo put it. Francesco was dragged into the streets, still bleeding from his thigh, tried on the spot, and hanged from the upper windows of the Palazzo Vecchio. Archbishop Salviati was given the chance to make his own confession: "Sacer, unctus, archiepiscopus sum" (I am holy, anointed, archbishop), he intoned, before he was hanged in his church robes, along with some close family members. Salviati had blamed Jacopo Pazzi for pushing him to the deed during the course of the past three years and claimed that he did not need any of this bloodshed, since he had an honorable archbishopric worth four thousand ducats a year and was waiting "in the name of the Holy Spirit to be pronounced cardinal." An epigram was circulated after the hanging, about Salviati wearing his sacred miter: in the tradition of Florentine gallows humor, the archbishop's skirt was said to be dangling like a bell. According to a gory urban legend, while the archbishop was hanging next to Francesco Pazzi, he bit him so violently in the chest in the midst of a furious death spasm that his teeth remained stuck in the flesh of his former friend.

Cardinal Riario, in the midst of this mayhem, had found refuge among the canons of the cathedral. By evening, however, two government officials had escorted the cardinal from the Duomo to the prison in the Palazzo Vecchio. Jailed as an invaluable hostage, he was forced to describe to the Holy Father, writing in his own hand, all that had happened. Jacopo Pazzi had fled through the Gate of the Cross, whose guards he had bribed beforehand. He was caught in the countryside and brought back on a stretcher, surrounded by shouting people, and hanged in Piazza della Signoria with all of his servants.

For a few days Montesecco's fate remained a mystery. He was the commander of fifty infantrymen and crossbowmen on horseback, some of whom had been killed during the riots, while others had fled with Jacopo Pazzi. No one knew whether Montesecco himself had been killed in the failed attack against the Palazzo Vecchio. Somebody did claim from *li indicij de li panni*—clues indicated by the clothing—that one of the corpses was his. But Giovanni di Carlo chillingly reports that the bodies had been disfigured to such an extent that many became unrecognizable.

In fact, Montesecco would not be caught until three days later. He was the only one of the plotters to be beheaded at the Porta del Podestà, the usual place for executions. All the others were hanged or torn to pieces by the populace. Jacopo Bracciolini, the treacherous humanist, had been caught, grabbed by the hair, and left hanging by his neck from the windows of the Palazzo Vecchio. The ropes were then cut and his corpse fell to the ground. Many of the other hired accessories were simply pushed alive from the upper floors of the building. Their remains were dragged around the piazza. About eighty people died altogether, including Stefano da Bagnone, the chaplain, and Antonio Maffei of Volterra, the apostolic secretary, the two priests who had tried to kill Lorenzo.

In the ensuing days, all the financial assets of the Pazzi banking dynasty, in Florence and elsewhere, were frozen. The few surviving male members of the family (among them Guglielmo, Lorenzo's brother-in-law, who was saved by his wife's pleading) were thrown into the dungeons of Volterra to serve life sentences. The tombstones of the Pazzi ancestors were erased, and the family portraits wiped out. As for the Pazzi women, they were forbidden to marry. Jacopo's daughter was deprived of all the jewels, clothes, rings, gems, and other ornaments that her doting father had given her. Her cloistered suffering after the attack was undoubtedly worsened by the fact that she had previously led such a pampered existence.

In the weeks following his hanging, Jacopo Pazzi's rotting corpse was disinterred twice. First the populace took it from the Pazzi Chapel in Santa Croce, and reburied it in unconsecrated ground outside the walls of Florence. Then they dug it up a second time and dragged it around the streets on the rope from which he had been hanged and threw it into the Arno. Reportedly, the bridges were crowded with people watching him float in the waters swollen by heavy spring rains. Then it was once again fished out and hung on a willow tree before being cut down, thrown back into the Arno, and left to drift all the way to Pisa and out to the sea beyond.

A BROTHERLY BURIAL

ON THE LAST DAY OF APRIL, THE FUNERAL OF GIULIANO DE' Medici was celebrated. The Duomo, site of the horrific stabbing, was hardly an appropriate location for the ceremony, so it took place in the Basilica of San Lorenzo, where the remains of the Medici ancestors rested peacefully behind the church's unfinished façade. In addition, the basilica was conveniently close to the Palazzo Medici.

This three-story palazzo looks like an elegant fortress, and its protective function now seemed more essential than ever. To get to the church for his brother's funeral, Lorenzo simply had to sneak out the rear entrance of the building, walk past the beautiful private garden crowded with bronze and marble statues, and cross the busy San Lorenzo piazza. Here he had only to climb Brunelleschi's stairway to reach the church. For such a short trip, less than a minute in length, Lorenzo was accompanied by twelve armed bodyguards. Fear was still hovering over Florence, and its surviving leader had to watch every step.

The service for Giuliano was remarkably modest. While many citizens wanted him to be buried with greater pageantry, Lorenzo wished his brother's funeral to be austere, like those of his father and grandfather. Through this understated approach to mourning, Lorenzo was reaffirming the continuity of the Medici dynasty. Giuliano's funeral was held at the same time as that of Lorenzo's friend Franceschino Nori, who had sacrificed his life to protect Lorenzo from the attack. This double ceremony signaled the rekindling of a mutual affection between Lorenzo and his people.

Cold-blooded politics, emotional tragedy, and refined taste coexisted to a shocking degree in the Italian Renaissance. Not long after his

Terra-cotta bust of Giuliano de' Medici, ca. 1475.

brother's death, for instance, Lorenzo commissioned the great sculptor Andrea Verrocchio to create three life-size terra-cotta busts depicting Giuliano, for display in the main Florentine churches. In one of them, Giuliano looks cheerful and cocky, dressed in an elegant breastplate of the sort that, had he been wearing it on the morning of April 26, would have protected him from his killers' knives.

A painted portrait that Lorenzo also commissioned shows Giuliano's image postmortem. His red robe blankets him like a shroud of death ready to be pulled over his dignified face. His eyes are almost shut, and his head is turned, giving him an appearance of sternness. The window behind him is ajar, as if the light of an Italian afternoon would be too strong for him to bear. This intimate, allegorical touch was painted by none other than the great Sandro Botticelli, a close friend of both brothers. At Lorenzo's request, this picture was not intended for public display, but was probably hung next to the portrait of Galeazzo Sforza in Lorenzo's bedroom, a work that seems to be its visual counterpart: by freezing the body, lowering the gaze, and casting the face in shadow, the active and celebratory image of the first portrait was transformed into one of contemplative mourning.

Ultimately, however, Lorenzo was a master of propaganda. A commemorative bronze medal that he had cast by Bertoldo di Giovanni was meant to reach the largest audience. The two sides of the medal show mirror images of the cowardly attack as seen from either corner of the Duomo altar. The plotters are dwarfed by the imposing profiles of the Medici brothers. The two Medicis resemble Botticelli's angels, in a slightly more masculine guise. Under the faces of Giuliano and Lorenzo are set the inscriptions "Public Mourning" and "Public Safety," respectively.

Lorenzo was an astute politician. But even as a political leader, he never gave up his literary ambitions. He was a prolific writer, composing light verse and serious poetry; he also compiled a collection of sonnets with his own commentary. Oddly, though, he did not leave us a single line commemorating his brother. It could be that writers were already officially at work on this task. Angelo Poliziano was in the middle of his poem *Stanze cominciate per la giostra del Magnifico Giuliano de' Medici* (*Stanzas Begun for the Joust of the Magnificent Giuliano de' Medici*) when

Portrait of Giuliano de' Medici by Sandro Botticelli, ca. 1478.

The Pazzi Medal, struck by Bertoldo di Giovanni in 1478.

the plotters left the subject floating in a pool of his own blood. The day of the attack, Poliziano approached the corpse lovingly and counted the stab wounds on it, as he touchingly reported in his commissioned account of the Pazzi plot. But the poet wanted to celebrate Giuliano's love of life and did not dare touch the *Stanze* after his hero's death. The poem describes the romance of young "Julio" and his mistress "Simonetta"— Simonetta Cattaneo—by means of a poetic transfiguration. There is, however, little psychological reliability in this idealized portrayal.

The stunning Simonetta, a married woman who died young in 1476, had received a state funeral that was actually more solemn and heartfelt than Giuliano's. But she had not been his only mistress. Before his death, it seems, Lorenzo's brother had left a sign of his mortal presence in the womb of a less lofty lady. Fioretta Gorini was seven months pregnant with Giuliano's child on April 26, 1478, the day of his murder. In late June she gave birth to a baby boy who was, not surprisingly, christened Giulio. This fatherless, illegitimate child, adopted by his grieving uncle Lorenzo, would be raised as a member of the Medici clan, eventually becoming a cardinal and finally a pope, under the name of Clement VII.

Le temps revient (time returns) was the Medici motto. Lorenzo expressed his brotherly love through clever patronage and the adoption of the deceased's illegitimate child. He also treasured the family memories of the brothers' childhood. In 1459 Benozzo Gozzoli had painted a gorgeous fresco cycle in the Medici Chapel inside the palazzo. This work depicted a large retinue accompanying the Three Magi as they paid homage to the newborn Christ child. In the midst of the multicolored crowd of noble Florentines and foreign guests from Europe and the Near East, three characters were shown: Lorenzo himself, his tutor Gentile Becchi, and his brother Giuliano.

Giuliano is the figure in the background, sandwiched between his brother's prominent nose and the teacher's protective gaze. The painter's subtle positioning of the figures provides insight into the Medici family dynamics. The firstborn, overwhelmingly bright and ambitious, would always cast his shadow on the younger, slightly less talented sibling. And now the shadow of death had engulfed him, at the age of twenty-five.

After Giuliano and Nori's funeral, Lorenzo did not set foot in the street for two days, remaining sheltered in the family palazzo. In the middle of the courtyard he could see Donatello's bronze sculpture of David, the graceful killer of the evil giant, an emblem of beauty, youth, and effortless physical skill. This slim nude figure stood on top of a column in the middle of the Medici courtyard, triumphant over Goliath's severed head. The short, bloody sword hanging from those delicate teenage hands might have now seemed like a chilling reminder of the recent carnage. And although Lorenzo swiftly recovered from the slight wound on his neck that he had received in the Duomo, the worst was still to come.

7

EXTREME MEASURES

ISTORIAN NICOLAI RUBINSTEIN OPENS HIS FA-
MOUSLY WELL-DOCUMENTED AND NOW CANONICAL
BOOK, *THE GOVERNMENT OF FLORENCE UNDER THE
MEDICI (1434–1494)*, BY WRITING: "The political régime which
was founded by Cosimo de' Medici and perfected by his grandson
Lorenzo differed from the despotic states of fifteenth-century Italy in the
preservation of republican institutions. Described as a tyranny by its enemies, its critics had to admit that the Medici acted within the frame-
work of the constitution."

The great challenge for Lorenzo, in the immediate aftermath of the
Pazzi plot, was to preserve the appearance of a republican regime while
defending his status as the wounded, unofficial leader of the Florentine
state. Since December 1469, when at age twenty he had taken over the
role of first citizen from his late father, Lorenzo had managed to walk a
fine line as both the guarantor of the people's liberty and the richest and
most powerful member of the community. If Galeazzo Maria Sforza, the
Duke of Milan, "thought, in January 1471, that Lorenzo, 'having begun
to understand what medicine he needed,' might make a bid for despotic
government, he was clearly mistaken," Rubinstein reminds us, arguing
that Lorenzo's ascendancy in Florence was enhanced by the fact that he
did not act like a petty tyrant. When he came under attack personally in
1478, a large part of the citizenry, which depended on the Medici goodwill, spontaneously rose to his defense not out of fear, as had been the
case after Galeazzo's murder in Milan, but out of rage and worry that

their freedom might be jeopardized. Lorenzo's survival in the wake of his brother's death paved the way for a new, insidious form of republican regime that justified some anticonstitutional, extreme measures to face the terrorizing urgency of the unexpected political circumstances. This was to be the new Medici medicine.

THE CONDOTTIERE'S CONSCIENCE

ON MAY 2, 1478, FLORENTINES WERE STILL BEWILDERED AND overwhelmed by sadness. *Calendimaggio* (the May Day Feast, a celebration of the coming of spring), traditionally one of the most colorful and cheerful occasions in the Florentine calendar, had been canceled due to the civic mourning for Giuliano de' Medici. That morning, just a week after his brother's assassination, Lorenzo received a letter that had been rushed overnight from the steep hills of Urbino. It conveyed Federico da Montefeltro's official condolences. The duke wrote that he had been informed, both by Lorenzo's letter (which has been lost) and "through many other channels," of the "horrendous and despicable attack" against Giuliano, for which he felt "deep displeasure and immense pain":

> *Nonetheless, things having happened in the way they did, through the divine grace and virtue of Your Magnificence and the extraordinary love and faith demonstrated by this magnificent people and by your friends, you have to be very content and thank God! And since things, God be thanked, happened in the way that they did, I do not consider it is necessary right now that I offer my assistance otherwise than by thanking Your Magnificence who with so much trust and love has communicated to me this adverse occurrence. I want to make sure that in the future Your Magnificence realizes that I am available to help you.*

As soon as you request my help, I will give it gladly and willingly, as I have done at all other times and to satisfy you in part with that charity and love that you require. I would prefer that Your Magnificence and the others who have to govern Italy chose a path in which the passions might abate, otherwise they will so easily lead to a disturbance. It is hard to overstate how much good springs from straightening things up in the beginning, and much more than could be fathomed; but on the contrary, when from the beginning one slides little by little into an uncomfortable situation, it picks up momentum, so much so that one could hardly remedy it. And Your Magnificence, by benefiting from your own prudence and potency, I believe that you should try hard to make it right by God and by the world; moreover, you are doing so well—by the grace of God—that more than anybody else you should desire peace and general quiet.

Most historians have never questioned the good faith and sympathetic intentions expressed by this letter. The recipient, however, must have read it very differently. Once he had penetrated the writer's intricate, contorted style, Lorenzo could hardly have believed his eyes. What was Federico talking about? *God be thanked, make it right by God and by the world, by the grace of God!* Lorenzo was still grieving for his brother, and now he was being asked to be patient and passive, and be grateful to the God who had not protected his beloved sibling in God's own house?

The tone, the content, and especially the closing sentences of the letter conveyed little in the spirit of condolence. On the contrary, this was, in fact, a threatening, implicit declaration of war. The offer of help was rhetorically empty. The message, once rhetorically decoded, stripped of its formalities, was clear: Lorenzo should consider himself lucky not to be dead, and if he wanted to live, he had better be quiet and do nothing to disturb God—God in this case being none other than the worldly and wrathful vicar, Pope Sixtus IV, and his henchman, Federico.

By the time he received the letter, though, Lorenzo was already aware that Montefeltro must have had a hand in the conspiracy. The Milanese envoy in Florence shared with Cicco concerned reports about the "son of the Duke of Urbino," the illegitimate Antonio, captain of the Sienese army, who had apparently been called from Siena to fight against Florence. And he had learned that eight soldiers, all but one in the Urbino uniform, had been captured on the outskirts of Florence and hanged on the spot.

Once he had read this friendly letter, Lorenzo's earlier suspicion that Federico had supported and perhaps even engineered the attack must have turned to certainty. Now he faced the difficult task of deciding how to respond to this offensive missive, one that wounded his personal pride as much as it threatened his political power. In the whole of Italy, there was only one person Lorenzo could still trust: his single true ally, Cicco Simonetta, the regent of the Milanese state. Already on May 3, the Sforza ambassador in Florence replied to Cicco, who had proposed "suspending the bargaining around the *condotta* [hiring contract] of the Duke of Urbino," that Lorenzo was "of the same opinion." They agreed to abolish his stipend, the *condottiere*'s livelihood.

On May 4, in the hours before his execution, Gian Battista, Count of Montesecco, the papal soldier and former subject of the Duke of Urbino, handed over the confession about the organization of the plot that his jailers had seen him writing. The document was an indictment of the pope and his clan, including Montefeltro. Yet when the Florentine chancery published Montesecco's confession later in the summer, they were careful to expunge the sections of the text relating to the Duke of Urbino. The doctored version of the incriminating document would serve the purpose of leaving the door open for Federico, so he might switch sides without losing face.

In Florence nobody dared say in public that the Duke of Urbino was directly implicated in the plot. However, some gossip was circulating widely, albeit prudently. An anonymous Florentine poem stated that involved in the plot were "others of great condition, / but it is better not to speak their names / although each of them was born of humble origins, / so that anyone can guess who they are." The reference to the fact that Federico was a bastard son (and so was Ferrante of Aragon, King of Naples) was quite obvious for anybody in Italy at the time. Another poem, attributed to Luigi Pulci and addressed to Giuliano's pious mother, Lucrezia Tornabuoni, attacked the Roman Church as underworld god Pluto's "new wife," as a poisonous Babylon, and as a "schismatic synagogue." There was no need to spell out Sixtus IV's name.

Once Montesecco's confession became known, Federico was not sure whether he would be accused openly and started to feel pressure. On May 8, he decided to write Cicco a wordy letter, filled with partial confessions and warnings, trying to prevent the impending rupture between them. This letter is an extraordinary blend of political dissimulation and truth, demonstrating how deeply Montefeltro was involved in the plot:

> From this situation in Florence, which you know about, I have felt and still feel a great displeasure for many reasons, as I have also conveyed to the Magnificent Lorenzo de' Medici, who wrote to me. And certainly, however horrendous the case was, it can better be seen through the great violence of offenses received which pushes others to put themselves at such risk, like these wretches of the Pazzi household did. They did not consider or fear death or the ultimate destruction of their lineage. To be fair, Lorenzo de' Medici in some instances has let himself go beyond reason, and not only against the Pazzi but also against the Pope, so that what has happened has happened. I am very sure though that this all occurred without the awareness of His Holiness, i.e. that he did not know or consent that anybody would be killed. However, I have known for a while that perhaps His Holiness would not have minded, or would have in fact appreciated and greatly liked a regime change in Florence.

So far, the letter seems amazingly sincere and straightforward; the writer wishes to establish his trustworthiness. Montefeltro claims that there would have been good grounds for the pope to complain about Lorenzo's behavior, because of his recent interference in business between Church and city-states both in Città di Castello and in Montone. He even comes close to confessing his own participation in the plot:

> Had I been told about this plot, it would not have been licit for me in any way to do anything but keep it to myself and secret, since I am mostly a soldier of the Pope and the King of Naples and being paid by

their monies, which makes me loyal and obedient to them. Nor should there be anybody who thought differently, since I would be a bad man if I propagated something confidentially communicated to me by my patrons. I say this because some footsoldiers of mine went from Castello with Lorenzo Giustini, whom I had sent upon his request to deal with some troubles he had in his town, and I have his letter which I can show upon request. I am very sorry for what happened, but now I tell you that if some remedy is not found to re-establish things easily in their proper balance, it will not be too long before things might get so bad they will be beyond repair and lead all of Italy into war, a situation that is not generally desirable, nor a situation that I would want at all. Having suggested to your Magnificence the proper remedy for this situation, you have, God Willing, the power and means to take care of it.

Federico seems to have thought hard enough about the justification he would use in case the attack went wrong. But his partial denial also spells out his awareness of the plot. He claims that his concern is to restore the lost balance of power by pretending that nothing has really happened. In fact, his pragmatic, soldierly talk is deceptive: between the lines, he is saying, "Let's deal with the consequences, no matter what the causes."

Federico's mention of Lorenzo Giustini's request for troops to sort out "troubles" in his town of Città di Castello is a revealing touch of insincerity. Federico had bothered asking Giustini for a letter he could "show upon request" to discharge himself from any wrongdoing. But it was a lame alibi. Giustini was a trusted member of the Roman clan and the bearer of the golden chain for Federico's son Guidobaldo that had sealed the deal with the pope's emissary back in February. The captain from Castello had in fact been in command of the six hundred troops sent from Urbino. He had also prevented Bernardo Bandini, Giuliano's killer, from being immediately captured and helped him flee toward the East.

The indirect evidence against Montefeltro provided by this letter might have been enough to close the case in history's tribunal. But a much more interesting story lies ahead. Federico's secretary sent to Cicco's son Gian Giacomo a less openly aggressive letter, in which the Duke of Urbino's awareness of certain plans (for regime change but not death) is conveyed in a slightly more nuanced form. Federico, in the words of his subordinate, did "not deny at all having known all these things for a while, that is, from the time when he was in Montone with his army." Federico is quoted as having prudently voiced some concerns about Montesecco's allegations against him. He is also said to have examined his "conscience" as a statesman and his "worldly honor" as a soldier, phrases pointing to the complex relationship with his two paying patrons. The secretary writes:

> *His Lordship says that in the beginning he tried to dissuade the King and the Pope from doing this deed for its evil and scandalous nature, but after seeing that this was taken badly and that the water was already running downhill he shut his mouth and his eyes, hoping and believing that the conclusion of his* condotta *with the League would sweeten the passions of some and would make them forget and throw aside this bestiality, mostly because they seemed to be so enthused about it. As you know, all the opposite has happened, since they have turned this* condotta *into a mercantile business, and under its banner they have committed this misdeed, and made him [the Duke] look like a beast, shaming him. He has relied on the Pope in order to justify himself to the King more strongly, but His Holiness has conferred on him the beautiful honor of shaming him.*

One could almost sympathize with Federico's irritation over the failed plan, but he also flatly denied that the condolence letter to Lorenzo contained anything reproachable or malicious. Responding to Cicco's charge of having received news

> *from Florence that the letter written by the Duke of Urbino to the Magnificent Lorenzo contained a coda or conclusion which could be interpreted in bad terms, the Duke of Urbino says he marvels greatly, since he has written to Lorenzo nothing but good and that there is no part in his letter which does what you say.*

The condolence message of May 1 had not gone unnoticed by the canny Lorenzo, and its insidious nature is now all too evident to the contemporary reader. Having failed to scare the Medici into silence, Montefeltro went on denying that his troops might have been spotted outside Florence. Here, the extent of Federico's shamelessness is truly exceptional. He has his secretary write further to Gian Giacomo:

> *I reply that it could perhaps be the case that somebody with our uniform has been seen around, since many who wear it are not men of my Lord or hired by him, as it can be clearly noticed, but that there would have been some of the Lord's country, that is, his soldiers or somebody else fighting for him. Rest assured that my Lord says that this is not the truth and that it will never be found out that he has been involved in any way in the aforementioned event.*
>
>

Urbino, 13 May 1478.

> *P.S. Some merchants and other people of ours who were there at the time of this event in Florence have returned here; they report that it is true that in Florence it has been said that somebody was wearing the Duke of Urbino's uniform, but then a comparison was made and it was found that it was not the one of the Duke of Urbino, and this is the actual truth.*

o   o   E   o   o

DID FEDERICO ACTUALLY EXPECT to be believed? Or, like many mobsters on trial in our own time, was he just refusing to admit the evidence of facts? The rhetoric of truth is most frequently adopted by professional liars. Federico was using the double Montefeltro code, which Simonetta had learned to appreciate during the previous thirty-five years of dealing with the fox from Urbino.

Cicco knew that the situation called for speedy action rather than hypocritical indignation. The chancellor faced a difficult diplomatic challenge, one worthy of his Machiavellian and "most excellent" brain. He did not hide from himself that this was the point of no return in his longstanding friendship with Federico, and, as usual, he acted swiftly and secretly. In a letter dated May 9, he had already implored Lorenzo to heavily guard himself, even though this might be a source of public gossip. Without naming names, Cicco then alluded to Federico as one of the various "authors" and "instigators" of the "horrific deed." Whether these people only passively knew about, or actively participated in, the "betrayal," in the event of a counterattack, warned Cicco, it was best in any case to *pretend* (the verb *fingere* is added by Cicco in the original draft) not to have "seen" or "understood" their role in the deed, "passing everything under silence and in the utmost secrecy."

Sometimes, playing dumb is the smartest political maneuver. Cicco had firsthand knowledge of this truth, having learned it the hard way in his long career under Francesco Sforza, a master of manipulation. One of the main rules in the game was never to let your enemy find out your true intentions. In fact, Cicco had already started playing the game and acted upon the first reports before Federico's letter to him of May 8. He personally wrote a sample letter addressed to Federico on Florence's behalf and shipped it to Lorenzo, who liked it "immensely," had it copied "word by word," and sent to Urbino and Rome, in order to suspend at once all the bargaining around Federico's stipends. Lorenzo's reply of May 12 to Cicco contains all the self-deprecating sarcasm that one might expect from him:

> the writing of the Milanese State . . . appears to me loving and pru-
> dent . . . I thank you for the affection, great prudence, grave coun-
> sel . . . I know well, given both the nature of those who offend in
> general and the particular conditions of those who have offended me,
> that we need to keep our eyes wide open and not to trust our innocence,
> since if that were enough, what happened would not have happened. I
> hope to God, who this time has saved me miraculously, that perhaps I
> will be worthy of His pity, so that He will have saved me for a purpose.

IN THE NAME OF THE FATHER

LORENZO'S SELF-PITY AND PLEA TO GOD WERE INDEED APPRO-priate. Keeping quiet in the poisoned atmosphere that followed the Pazzi conspiracy was almost impossible. Florentine ambassadors and merchants in Rome were threatened by the pope with jail or murder, in open disregard of treaties between the states. Sixtus was furious about the arrest in Florence, shortly after the attacks, of his young nephew Cardinal Raffaele Riario, who was held captive for about a month. After a series of intense negotiations, the cardinal was finally released. But the irate pontiff excommunicated Lorenzo and indicted the entire city of Florence under the pretext that its citizens and officials had hanged members of the clergy, including the archbishop of Pisa and the apostolic secretary Antonio Maffei of Volterra, Lorenzo's attacker. The only way for the Florentines to save their souls was to get rid of the God-defying Medici leader, or at least so said the pope.

Cardinal Riario was released from prison on June 7. The Florentine magistrates and many citizens accompanied him on his walk from the Palazzo Vecchio to the Annunziata church. He was "in dread of being killed by the populace," as the contemporary diarist Luca Landucci noted. One can only imagine what the angry Florentine mob, notoriously loudmouthed, shouted at the pope's young nephew. He was escorted by forty guards but the terror he experienced that day would remain with him for the rest of his life: a legend describes him as permanently pale. It was on that very day, as Landucci records, that "the Pope excommunicated us" (that is, the Florentine people). The shameful papal bull had in fact been published almost a week earlier, on June 1, but its terrible content was not immediately divulged to the people.

On June 12, once his way out was secured, Cardinal Riario finally left Florence. The most influential citizens called for an immediate emergency meeting. Lorenzo knew this was the moment of truth: it was also the supreme test of his statesmanship and of the cohesion of the regime. He gave a memorable speech, reported by Giovanni di Carlo in the *History of His Times*. Giovanni began his account by describing the three civic parties in attendance. At the meeting, the angriest citizens blamed the pope and his priests, who must not only have been aware of the plot but also involved in it. Others, Giovanni tells us, expressed sorrow and some pushed for a diplomatic solution by sending envoys to the pope and the King of Naples to avoid war. At that point, Lorenzo rose to his feet and waited for silence in the crowd. Then he spoke in his nasal voice:

> On this public occasion, Sworn Fathers, if I were not struck by a private mourning in my soul and body, perhaps I would talk at more length, deploring it along with you, acting like an eloquent orator and taking on the role of the good citizen. However, the indignity and impiety of the case burdens and hampers me. Words fail me, and my teeth impede the movements of my tongue.
>
> It is customary for mortal men, when they experience something bad or evil, to seek refuge with their relatives, friends, and in extreme need with priests and holy bishops who, if unable to provide help, can at least alleviate pain and ease sadness with their words. As the philosopher says, we are born not only for ourselves, but also for our fatherland, for our countrymen and even more for our neighbors, in order to assist them and favor them as much as we can. For the same reason, matrimonies, pacts and agreements are made in every business, whether civil or military, especially at a time so full of troubles and calamities.

Lorenzo was appealing to the strong sense of the Christian and communal bonds among the Florentines. In the most charged moment of what in effect was his survival speech, he addressed himself to his dead sibling, in a low, moving voice:

Dearest brother, whose wounds are still under my eyes, how should I talk about your undeserved death? Perhaps I should look for priests or churchmen, who were not only present at this horror, but even participated in it? In pagan Rome, divine temples used to be refuges for safety, whereas in the greatest Christian temple consecrated to God my brother was killed and I was hit, pulling through by a hair from the hands of impious killers . . .

Lately, I have been reconsidering my situation, and I think my brother's fate is preferable to mine. I have preserved my life, which turns out to be damaging for you and for the city.

Sworn Fathers, you are my friends. I owe you everything. All citizens must place the common before the private good, but I more than anyone else, as the one who has received from you and the fatherland more and greater benefits. Therefore, use my wealth as you please, I am ready to go into exile or to die. I am ready to go off to the farthest islands on earth or migrate from this life altogether. You have fed me and raised me, and you can take everything from me. If you find it is of use to the Republic, kill me with your own hands, since I am in your hands anyway, as are my children and my wife. If you want, let them have the same fate as mine, the most honest death. It will be to the eternal decency and praise of yours that you have submitted us to exile or death for the good and safety of the people and city. For the state and the city and the people, there would be no better divine and more tolerable goodness than to let us die at your hands—the hands of my parents, my citizens and friends. But my brother was innocent and nonetheless he was killed in the spring of his life . . . If they attacked him in our great and famous church, during the celebration of divine rites, can you trust the Pope's most secular promises? . . .

So, decide of me and my children what you think is best for the welfare of the Republic, and whatever your decision I will consider it the best and safest.

In his *Florentine Histories,* Machiavelli reports that the assembled audience could not hold back tears. No such melodramatic outcome is recorded by Giovanni di Carlo, who was present at the oration and wrote it down only a couple of years after it was pronounced. His version is therefore slightly more reliable than the one reinvented by Machiavelli half a century later. And while, in Machiavelli, the political reasoning that followed this emotionally charged moment remained in Lorenzo's speech, Giovanni left it to an unnamed citizen. But then Machiavelli's *Florentine Histories* were commissioned by Pope Clement VII, son of Giuliano de' Medici, and to present Lorenzo performing a one-man show of political bravura was appropriate to a Medici pope. For Machiavelli, Lorenzo was being an astute politician when he fashioned himself as a sacrificial lamb offering to give away all his power and even his life: he was really aiming to preserve his position and his family, with all his money and influence intact.

In Giovanni's account, on the other hand, the nameless Florentine orator who stood up after Lorenzo's speech mentioned the approaching "Urbino phalanx," the scary proximity of Federico's army, and then launched into a general wake-up call to the sleeping city of Florence. After listing a series of popular proverbs, such as "only the good fighter gets a good peace" and "don't let the wolves in among the sheep," he asked a rhetorical question: "Who would think that a wolf dressed in sheep's clothing can be anything other than a wolf?" (a clear reference to Sixtus, who had shown himself more of a wolf than a sheep, or shepherd for that matter). Eventually, the speaker came to his point:

> They want to invade the whole city. They are not after Lorenzo and his acolytes, but they want to put a yoke on the entire state. If they wanted only Lorenzo, why would they move so many troops and occupy our public buildings? . . . It is an extreme measure for Popes to call on secular armies . . . I know for a fact I am hated by priests, who lack piety and religion and respect for God, and who are greedy and corrupt . . . Let's send envoys, even clerics, to the farthest corners of the earth to get money to fight this war. If we should lose, at least we will lose not like nervous women, but like strong men . . . In such extraordinary circumstances as ours, it is not necessary to respect the status quo.

Lorenzo made a masterly use of counterpropaganda. To fight the war of words against Sixtus IV, he hired an army of lawyers who argued that the crimes against clergy members had been committed in self-defense. How indeed could the pope forget that the archbishop of Pisa had attempted, weapons in hand, to seize the Palazzo Vecchio? Who could deny that the plotters had paid killers to attack Florentine citizens in the main cathedral? The case for the excommunication of Florence hinged entirely on the faint assumption that Sixtus was acting in good faith. But after the plot, it was far easier to claim that the pope was a tyrant and a crook.

THE BLOODY BIBLE

THE FLORENTINES REACTED TO THE POPE'S THREAT WITH A most violent pamphlet. Longtime Medici supporter Gentile Becchi—who had been the brothers' tutor before becoming bishop of Arezzo—took charge of the response to the excommunication: in the fiery, sacrilegious *Florentine Synodus,* he reported that all the Tuscan bishops had gathered and attacked the pope as an arch-assassin, "Vicar of the Devil" and "Pimp of the Church." This counterexcommunication was meant to ruin the Holy See's reputation in Italy and across the Alps.

Sixtus IV saw the dangers involved in this defamatory campaign and commissioned a quickly printed attack for circulation in Germany, France, and other countries. This document, entitled *Dissension Arisen Between the Holy Pontiff and the Florentines,* survives in only a handful of copies around the world, and it has never been studied until now. The anonymous author uses all the nasty arguments he can find to show up Lorenzo's weakness, mocking him for being incapable of opposing the military might of King Ferrante of Naples, and at some point bursts out: "If God is with us, who is against us?" The use of Mark's Gospel is a powerful piece of counterpropaganda from the righteous defender of the faith. The *Dissension* lists all the Florentine misdeeds, discredits the "heretical and sodomitical *Synodus*" (its author, Gentile Becchi, bishop of Arezzo, was rumored to be homosexual), and avoids mentioning Giuliano, until suddenly declaring that he died "by God's will" and because of his wretched life. Then it offers a twisted biography of Lorenzo as an early apprentice to the ways of evil and tyranny.

Gentile Becchi had plenty of motivation. He was a native of Urbino, and his family possessions were being seized at the duke's will, even as the excommunication against the Florentines was destroying his revenue as bishop of Arezzo. And Arezzo was the town southwest of Gubbio that would likely have been awarded to Federico if the Pazzi operation had gone well. Without mincing words, in his typically biting style, Becchi wrote to Federico's secretary: "You say to me that I should become like the angel of peace. Who is waging war, you or we, who have been cut into pieces in church? Attacked by a huge army, we even have to feel guilty. If you asked anybody involved: 'What have we done against you?,' what would you answer in good faith?"

In the midst of this theological turmoil, Federico was absorbed by a personal, seemingly petty concern. Over the preceding years he had invested several thousand florins in the making of a gorgeously illuminated edition of the second half of the Bible (from the Book of Job to Revelation), which he had commissioned from the most famous manuscript dealer of the time, Vespasiano da Bisticci. Vespasiano, who ran the largest workshop in Florence, was also a writer in his own right, and left us a series of biographical medallions of the illustrious men of his day. Unsurprisingly, he had only praise for Federico's virtues as a soldier and as a humanist, and for his expensive taste in richly decorated books.

The Bible was to be the jewel in Federico's sumptuous collection, and the duke could not bear the thought of possibly losing it to the Florentines. The huge manuscript had been completed on June 12, the day of Lorenzo's survival speech. It was dedicated to the "Church's Commander, engaged in defending the Christian religion no less than adorning it." Lorenzo, the "Son of Iniquity and Perdition" according to Sixtus IV's bull, must have appreciated the irony of the situation: the pope's captain depended on his excommunicated enemy to release the

*The opening page of the second volume of the Montefeltro Bible,
produced in Florence and finished on June 12, 1478.*

most precious Bible ever made. But Lorenzo politely had the lavish folio sent to Federico.

On June 21 Federico thanked Lorenzo for his kindness, but by then war planning was already under way. A Florentine agent in Urbino informed Lorenzo that the duke was preparing for battle, although in late June he was still recovering from the November injury to his leg. Federico had an "ingenious" saddle-chair built to allow him to ride with the injured leg around his horse's neck. The horse was paraded daily in the streets of Urbino to demonstrate that the duke intended to keep his promise to lead his own troops. But in a confidential letter, the agent wrote to Lorenzo that, one day, while Federico had proudly mounted his horse, he had not been able to restrain muffled cries upon dismounting. The duke was reportedly furious that his moment of weakness had been witnessed by Lorenzo's man.

According to the courtly poem written by Giovanni Santi, the mission of the unnamed Florentine envoy in Urbino had been to complain unofficially to Federico about his complicit silence about the conspiracy and to question his moral integrity. Apparently, Federico had replied to the envoy's line of questioning with the same arguments he had used earlier in the letter to Cicco: it is not reasonable to alert an enemy (such as Lorenzo) and offend your good patrons, so if he had known anything, he would have kept his mouth shut. In the past he had had many offers from people willing to discreetly rid him of his foes (such as his late archenemy Sigismondo Malatesta), but he would rather fight a "nasty war" even if he could not even stand on his feet.

In the meantime, Federico's papal *condotta* was finally confirmed and paid in full, making the loss of Florentine and Milanese money more bearable. It amounted to the fantastic sum of 77,000 ducats for commanding four hundred men-at-arms and four hundred foot soldiers. The cash was brought to Federico by the pope's usual intermediary, Lorenzo Giustini. After their three-hour-long secret meeting, rumors spread in Urbino that everybody in the ducal army would be paid immediately: fifteen ducats to the cavalrymen and eight ducats to the foot soldiers. The generous and immediate pay to 370 *huomini d'arme* (men-at-arms) showed the duke's readiness. There was still some debate about whether his recovery would be speedy enough for him to command his troops. Federico also put in place some extreme security measures: he had left his palace only twice in June, each time surrounded by cross-bowmen carrying swords and Bolognese machetes, and the gates were guarded so closely that no one was permitted to enter. Paranoia and fear of being killed were unusual characteristics for a professional soldier, especially a mercenary like Federico. It was not a pretty sight.

The spy who provided this detailed information was Matteo Contugi, a calligrapher from Volterra who had been hired in Urbino to copy some of the most beautiful manuscripts in the famous Montefeltro Library. This is only one of many entertaining reports from this educated and clever man, who held a respectable post in the court of Urbino. He was above any suspicion there, although since he was from Volterra, the city that the duke had sacked, Contugi had good reason to hold a secret grudge against him.

Contugi added that Federico had also received some gifts from Cicco. They were probably wrapped into cheese shapes, so that nobody would see or steal them. The well-informed agent writes that they consisted of a rich cover for a horse's head, a beautiful helmet, and a sword. One may wonder why Cicco was bothering with these gifts. Apparently, he was still hoping that the war machine would stop, and that Federico would switch horses.

In early July 1478, Cicco wrote to Lorenzo that Florence and Milan were *unum velle et unum nolle* (united in willing and unwilling) and that they would be made or unmade together. When Lorenzo received this letter, the excommunicated but still devout Florentines were celebrating the delayed Feast of San Giovanni (which was really on June 25) "as if it had been the real day." The people tried to find some relief and distraction in the usual *passatempi*. But just a week later, on July 13, the city had to wake up to the bitter reality: the King of Naples had sent a herald with the papal ultimatum. The most influential citizens of Florence agreed that expelling Lorenzo from the city would not solve their problems. And so the Pazzi war began.

8

LIVES AT STAKE

WARFARE IN RENAISSANCE ITALY WAS OFTEN MORE A MATTER OF SHREWDNESS THAN BRAVERY. The rules of engagement were to avoid confrontation and play with strategic delays—unless the use of brutal force became necessary. Federico did not hesitate to resort to violence. He was a steadfast commander and also an expert in military technology. His engineers and architects were the best brains in Italy. His tactics included the use of devastating artillery devices as well as the construction of strongholds.

In his youth he had displayed his military skills when he took by a nocturnal attack the Castle of San Leo, a virtually impregnable fortress built on a tall, precipitous rock. Federico had some long ladders made, and his men successfully climbed all the way to the top—when they were having second thoughts midway, he threatened to pull the ladders away. This act of bravado had persuaded Federico's archenemy Sigismondo Malatesta, the lord of neighboring Rimini, to accept a truce with Urbino.

In his dialogue on *The Art of War* as much as in his *Florentine Histories*, Machiavelli poked fun at the virtually bloodless battles featured in the last decades of the fifteenth century. The main purpose of fighting, for largely mercenary troops, was in fact to loot more than to win. And the civilian population, as usual, would pay the highest price. One should keep that in mind while reading this brief account of the Pazzi war, which lasted almost two years—that is, two springs and summers, until the fall of 1479.

The army hired by Florence and Milan against Pope Sixtus IV and King Ferrante of Naples seemed strong at first, but internal feuds weakened its power. Since the start, Lorenzo and Cicco had employed two expensive mercenary captains, Ercole d'Este, Duke of Ferrara, and young Federico Gonzaga, Marquis of Mantua, but the two fought over leadership, slowing down their own military operations. They ended up pillaging each other's military camps. This was a perfect environment for a ruthless veteran like the Duke of Urbino, who took advantage of every opportunity offered to him by his enemies.

The battles of the Pazzi war were relatively bloodless for the armies, but the war has remained notorious as a testing ground for innovative siege weapons, including chemical artillery. Federico was particularly keen on new, deadly devices. He boasted in a letter to Matthias Corvinus, king of Hungary, about his five field-pieces, called bombards, distinguished by startling names such as the Cruel, the Desperate, the Victory, Ruin, None of Your Jaw. One of the largest consisted of two portions weighing 14,000 and 11,000 pounds each. It discharged balls of stone, varying in weight from 370 to 380 pounds. Federico was eager to see it at work.

A DIRTY FIGHT

ON JULY 25, AN ANGRY AND ANXIOUS POPE SIXTUS IV WROTE in his own hand to Federico a letter half in inelegant Latin, half in uncultivated Italian:

> We trust that God, whose honour and glory are at stake, will grant you victory in everything, especially as our intentions are straightforward and just. For we make war on no one save that ungrateful, excommu-

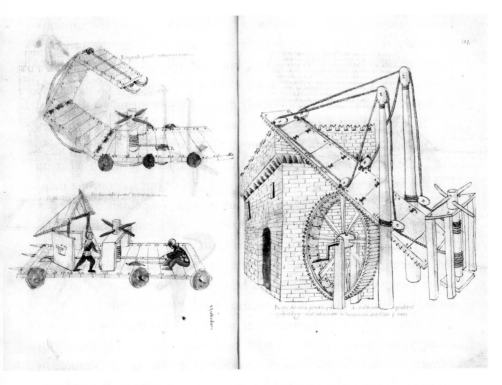

War machine, in Roberto Valturio's volume, De Re Militari. *This work was composed for Federico da Montefeltro's enemy Sigismondo Malatesta, lord of Rimini. Federico eagerly studied the military techniques of his adversary.*

nicated and heretical Lorenzo de' Medici, and we pray to God to punish him for his infamous acts, and to you as God's minister deputed to avenge the wrongs he has iniquitously and without cause committed against God and his Church, with such ingratitude that the fountain of infinite love has been dried up.

The Duke of Urbino hardly needed the pope's blessing to be encouraged in his bellicose enterprises. Before the beginning of the hostilities, Federico—who was still recovering from his leg wound—predicted in a speech to his soldiers, who were eager to loot rich prey on Tuscan soil, that within three years the bold Florentines would be reduced to nothing. "Naked and on their knees," embellished Giovanni Santi, imitating

Federico's oratory style in the poem he wrote to celebrate the captain's successes, "they will come to plead for mercy and will lower the lofty pretenses of their ancient freedom (if one can still call it that, I do not know). They will be brought down to their knees for a long time, and their ancient glory will be hopelessly dressed in a mourning suit!"

The prose of war was even more disagreeable than these gloomy, versified prophecies. When in the summer of 1478 a plague struck Tuscany, the Duke of Urbino reportedly said that the disease achieved what he had not yet hoped to obtain through war, wiping out most of the men. Federico's ally Alfonso of Aragon, who led the Neapolitan troops, was renowned for his ferocity on the battlefield. A Florentine official who was trying to resist Alfonso's siege in Castellina, in the Chianti valley, sent a message to him complaining that he had found some poisoned arrows thrown at the defenders, and he warned Alfonso that if that continued he would attach toxic substances to the Tuscan artillery.

But the relationship between Federico, now old and crippled, and the younger, impulsive Alfonso was not all that smooth. The malicious calligrapher-turned-spy Contugi reports that the allied Neapolitan troops nicknamed the Duke of Urbino Cain: the rumors that Federico was behind the killing of his stepbrother Oddantonio were still very much alive thirty-four years after he had seized power over the Montefeltro region. In some ways, the troops were justified: over the decades, the duke had remained as ruthless a field commander as he was a politician, and the Pazzi war presented him with a good opportunity to show off his military prowess.

The true soldier knows when he must use force and when he must resort to fraud—that is, when to be a lion and when to be a fox. And Federico was a true soldier. The first serious strategic challenge that he faced was the siege of the virtually impregnable Florentine Castle of Sansavino, not far from Siena. At a point when his camp was floating in mud and his army was demoralized, he delivered such a galvanizing speech that he pulled his forces back together. According to Santi, he paraded "more than a thousand horses" and his famous bombards in front of the castle's walls, just to frighten the besieged. Then he obtained a general ceasefire, approved by Ercole d'Este, commander in chief of the Florentine and Milanese army, pretending that he had not sought it.

During the eight-day ceasefire Federico received money and ammunition from Rome and fresh crossbowmen from Urbino. As soon as the hostilities were about to resume, he made such a show of force that he did not need to use it against Sansavino. The castle's captain simply resigned, keys in hand. "Sometimes a captain needs to be a lion, sometimes a fox"—Santi had him say in his celebratory poem, adding: "A single eye has seen more than a hundred-thousand!" Federico was amused by the astute Florentines' outcry that they had been tricked by a shrewdness greater than theirs. This dirty war quickly began to wear down the Florentine forces and their close Milanese allies.

CICCO'S WAR

LORENZO WAS NOT THE ONLY TARGET OF THE PAZZI WAR. FOR Roberto da Sanseverino and the exiled Sforza brothers Sforza Maria and Ludovico, who had naturally sided with the enemies of Florence, Cicco was still enemy number one. Cicco's age was taking its toll, and he had begun to resemble other powerful gout-stricken figures such as Pius II, or Piero de' Medici, who had often governed from their bed. With the incompetent Duchess Bona and the child-duke Gian Galeazzo utterly incapable of governing, and with Cicco struggling with his health, Milan was particularly vulnerable.

Since his exile in May 1477 the hot-tempered *condottiere* Roberto da Sanseverino had been restlessly pursuing his vengeful return to Milan. He had visited the king of France to look for foreign support, and then had conducted bold actions of disturbance aimed at weakening the regency. In early August 1478, for example, he helped Genoa in its second rebellion against Milan and scored his first major victory. The Milanese were at a disadvantage in any case: unlike the punitive expedition that the Sforza brothers and cousin had conducted against Genoa in March

1477, this one had no strong military leadership. Against the large ducal army sent by the regency, the former captain and now foe Roberto made the canniest use of the Genoese defensive strongholds, which he himself had attacked once before. He easily humiliated the Milanese troops and sent many of them back half-naked, after seizing their weapons and armor. The fiasco was a big blow to the credibility of the regency in Milan.

The growing isolation of Lorenzo and Cicco brought about an increasing tension between the allies. On December 29, 1478, Cicco wrote a compelling letter to Lorenzo stating that their enemies clearly believed that the elimination of them both would be a complete success. Although Cicco's library was filled with secular, humanistic books, in official documents he often resorted to religious texts, quoting lines especially from the Gospel of Matthew: he compared the hatred of his own adversaries to the prophecy of the blood that would befall the architects of Christ's condemnation, and his citing the response given to Peter when Christ walked on water—"Oh, ye of little faith . . ."—signaled his awareness of the imminent danger in which he lived. In this most tragic moment of his career, Cicco saw himself walking in Christ's footsteps, and in doing so, he assigned Lorenzo the role of Peter.

Pope Sixtus IV would have been amused by the pious references made by his political enemies. The pope and the King of Naples, fully aware of the fact that Milanese money and its army were keeping Lorenzo afloat, decided to create as much trouble as possible at the borders of the Sforza duchy. They sent a man called Prospero Medici (no relation), an agent provocateur who hated Cicco, to buy out and rouse the Swiss mercenaries against the regency. These wild and greedy troops crossed the Alps and penetrated the Milanese state, raiding mountain farms with a violence that was, as Cicco's son Gian Giacomo Simonetta wrote to Lorenzo in a letter dated January 9, 1479, "scarier than that of the Turks" (the Turks were permanently on the verge of attacking the peninsula, and in fact they would invade its southern tip in 1481). Some Sforza soldiers were dispatched on a retaliating mission, but they were caught in a bloody ambush and humiliated in a serious debacle. This earned the Swiss fighters a good name, and they eventually became the official bodyguards of the popes (from 1506, under Julius II).

Florence and Milan were also weakening financially. In Florence, Lorenzo had a hard time extracting taxes from his citizens, so much so that police officials had to be sent to people's houses to collect them. In Milan, the destabilizing wars sucked up all the state funds. In his January 22 letter to Lorenzo de' Medici, Gian Giacomo Simonetta reported that since Galeazzo's death the Milanese duchy had already spent the mind-boggling sum of 1.6 million ducats on security and wars.

Access to the ducal treasury, which contained over two million ducats, was a privilege of the duchess alone. Therefore, the governors were forced on a daily basis to borrow cash from moneylenders at a high interest rate, and in order to guarantee a repayment they had to compromise all the present and future state tax revenues. To avoid bankruptcy, Cicco had to accelerate negotiations toward a peace process. He probably had too much faith in its feasibility. He did manage to have a treaty between Florence, Milan, and Naples drafted in June 1479, but it came too late.

Back in the summer of 1478 King Ferrante had sent to Bona and young Duke Gian Galeazzo Sforza a long, nasty invective against regent Cicco, who was, he said, "forgetful of fortune and of himself" and the "dictator of your letters." Ferrante did not actually mention Cicco's name, referring to him instead as the Milanese *Dictator*; the biting and vicious double meaning was perhaps too subtle. But in a letter dated January 12, 1479, Ferrante explicitly expressed his hatred for Cicco, calling him a "worm coming from the earth" (as a native of Calabria, Cicco had been born a subject of the Aragonese king). Such statements were designed to create a wedge between Duchess Bona and the regent, and to convince her that he was untrustworthy.

o o L o o

SFORZA MARIA AND LUDOVICO had been exiled by Cicco after the attempted coup of May 1477. Since then, the two troublemakers—who had also been suspected of being behind Duke Galeazzo's murder—had been kept relatively quiet by the duchess's threat that they would lose their allowance if they caused any trouble. Sforza Maria, Duke of Bari, was first exiled to his remote duchy in Puglia, at the southeastern tip of Italy. He then managed to move from there to Naples, under the wing of King Ferrante of Aragon. And it was from Naples, in January 1479, that Sforza Maria took off by sea in a few galleons eagerly provided by Ferrante, eventually to fight his way back into Milan.

Ludovico Sforza had been confined in Pisa, having managed to remain on neutral terms with Lorenzo. He then joined his brother on the coast of northern Tuscany and they reunited outside Genoa with restless Roberto da Sanseverino, who had not ceased for a minute to create military mayhem for the Milanese government, by siding with any potential insurgents and raiding the Lombard countryside with his troops. The three exiles were aiming to discredit Cicco as a usurper of the duchess's trust.

Supported by their powerful Aragon ally, Roberto and the Sforza brothers made several attacks against the regency. Roberto started marching toward Milan; surprisingly enough, he did not find any real opposition on his way. Many ducal towns surrendered in the name of the Sforza heritage, denied them by the evil governor Cicco. Unlike Roberto, though, the brothers were not trained for the hardship of military life. Sforza Maria fell ill in the summer of 1479, and died in late July "because of his unbelievable fatness." But the only other legitimate Sforza, Ludovico, also known as Il Moro, the Moor, for his dark complexion, showed the strength of his survival instinct.

"THIS NEW STATE IS LIKE GLASS OR A SPIDER WEB..."

DUCHESS BONA, GALEAZZO'S MERRY WIDOW, HAD BECOME even more ineffective in state matters under the influence of her lover Antonio Tassino, a young and handsome man. He was jealous of Cicco's power and persuaded her to readmit her exiled brother-in-law, Ludovico, with whom he had had a confidential correspondence not intercepted by any spy. It was a sign that Cicco was losing his grip. On the night of September 7, 1479, Ludovico secretly entered the Sforza castle in Milan, via the large park at the back. He was welcomed by Duchess Bona and was lodged in a beautiful room. All she wanted, admittedly, was *vivere allegramente,* to live without any worry. It was a very naïve hope. She and Ludovico agreed on a peaceful reentry for himself and Roberto da Sanseverino.

As soon as Cicco realized what was going on, he went to Bona and told her that she had made the worst mistake of her life: "Madonna, in little time I will lose my head, and you will lose your state." These words, later reported by many historians, would reveal themselves to be prophetic. There was no point in hiding in one of the many secret chambers of the castle, which had provided a safe haven for the chancellor for so many years. Cicco patiently awaited his fate. During the night of September 10, Cicco and his brother Giovanni were captured by ducal guards and hidden in a carriage escorted by one hundred cavalry. They were brought to the dungeons of the Castle of Pavia, near Milan. Their palaces in both countryside and town were left exposed to the looting of the people. A large number of soldiers had to be sent into the streets in order to prevent any more public unrest.

Cicco's enemies were jubilant. Sixtus IV and Girolamo Riario in Rome and King Ferrante in Naples all expressed their satisfaction at the arrests. Now that Milan had been liberated from the "usurper's tyranny," Florence would soon follow. Federico, however, did not send any congratulatory letter to Bona. Just two years before, in the summer of 1477, he himself had warned the chancellor against falling into an abyss of "dangerous dangers." That the downfall had come to pass did not thrill him. After all, they had never been enemies. He also realized that the new regents were rather unreliable. "These Sforza heirs"—as Mantuan ambassador Zaccaria Saggi put it—"play hard at being inscrutable." The traditional allies of Milan would come to realize this all too soon.

When Lorenzo received the news about Cicco's imprisonment, he immediately wrote to Ludovico Sforza, appealing to their long-standing friendship. Without ever mentioning Cicco, he emphasized that he himself had never done anything against Ludovico and had actually been helpful to him during his exile in Pisa. But Il Moro's response was supremely noncommittal. Although formally deprived of any power or title, Ludovico was already acting like a duke-to-be, garnishing his chancellery's letters with solemn and empty words. He immediately created a clique of courtiers who would praise and please him. While the Simonetta brothers were rotting in the dungeons of Pavia, he asked that Giovanni Simonetta's *Life of Francesco Sforza* be read aloud to him, chapter by chapter. This elegant Latin biography celebrated the glorious deeds of Ludovico's father, who would remain an unattainable model of virtue for his ambitious son. Zaccaria Saggi was startled at the "new things" that were unfolding in Milan, and commented: "This new State is like glass or a spider web . . ."

Lorenzo realized how dangerously defenseless he was without the Milanese protection. He urgently dispatched the Florentine poet Luigi Pulci to meet Roberto da Sanseverino in Milan, just as he had done in February 1477, under very different circumstances. Roberto was requesting that the duchess pay him the money she owed him for the services he had performed before his exile and that she return to him the properties he had lost since then. He also requested that this time around his stipend should be not equal to but higher than that of Federico da Montefeltro. Pulci's mission in Milan was not to deal with such economic details, however. A plan of attack against Tuscany was afoot, and Pulci had to steer the greedy *condottiere* away from it.

Florence was in fear—and justifiably so, as is made clear in a series of partially coded letters that have recently come to light. Count Riario had sent to Milan his envoy Gian Francesco da Tolentino, the captain who had been in command of the papal troops enlisted to seize Florence after the botched Pazzi conspiracy. Tolentino's semiciphered letters, written during the month of October 1479 from Milan, contain some shocking information. Tolentino reported with sadistic enjoyment that Cicco was about to be tortured (only his old age and bad health had prevented him from being tormented until then, though his military advisor Orfeo da Ricavo had not had such luck). Then he added that the usual source, Lorenzo Giustini, had informed him that the Duke of

Urbino thought it was time to tighten the rope around Lorenzo's neck. Tolentino also laid out for Riario a plan to raid the rich Tuscan villas of the Mugello valley:

> We will *sack* all those palaces and we will raise terror in Florence . . . For God's sake, my lord! *It is the fear of being touched in their properties* that really throws that *people upside down!* Please consult the Duke of Urbino on this matter and inform me as soon as possible. Once I put these troops together I will go to Imola to take care of the business . . . *[words in italics are ciphered in the original]*

The same mercenaries who had participated in the failed Pazzi operation still hoped to redeem themselves with a spectacularly violent exploit. If only they could manage to get the impetuous Roberto da Sanseverino on board, their plan would finally go through. Pulci, ever the buffoon, somehow managed to dissuade Roberto from leaving Milan at such a perilous juncture, just at the time when Ludovico was gaining momentum: the poet might have reminded the *condottiere* of the many treacheries that Gano, the archcourtier in his chivalric poem *Morgante*, had been performing in the absence of the great Orlando, the bravest of all of Charlemagne's paladins.

SEIZING THE MOMENT

IN THE MEANTIME, ANOTHER VALIANT SOLDIER WAS ENJOYING the fruits of his successes. Thanks to his ruthless and shrewd strategies, Federico had seized all the key Florentine fortresses, Castel Sansavino, Poggio Imperiale, and Colle Val d'Elsa (this last bastion fell on November 13, after weeks of murderous artillery fire). Now that he dominated the Tuscan territory, it would have seemed easy enough to seize its flourishing capital. Unexpectedly, though, he decided against the enterprise. One biographer of Federico reports the eloquent speech he addressed to Alfonso of Aragon and his troops, advising them not to attack Florence:

> Willingly, O Lord, would I go along with the opinion of those who advise you, if I were not still crippled, and since they proceed with reason and prudence and consider the beginnings and ends of things—there is nobody with so little intellect who would not judge that it is right, at first sight, to enjoy victory and to silence whoever said that such a great, juicy occasion should be neglected. What would be easier than to march in at full speed, enter the city with all our forces, end the fight and obtain at once what has been so talked about? This would indeed be the ideal end to a war. But let us please consider the downsides: how could we stop the soldiers, libidinous and eager from the fresh victory, thirsty of prey both by nature and by custom, to sack, pillage and destroy that delightful countryside? Would they listen to any order or command? And even if they were obedient, and follow the orders, what then? Is Roberto Malatesta, the young and fiery captain hired by the Florentines, that far away? Does he not have enough troops to give us trouble? Does he not wait for any little opportunity to double his victories, and acquire for himself the title of liberator and defender of Florence?
>
> But even if we do manage to control the city, and assuming that nobody falls short of his duty, when we find ourselves among so many enemy strongholds in a foreign country, won't everything be full of dangers, and suspicions? Will our adversaries behind our backs go to sleep, and give us the comfort of living, and of fighting? We will be closed in on every side, and besieged while we believe to be besieging. Our enemies will be laughing at our expense, shaming us, and we will be doomed more by distress and hunger than by swords or by their forces. Haste makes waste, so if I am not mistaken it can only be a good thing to consider this matter prudently, before rushing into such an important, dangerous resolution.

This impressive piece of rhetoric might have been entirely fabricated by a complaisant biographer. But even assuming that there is no historical truth to it, the oration contains strategic wisdom about occupying foreign and unwelcoming states that is still valid today. It also shows that when Federico agreed to contribute to the conspiracy against the Medici, he had been banking on popular support for the conspirators' party, which would have allowed his troops to control the city without too much bloodshed. In a way, he had been preparing himself to become the savior of Florence. But things had turned out very differently. Here was another opportunity to attack the city, and if Federico refused to take it, that was perhaps because he did not want to turn Florence into another Volterra. Certainly his legacy as a lover of *studia humanitatis* would have been forever tarnished by a sack of Florence—and he must have realized that. Was it possible that, at the time of the Pazzi conspiracy, he had agreed to send in his troops against Lorenzo in order to *prevent* the pillaging of the beautiful city that he wanted to control and the destruction of all things he held dear?

Another biographer of Montefeltro wrote about a "stratagem used by Federico against the Medici" during the Pazzi war: "In order to make them look suspicious to their state, he ordered that all of their possessions be safeguarded under the most severe punishments. Although the citizens could not do anything against this provision, since the Medici were very powerful, the rulers of Florence fell under suspicion in that city so naturally suspicious. It is no surprise, then, that after Federico's death Lorenzo blamed this excellent captain."

Ultimately, Federico was a strategic thinker who could play both sides of a chess game. He knew that an occupying army could successfully execute a regime change if it was perceived by the population as a liberator rather than an invader. Deterrence and threat worked in its favor, not violence and aggression. Federico also knew that he would achieve his ultimate goal of ridding Florence of Lorenzo not by occupying the city—aggression had failed once—but by forcibly undermining Lorenzo's authority from without. Federico was killing Lorenzo by a slow death, in some ways perhaps more painful than the one that was inflicted on his brother. Or perhaps his inaction was another sinister oblique message to the Florentine leader. Politics is all about seizing the moment: new opportunities open up new scenarios for the Machiavellian mind.

o o L o o

EVIDENCE OF FEDERICO'S shifting plans comes from the confession made by the jailed Cola Montano, the humanist and "teacher of evil" who had indoctrinated the killers of the Duke of Milan. Montano, caught years later while he was engineering yet another conspiracy against Lorenzo—he was swiftly put on trial by Florentine officials and hanged for treason in March 1482—recounted fully his participation in the Pazzi war, recalling some key conversations among the fighters.

Having left Urbino with Federico in July 1478, Montano followed him during the early stages of the Tuscan campaign. When he informed Federico that Pistoia (a city southeast of Florence that functioned as one of the key bastions of its defense) was ready to surrender, the Duke of Urbino reportedly said that this would end the war and annihilate Florentine power. According to Montano, Federico was not enthused by such a quick triumph, since he wanted Florence "to be downsized, not destroyed altogether."

Both Count Riario and Lorenzo Giustini told Montano that Arezzo (the southeastern bastion of the Florentine state, but also the southwestern doorway to the Montefeltro duchy) could also fall with ease into Federico's hands, but, Montano went on, "the Duke of Urbino was a man so prudent that he would never try an enterprise whose outcome was not more than certain." In a closed-door meeting with Montano, Riario then burst out: "Is it not amazing that we still have not managed to get rid of Lorenzo?" Montano replied: "Although many consider the Duke of Urbino Lorenzo's enemy, he is not." They debated the issue heartily, and finally Riario said: "I command that you, Cola, believe that the Duke of Urbino is an enemy of Lorenzo no less than I am! And if you don't agree, it means that you are a no-good, born to be disobedient!"

No other written record of these exchanges exists, since Riario forbade that Montano write to him, even in code. In fact, when Cola was

caught, he was found to possess sets of ciphers for use with the other major players, but not with Riario. Perhaps because he was trying to save
his own life, Montano did not convert to Riario's opinion that Federico
was a committed enemy of Lorenzo. But in just a few months, Riario
himself might have changed his mind about Federico's ambivalent stance
toward Lorenzo de' Medici.

9

TRAVELING SOUTH

THE ONLY ITALIAN RENAISSANCE CITYSCAPE THAT HAS BEEN DEPICTED IN ITS ENTIRETY IS NOT FLORENCE, ROME, OR MILAN, BUT NAPLES. The beautiful snapshot of the seaport's skyline, captured from the bay, can be seen in the Strozzi wood panel, which was made in Florence by Giuliano da Maiano's workshop for the successful Strozzi merchant family. On a background of Naples's fortified coast, the main Anjou castle, or Maschio Angioino, stands tall, dominating the bustling harbor, where a fleet of parading ships are entering.

The Aragon dynasty had been ruling Naples since 1444, the same year in which Federico da Montefeltro had become lord of Urbino. The first king, Alfonso "the Magnanimous," had restructured the Anjou castle and made it into his royal home. After Alfonso's death in 1458, his illegitimate son Ferrante had to fight his way to the throne, which he did with the help of the Duke of Milan, Francesco Sforza. He eventually succeeded in defeating the rival Anjous and celebrated his triumph on the majestic bronze gate of the castle itself.

To the extreme left of the Strozzi panel is also Castel dell'Ovo, a defensive fort that was used as a jail, while the Castel Sant'Elmo, on top of the city hill, watches over its palaces and churches. Naples was the capital of the kingdom, which extended over all the southern part of the Italian peninsula, including Sicily. The powerful Ferrante, who, like his father, had employed Federico da Montefeltro as one of the captains of his army, was the man behind the scenes who could make or break anybody's fate in late-fifteenth-century Italy. And Lorenzo de' Medici knew that very well.

DIFFICULT DECISIONS

EVEN BEFORE FEDERICO DA MONTEFELTRO AND ALFONSO OF Aragon had so effectively used their united military might to overwhelm Florence, Lorenzo knew he had no allies left. Two weeks after Cicco's fall from power, on September 25, 1479, Lorenzo wrote to the Florentine ambassador in Milan that he was ready to follow Alfonso's advice and "throw myself into the arms of the King of Naples, Ferrante of Aragon, showing that this is the only way in which I can save the city and myself." Lorenzo decided to go to Naples and plead his case at the feet of its king.

For months the young Medici had been feeling not only the pressure from his outside enemies, but an increasing heat from within Florence. Early in 1479 a spy in Urbino had reported to Federico on the difficulty faced by the Florentine Republic in collecting taxes—and on the intervention of officials appointed to do so forcibly. Internal freedoms were being curtailed. To voice any criticism of the government even in the streets was now punishable: complainers were to be administered the traditional torture of the rope.

Before Lorenzo could arrange a trip to Naples, one of Florence's prominent citizens addressed to him in public a short, sardonic speech that expressed the common unease. Giovanni di Carlo recorded it: "Your grandfather overcame the nobles and the powerful; your father won over the wise and learned; you have vanquished the Pazzi [pun on madmen]; now you have to deal with the angry! . . . Cosimo and Piero—with half

of the money you have spent on this war—would have gained much more than you have lost."

Among Florentine citizens, hostility toward the Medici leader was rising. At such a fraught moment, Lorenzo resolved to turn to the man who had been his old ally and had become his deadly enemy: the Duke of Urbino. At the beginning of the Pazzi war, Federico had publicly predicted that the Florentines would be bold the first year of fighting, weak the second, and near dead the third. Two-thirds of the way through the fighting, the prediction was spot on. The coalition of the pope, the king, and the duke was bringing Florence to its knees. Sometime in the fall of 1479, Lorenzo sent a secret envoy to Urbino to beg for mercy. With undisguised satisfaction the court poet Giovanni Santi claimed that "just as the [prodigal] son returns to the father," so the Florentine leader was finally coming to his senses. The messenger expressed Lorenzo's regret at not having followed Federico's "prophecies" and "straightforward advice," and declared that Lorenzo was ready to do whatever it took to save the day. Federico, "moved to great pity," replied to the envoy that the only way to give hope to Tuscany was for Lorenzo to "bury his arrogance at the feet of his enemies." Federico thoughtfully added that if Florence had lost her freedom, Italy would have lost one eye. It was a double-edged metaphor, considering that Federico himself was one-eyed.

Federico's message was his oblique way of announcing either a sudden change of mind or a long-meditated decision. At this point, it was better for Federico to deal with a humbled Lorenzo than with the ever more arrogant Count Girolamo Riario, who was keen to paint himself as the most influential man in Italy. The Duke of Urbino knew that if Florence—where the interdict was still in effect—lost all of her power, the whole center of the peninsula would become free game for the papacy, and the next target on the list might be Urbino itself. The Montefeltro dynasty depended on the pope's legitimization, which could always be withdrawn. The delicate balance of power was shifting once again.

On December 4, 1479, Alfonso of Aragon wrote to his "dear and much loved Lorenzo" that two galleys were ready to sail to Naples at his

 LEFT PAGE: *Strozzi panel.*

will. On December 6, Lorenzo replied to Alfonso and to Federico—addressing them both at once—stating that "following the given order" he would leave Florence and head for Pisa, from where he would transfer himself by sea "at the feet of His Majesty the King." Then he added: "Here I leave things well in order, the way I hope I will find them when I return."

The next day, after a tearless goodbye to his family members, Lorenzo discreetly left Florence on horseback. He was already on his way to the Tuscan coast when he wrote a hard-thought, well-calculated letter to the Signoria, meant to strike a solemnly dramatic tone:

> *Most Illustrious Lords. Given that all other endeavors have been fruitless, I have determined to run some peril in my own person rather than expose the city to disaster. Being the one most hated and persecuted by our enemies, I may by this means restore peace to our city . . . Perhaps our Lord God desires that this war, which began with the blood of my brother and my own, should be put to an end by my hands. My ardent wish is that either my life or my death, my misfortune or my well-being should contribute to the good of our country.*

While Lorenzo was already traveling to Naples, Giuliano's killer Bernardo Bandini had been captured far away in Constantinople by the sultan and sent back to Florence as a personal homage to Lorenzo and the Florentine merchants with whom the Turks dealt. Bernardo was hanged on December 29, 1479, dressed as a Turk in mockery. A young and still relatively unknown artist called Leonardo da Vinci drew him in this undignified pose, in the hope that he would be commissioned to paint the traitor in larger scale.

Lorenzo knew that Bernardo was on his way to the gallows, but he was not there to witness the execution of his brother's killer. He must eagerly have awaited it. The macabre staging was a warning to anyone who might think of acting against him during his dangerous mission.

Leonardo da Vinci, sketch of Bernardo Bandini hanged, 1479. Leonardo noted the colors of Bernardo's clothes in the margin, in order to be able to reproduce them in a large-scale fresco.

A TRIP TO HELL

THERE WERE SOME HISTORICAL PRECEDENTS TO LORENZO'S visit. In 1435, the King of Naples had fallen into the hands of the Duke of Milan (it is the story on which Shakespeare's *The Tempest* is loosely based). Machiavelli explained why the king was not slain by his enemy: not out of exemplary magnanimity, but in order to preserve the balance of power throughout the Italian peninsula. More recently, in 1465, there had been an episode involving an ambitious *condottiere* called Iacopo Piccinino, who had made no secret of his aspiration to become lord of a city-state—like Federico da Montefeltro and Francesco Sforza. Invited to the Neapolitan court by Ferrante, Piccinino had been his honored guest for a few weeks. But his ambitions were not welcome in Naples. During a lavish banquet, his bodyguards were neutralized and then eviscerated by the king's men, and Piccinino was thrown into jail in Castel dell'Ovo, accused of harboring secret plans against the Crown of Naples and the Duchy of Milan. Eventually, Piccinino jumped, or more likely was helped into the harbor, where his dreams of glory were drowned.

When Lorenzo had first come to Naples, in March 1466, the memory of the Piccinino scandal was still very fresh. The "immortal" Francesco Sforza had just died. Lorenzo's father, Piero, profoundly saddened and concerned about the loss of his powerful ally, had sent Lorenzo to Naples from Rome, where he was visiting Pope Paul II, telling his son that he must now become "old ahead of time" and represent the family as the Neapolitan court mourned. Piero was proud of Lorenzo when he heard how well the seventeen-year-old had conducted himself as part of the royal elite.

Thirteen years later, the situation was rather different. On a cold and rainy day in midwinter, Lorenzo arrived in the Bay of Naples after having spent some sickening nights on board a pitching galley. Sailing with an escort of Aragonese noblemen, he had managed to avoid Rome and the pope on his way from Pisa to Naples. The city did not appear in the welcoming bright colors of the Strozzi wood panel. Still, just as in the painting, the Anjou castle dominated its skyline. The king loved to boast that, from its menacing towers, he could control every corner of the city. (According to a popular legend, the king also kept the embalmed corpses of his enemies in its basement.) Only a few miles to the south rose the threatening, dark silhouette of a sleeping giant: Mount Vesuvius was the undisputed ruler of the bay and as unpredictable as its human counterpart. Vesuvius stood as a warning of possible things to come when Lorenzo finally set a shaky foot on land.

The king welcomed his royal guest Lorenzo in the grand Sala dei Baroni, or Hall of the Barons. Lorenzo knelt at Ferrante's feet and then gave a speech, probably an extended apology for his arrogant and provocative behavior. Ferrante was a somewhat imposing man, heavily built and with a massive jaw, who had famously mastered the arts of simulation and dissimulation and would never betray an emotion. But, as Machiavelli later wrote, he was impressed with Lorenzo's boldness and gravitas: the Florentine leader had been able to survive the Pazzi war virtually on his own, and "the greatness of his enemies had only made him greater."

In Naples, Lorenzo was at once watched and protected. He was not hosted in the castle itself, but most probably in the Palazzo Carafa, where it was easier for the king's men to keep an eye on him. In his later confession, the scheming Cola Montano, who was in Naples at the time, claimed that he had spoken to a Florentine exile who was planning to kill Lorenzo while he went to pray in the Piedigrotta convent. Even though the king's secretary had reportedly remarked, "May that be done!" this rumor is most likely unfounded. Nothing that the king himself had not approved could be carried out in Naples.

Lorenzo's fear of being disposed of like Piccinino gradually faded and was replaced by sheer disquiet. He now had to endure a long wait before the king came to a decision regarding the pursuit of the war, and he was increasingly anxious about the restlessness of the Florentines, who were perfectly capable of organizing a coup in his absence. A contemporary

Bronze bust of Ferrante of Aragon. He is wearing the Collar of Ermine, which he also granted to Federico da Montefeltro in 1474.

Medici biographer reported that Lorenzo spent so much cash during his Neapolitan sojourn that he did not dare report the actual amount. He provided dowries to women from Calabria and Apulia and lavished expensive gifts on anybody who asked for them. One can only imagine how thoroughly the elegant Tuscan gentleman loathed the expansive southern mannerisms, but he had to play along with the local mores. Lorenzo had two personae in Naples; he was reportedly "gay during the day and desperate at night."

The only leisure for Lorenzo probably consisted of walks in Castel Capuano, also known as Villa Duchesca, the sumptuous gated garden built for Ippolita Sforza, Princess of Calabria. When Lorenzo arrived in Naples, Ippolita received him generously, as befitted a lady who was the daughter of the illustrious Duke Francesco. She was a refined woman, the first in the Renaissance who had a library and a private *studiolo* built for her. Lorenzo and Ippolita could have talked easily about their favorite poets Petrarch, Poliziano, and Pulci. Her tastes were rather different from those of her brutal husband, Alfonso, the *condottiere,* son of Ferrante.

Ippolita's father-in-law, King Ferrante, was not an erudite man, either. Like Federico, he was highly superstitious, ever attentive to signs from the heavens. In February 1480, such signs appeared in the form of an ambivalent piece of astrological prose sent by Florentine philosopher Ficino. Entitled *A prophecy of King Alfonso to King Ferrante, first arising between them in the angelic tongue and later translated into human language by Marsilio Ficino of Florence,* it was written in the voice of the "divine author," who stressed "how pleasing is Peace to those above" and that "devotion to God and mercy to men" are key virtues of a majestic ruler, as Ferrante's father Alfonso "the Magnanimous" had been. But beyond these otherworldly concerns, Ferrante had a very solid grasp of reality, and his main strategic concern was his maritime power. As a result of the ongoing negotiations with Lorenzo, the Aragon fleet was to be hired by Florence in 1480 as down-payment for peace. It was a very costly deal for the Republic, and it was not to be the only one.

The negotiations lasted for weeks. One of the worst diplomatic hurdles Lorenzo had to face during his stay in Naples was a confrontation

Marble bust by Francesco Laurana of Ippolita Sforza. The identity of this woman is disputed among scholars; some think it portrays Ippolita's daughter Isabella, future wife of her cousin Gian Galeazzo Sforza.

with Giustini, lord of Castello, the man who, on the bloody Sunday of the Pazzi conspiracy, had been waiting outside the gates of Florence with Federico's troops. In the aftermath of the bloodshed, Giustini had been condemned to death in absentia and was therefore extremely hostile to Lorenzo. But now in Naples, as the pope's envoy, he was sneaky enough to make an effort to hide his personal dislike for the Medici survivor. Lorenzo had no choice but to put up with Giustini. He knew that the pope was trying to crush him, and he could only hope that the king would see a political advantage in keeping him alive.

On February 28, 1480, Lorenzo abruptly decided to leave Naples. No agreement had been committed to paper yet. Giustini followed Lorenzo to the nearby port of Gaeta, in an effort to convince him to go back to the king and conclude the peace negotiations. But Lorenzo, who had been born into a family of merchants, knew that to close a good deal one should not show too much interest in the merchandise. This was precisely why he left: it was the only way to get what he wanted.

His strategy bore fruit. On March 6, Giustini wrote the legal agreement between Ippolita as a representative of the Aragon family and Niccolò Michelozzi, Lorenzo's faithful secretary, who had stayed in Naples in his stead. The treaty was written up on March 13. Among the Florentine concessions was the revocation of the capital sentence against Giustini himself. By pardoning Giustini, Lorenzo had preserved his own safety. But in Rome, Sixtus IV and Girolamo Riario felt betrayed by their henchman, who had mediated a peace disadvantageous to the Church's interests.

THE COST OF FREEDOM

Upon Lorenzo's return to Florence on the night of March 15, a small crowd of his supporters feasted loudly. But rumors of discontent spread around the city. The peace seemed overly costly. Giovanni di Carlo gave a firsthand account of the city's reactions to the secretive, nocturnal deal struck in Naples: moles and bats, he observed sardonically, had been the only witnesses at the negotiating table.

The Florentines, always very careful with their money—or with their tax florins—were worried about the cost of peace and were probably eager to discount Lorenzo's bargaining abilities. Peace was indeed expensive. One of the conditions imposed on Lorenzo was the payment of a large sum of money to Alfonso, Duke of Calabria. The total amount was not made public, but it was at least sixty thousand ducats. Another clause that could only incur the people's wrath was the liberation of the surviving Pazzi prisoners from the Volterra dungeons. But what was most infuriating to the Florentine citizens was the fact that, in order to make good on his promises to the King of Naples, Lorenzo had to tighten the reins on the Republic.

Florence was now a political inferno. Lorenzo gave up using any hypocritical means to soften the harsh discipline he imposed. On April 10, with the creation of the College of the Seventy, consisting of men all chosen for their proven Medici loyalty, a tyranny was born. Lorenzo had to resort to state funds for his political survival: he had no money left in the bank. The economy was in very bad shape; taxes were shooting through the roof. And the exact amount of money owed to the King of Naples was still not known.

During those difficult months Lorenzo received a long letter from Elisabetta Visconti, Cicco Simonetta's wife:

Most obsequient Father Lorenzo Magnificent. If I had to write about something other than your own business, I might open my letter with nice words and conceits, in order to incline You towards my desire, but since I am writing about your own business, I think it is superfluous and useless, especially since I am addressing somebody very prudent and grateful. Your Magnificence knows what we are going through, how our possessions and ourselves have been treated. You also know that this is happening not from our lack of loyalty towards our friends, but because we had too much faith in them . . . There is little left for me to say to Your Magnificence, but to remind and recommend You have memory

*of your friends in deeds and not in words, for what they did and what
they would have done in the future for the love of Yours, because in
truth I do not know whether Damon and Pythias were as close and constant in their friendship as you were with Cicco and my sons, and especially Gian Giacomo . . . who escaped from jail thanks to an apparent
miracle of the Santa Annunziata of Florence.*

The letter went on pleading that Lorenzo try to clear up the superfi-
cial "rust" existing between jailed Cicco and the King of Naples, reminding him of Pompeius's clemency toward the Armenian king Tigrane,
"who was not allowed to go on begging, because [Pompeius] deemed it
beautiful to be the winner who gave back to kings their crowns."
Elisabetta ended by calling herself "a wife and a mother full of concern
and anxiety," and she signed: "Yours like a daughter, Unhappy Isabetta
Simonetta and Visconti."

It is said that Cicco's wife went mad with the pain of her husband's
imprisonment, and it is possible that this lucid entreaty was not written
by her but by her well-educated son Gian Giacomo. In truth, the erudite touches do sound somewhat suspicious. But its literacy did not
help: Lorenzo never answered the letter. Elisabetta Visconti's appeal to
an old friendship fell on deaf ears. Perhaps Lorenzo was too embarrassed
to respond. There was little he could have done in any case—although
he did act on behalf of Florentine Orfeo da Ricavo. Renaissance politics
were ruthless; loyalty took second place to opportunity, and it was better to lose a friendship than to lose power. Lorenzo might even not ever
have been a real friend to Cicco; after all, in July 1477 Federico had
warned the chancellor of the "dangerous dangers" that Lorenzo posed to
him. The words had seemed self-serving then; now they seemed wholly
prescient.

o   o   T   o   o

IN ROME, THE ANNOUNCEMENT OF the peace in the Sistine church
of Santa Maria del Popolo was far from triumphant. The peace conditions had been weighed, treated and signed in Naples with minimal concern for the Church's interests. The Urbino poet Giovanni Santi pointed

out that the king's joy was counterbalanced by the pope's fury: "if Lorenzo went to kiss the crown," he asked rhetorically, "why did he not trust the much greater successor of Peter? Was not this a clear sign of a lack of sincere faith?" It was true, added Santi, that Lorenzo "did not wish to fall into the hands of any priest," and certainly not into those of the "arrogant Count" Riario. There was now a serious rift between the two major "confederates"—Rome and Naples—because the pope felt slapped in the face by the king, and he contemplated revenge.

In this new balance of power, Federico suddenly found himself in the untenable position of being a servant of two estranged masters. In May 1480 the spy Contugi reported that reciprocal suspicions had arisen between the veteran Federico, captain of the Church, and Sixtus IV, who, not unreasonably, considered him to be the cunning backstage deal-breaker of the peace agreement, since he had supported Lorenzo's trip to Naples. Sinister warnings were coming from Rome to Viterbo, a papal city north of Rome where Federico was then stationed. The threats against Montefeltro, Contugi wrote, included the use of "poison or knife" as a "holy man" had revealed to the pope. Watchful bodyguards were deployed in order to prevent either of these "excesses." But even an influential informant thought that the Duke of Urbino would not part from the Church: he claimed that he "will be the reason why there will be universal peace in Italy."

On May 22, Contugi reported a manipulative monologue that Federico, ever the histrionic orator, delivered in front of a large crowd in Viterbo. He told them about the warnings, and then, addressing himself, he pleaded: "O Federico, what have you done, either betrayals or murders, that you would deserve to be assassinated?" He wept abundantly and then cried out: "O God, help my innocence!" Everybody started sobbing "so much that it looked like Good Friday night." Then he stopped abruptly and said: "Folks, don't weep! Perhaps this threat was not true!" The crowd cheered.

THE SCAPEGOAT'S TRIAL

MEANWHILE, IN A RATHER LESS MELODRAMATIC FASHION, Cicco was undergoing a tough trial in Pavia. He had been offered a way out by the new Sforza rulers. If he gave them all the money that he had accumulated over thirty years of service under the Sforza family, he would be granted a safe exile. He refused—concisely, as always had been his way. Having written so many letters, taken thousands under dictation and later himself dictated thousands more dispatches, and encoded or decoded hundreds, he knew about verbal economy. Without even addressing Duke Gian Galeazzo, who he knew was a puppet in Ludovico's hands, he wrote:

> *I have been jailed, robbed and disgraced undeservedly, since I have constantly worked for and loyally attended to the State of Milan. What are my rewards and remunerations? If I have erred, let them punish me. I want my money, which I have earned with so much labor, to belong to my children. I owe a lot to God for having given me a long life. I do not fear death: I do not desire anything but to be deprived of this life. Farewell.*

So the trial began. The judges and jurors were all Milanese nobility who had felt slighted by the chancellor's power during the previous three decades. They were handpicked by Ludovico Sforza and Roberto da Sanseverino, both of whom held more than a grudge against Cicco. The list of charges amounted to forty-two. The former chancellor was convicted of having performed each and every one of the crimes, excesses, and malfeasances attributed to him, and according to the trial records, he had confessed to them under torture.

He was called an assassin, a forger, a heretic, a sodomite. "Inspired by devilish spirit and shrewdness," he had ascribed to himself majestic powers. He had masterminded the imprisonment and assassination of Donato del Conte, the *condottiere* who had been part of the May 1477 Sforza attempt at overthrowing him and Duchess Bona. "Not content with the aforementioned things," he had exiled the Sforza brothers and Roberto da Sanseverino. Because of his "evil and tyrannical nature," he had refused an honest truce offered by King Ferrante of Aragon and had provoked a war in all of Italy; he had written letters to the Duke of Urbino that had interrupted the smooth peace process. He had treated with disrespect his Holiness the pope by sending ambassadors to Rome who had threatened him with creating a schism. He had single-handedly engineered with "brainy, obstinate and enduring devilishness" the Pazzi war, provoking Milan's loss of Genoa. He also had personally incited Milanese troops to attack the Swiss rebels, purposely causing their disastrous defeat. When the Duke of Urbino had sent his son Gian Giacomo an envoy to offer a peace, Cicco had not let anybody know about it, because this treaty did not include the Venetians. He had thrown into jail several Milanese citizens who had meant no harm to him. One of them was Ettore Vimercati, unjustly charged with having attempted to stab him to death. "Not content with the aforementioned things," he had offended the ambassador of the King of Naples in Milan and had used outrageous and stinging words against the king himself. He had fired, out of falsity and arrogance, the "faithful" Ambrogino di Longhignana, former captain of the Sforza castle. He had caused Ottaviano Sforza's drowning, and he had also taken control of Sforza Maria's house in Milan. He had stolen from the chancellery twenty-four files of letters and burned them. He had written and dictated many sections in his diary blaming unjustly and falsely the Sforza heirs. He had written letters in the name of Gian Galeazzo Sforza and called them ducal. He had reported false and untrue news to Duchess Bona. Finally, he had practiced sex "against nature" with other males, "and sodomy being a most horrific and detestable sin, not only did he enjoy it but he even said that nobody could call himself an honest man if he did not engage in it. Under which charge, he also sinned greatly against the Christian religion."

In short, Cicco was blamed for everything that had gone wrong not only in Milan, but in all of Italy in the last three years. It was convenient to unload everyone's faults on the shoulders of one politically expendable culprit. Most of the charges included partial truths and twisted facts, arranged to secure a spectacular conviction. Accusing Cicco of having abused the chancellery (which he himself had created) or of having forged many ducal letters (as if his job since 1450 had not been exactly to do this) was rather ludicrous. So was attributing to him the rupture of the peace in the whole peninsula, which had been, of course, far from peaceful in any case. Cicco had simply been the financial and military bulwark that had kept Lorenzo alive for two years. That was justification enough to hate him. Alas, poor Cicco!

It is certainly possible that he did practice sodomy, despite his love for his wife and for his many children. Bisexuality was not uncommon in Renaissance high society. Lorenzo and his circle, including Pulci, Poliziano, and Ficino, were rumored to conduct homoerotic affairs, as was Galeazzo Sforza (who favored younger flesh). Obviously, in the context of the trial, this charge was instrumental in proving Cicco's perverse personal habits. The language of the entire trial, which historians have considered a juridical scandal, sounds very much like the one systematically adopted by the Inquisition later on. The verdict was capital punishment. Surprisingly, though, Cicco was not condemned to be hanged, as a man charged with such treacheries would customarily be, and he was not denied holy burial in a convent in Pavia.

10

RESTING IN PEACE

PAVIA LIES ABOUT FORTY MILES SOUTHWEST OF MILAN. It is an elegant city, with beautiful palaces and some of Italy's oldest medieval churches. Next to the well-guarded bridges on the Ticino River stood one of the first universities of Europe, which the Visconti family, under Petrarch's supervision, had turned into one of the continent's greatest in the mid-fourteenth century. The Visconti also built a castle with large hunting grounds. The new Sforza dukes took over the property in 1450 and transformed it into their palace. This is where Galeazzo had spent much of his time pursuing various leisure activities.

It is also here that Cicco Simonetta was beheaded in 1480, after being convicted on state treason charges, just as, nearly a millennium before, had been Boethius, the author of *The Consolation of Philosophy*, which he wrote in a tower in Pavia while awaiting his execution. (Boethius's bodily remains are kept in one of the city's crypts; so are those of St. Augustine.) The *rivellino*, or gated bridge, on the side of the park where Cicco was executed does not exist anymore. After the French lost the battle of Pavia in 1525, they destroyed the whole wall to punish the Milanese who had fought against them. But the rest of the castle is still standing, with some of its frescoed rooms, including the marvelous Visconti-Sforza library, the chancellery, and the kitchen, aptly placed next to Cicco's office outside Milan. Here, too, he had worked long hours, for almost thirty years, before being imprisoned.

CASTLE OF PAVIA

OCTOBER 30, 1480

STATELY AND PLUMP, CICCO SIMONETTA CLIMBED UP THE stairs of the Castle of Pavia's main tower. On this early morning it was chilly and humid, as it tends to be on the flat Padanian Plain. Having spent about one year and one month in the dark dungeons, as the air pinched his skin he must have felt somehow relieved to see the light of dawn bouncing behind the gated walls. He had become heavier during his captivity, although he had not eaten any of his favorite food, the baked fat capons from his farm in Sartirana Lomellina. Gout had been tormenting him all along, and worsening day by day. All dressed in black, Cicco knew he was walking toward his death. He was extremely calm, not a muscle on his face betraying the pain in his feet. He proceeded slowly but surely, followed sheepishly by two armored watchmen. He reached the *rivellino,* the small bridge's gate on the north side, facing the ancient, still intact Visconti park.

Cicco must have thought now of his wife, Elisabetta Visconti, who had reportedly gone mad after his imprisonment. Ever since he was jailed, he had been denied the right to see her. But it was for the better. Had she seen him in that decaying state of health, she probably would have died of despair. Their seven sons and daughters were already safe, either in the Alps or in Florence. His brother Giovanni was still incarcerated, though he had not been charged with anything, and would likely be released after the foes had satisfied their need for revenge.

In the small cheering crowd (the spectacle of death always had entertainment value) perhaps he glimpsed the face of an old friend, the poet

Bonino Mombrizio, who had dedicated to him a *Lives of the Saints* that he edited. When in 1477 Cicco had received the first thick volume from the pious humanist and seen the dedication to the "magnificent magnate" who had made its printing possible, he certainly did not expect to become a martyr himself. And he was not. His long, eventful life, though always respectful of the Christian faith, had been so filled with wars, murders, betrayals, petty rivalries, and personal struggles with popes, that he was not expecting any special treatment in the next life. In all his time in the tower's dungeon, he had chosen to read only the Book of Job. The night before, he had confessed his worldly sins to an Augustinian friar, with great simplicity.

The chancellor had enjoyed many successes, joys, and generous patronage—often generously returned; he had practiced smart politicking, until a weak woman had given away all he had worked for over so many years. Cicco had met and often sided with or fought against all the greatest of his contemporaries, such as Francesco Sforza, Cosimo de' Medici, Pope Pius II, kings Alfonso and Ferrante of Naples, the Venetian doges, King Louis XI of France, Federico da Montefeltro, and, last but not least, Lorenzo de' Medici, "the Magnificent." But those associations were worth little now that his career was over.

Cicco slowly approached the high tribune, where the executioner was waiting for him, the ax shining at his side. Many took Cicco's slow gestures for solemnity. It was just the gout that made it harder for him to bend his knees. No complaint from him was heard.

The decapitated body was buried in the nearby cloister dedicated to St. Apollinare, a noted miracle worker especially effective against gout, poignantly. A few epitaphs composed by anonymous friends were carved on his tomb:

> *I was faithful to the Prince of the Milanese people; I protected his*
> *sceptre*
> *Though the foes gave me a headless tomb.*
> *They say I am Blind [pun on Cecus]; but I saw many things ahead*
> *of time.*
> *Trust me, the fatherland remains blind without me.*

While I stayed loyal to the fatherland and to the duke
I was killed by the insidious tricks of many who betrayed me.
But he who deserves to be celebrated with greatest praise
Is the one who cared more for his faith than for his life.

The day after the execution, a Milanese official gave a speech to all the ambassadors to justify the Sforzas' action against Cicco, lest it be perceived as ungrateful or unjust. Two days later, Duchess Bona found out that the temporary exile of her greedy lover Antonio Tassino, who had been sent back to his native Ferrara by Ludovico with a large bribe, was now irrevocable. Desperate, or "demented," in Bernardino Corio's words, "forgetful both of honor and maternal duty," she left Milan in a rage, not to return for at least two years. She must have remembered Cicco's prophecy then: he had lost his head and she had lost her state. Everything in Milan was now decided by Ludovico "Il Moro," who, once again, gradually managed to exclude his politically unwise cousin Roberto da Sanseverino. Duke Gian Galeazzo, young and shy, became a mere instrument in his uncle's hands. Fifteen years later "the Moor" poisoned Gian Galeazzo and grabbed the long-coveted title of Duke of Milan. But a mere five years after that, he lost everything to the king of France.

PAPAL PARDON AND ANGER

As Cicco's death was placating the Sforzas' vengeful desires in Milan, in Rome Pope Sixtus was still angry about the peace arrangement reached behind his back between Lorenzo and the King of Naples. The pope's excommunication of the city of Florence was still having dire effects on commerce. Lorenzo knew the Republic had to ex-

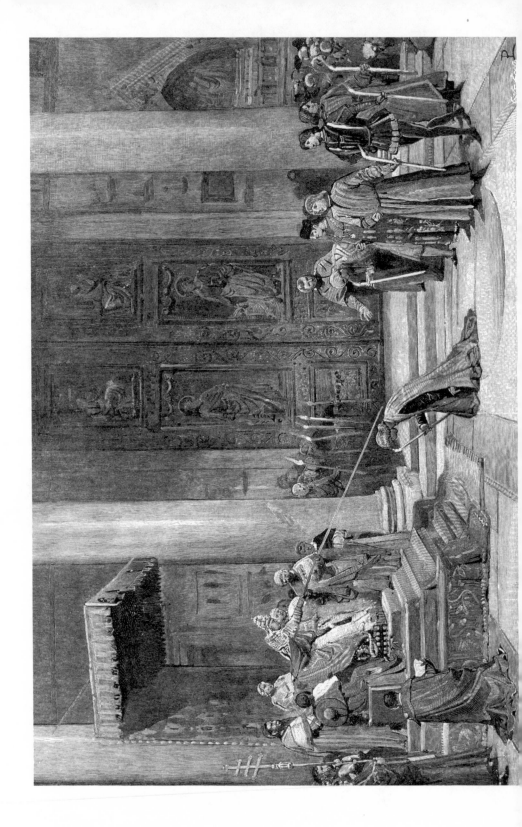

tend a formal apology to the pontiff in order to obtain a repeal of the holy indictment. Twelve Florentine ambassadors from the most notable families were finally dispatched to Rome. They arrived on November 25, 1480, but were received by the pope only on December 3. They justified to him their Christian disobedience by describing it as political self-defense, reminding the pontiff that they had been desecrated and violated in their own cathedral and government palace.

Sixtus did not respond straightaway to the apologetic oration delivered by the chief envoy. He retired into his chambers until the next day, when he summoned the delegation and delivered a wordy reply: "Which kind of patriotism are you invoking? What does it mean to be fighting for your fatherland?" he asked, adding that one should respect the law and honor religion. It is in this context that he formulated what is known as the most eloquent definition of liberty up to that time: "What greater servitude could there be, O Sons of mine, than to have no one in Florence able to say: 'this is good,' 'I want this,' 'I like this,' 'this suits me'?" In other words, the pope was deriding the propensity of Florentines to embrace relativistic judgments of value: their rejection of the absolute moral rules embodied by the Church made them less, not more free.

The pope's oration went on for a long time. In the end, though, Sixtus granted the absolution in a ceremony where a choir chanted a Miserere and he—symbolically—beat the chief Florentine envoy with a long stick.

The sealed absolution was sent to Florence on March 21, 1481. On April 13, the pope proclaimed a "jubilee of guilt and punishment" in Florence, that is, an indulgence, which citizens could obtain by attending six services in six different churches until Easter Sunday. Whoever visited these churches on the three holy mornings of the Christ's Passion, after confession and penance, and contributed to the Crusade against the Turks, would be cleansed of his sins. The Florentine Republic agreed

LEFT PAGE: *Sixtus absolves the Florentine ambassador, beating him with a long stick while the papal choir chants a Miserere in December 1480. A twentieth-century etching.*

to hire on the Church's behalf fifteen expensive Catalan galleys to be sent off to fight in the east. But the unofficial letter sent by the pope's secretary to Archbishop of Florence Rinaldo Orsini (Lorenzo's brother-in-law) included, along with the absolution, written permission to continue mercantile exchanges with the Turks. (Wood and iron only were excluded from the authorized exchanges, since they might too easily be used to build instruments of war.)

о о R о о

WHILE THE WOUNDS of the Pazzi war were still fresh, and Sixtus seemed finally to forgive the Florentines, the Duke of Urbino became the next entry in the pope's black book. By the summer of 1481, the relationship between Lorenzo and Federico had become dangerously friendly again. They first exchanged ciphered correspondence, then a beautiful horse and some precious symbolic gifts, in preparation for a secret visit Lorenzo paid to Federico in late November—but so discreetly that it has almost escaped historical detection.

This visit was recorded only by the well-informed spy Matteo Contugi, but he described it in such detail that there is little doubt about its actual occurrence. On November 28, he wrote: "Moreover, to strengthen his position, Lorenzo makes a show of having forgotten any offense and to have set aside everything, and has come to talk to this Lord placing himself in his hands. It is clear that under the circumstances the Duke would not have harmed him . . . It is known in Urbino that, with or without the Lord's awareness, during the Pazzi plot he had sent to Lorenzo Giustini from Castello thirty cavalrymen and five hundred crossbowmen, although he declared that he knew nothing about it. Lorenzo has made believe that he believes this. He is not a vindictive man . . ."

Lorenzo had decided to seduce Federico. Forgetting is the best way of forgiving: although he knew very well that Federico had been more than aware of what was going on at the time of his brother's murder, he pretended not to care. And the Duke of Urbino seemed to be pleased with this elegant and courtly attitude. In a letter he himself wrote to Lorenzo on November 29 Federico took pains to address his erstwhile opponent in the most amicable of tones: "You can be most certain that the confidence that Your Magnificence has said to have in my labors would not have been in vain . . . you can make good use of my possessions as if they were your own." Lorenzo's sly overtures had paid off.

Contugi, however, would not be so easily persuaded by Federico's assurances. On December 13, referring to the duke, he even quoted Dante:

Et quando l'argumento de la mente
S'aggiunge al mal volere et ha la possa
Nessun riparo ci può far la giente.

For when the power of thought
is coupled with ill will and naked force
there is no refuge from it for mankind.

The lines are taken, appropriately, from the circle of the traitors in the pits of the Inferno. In the same letter Contugi insisted: "When I found myself in Federico's chamber, he expressed his opinion—either dissembling or sincerely—that there would be no war, although sometimes he says exactly the opposite of what he truly means."

Regardless of how unreliable the Duke of Urbino seemed to be, there was a price to pay for his rapprochement with Florence, which could not make Sixtus IV happy. Bad feelings between the two only grew. Count Girolamo Riario, the pope's nephew, was becoming more ambitious than ever. Having failed to obtain Florence, he now set his sights on the city of Ferrara. With the help of the Venetians, who were no less upset than the pope for being excluded from Lorenzo's sudden entente with the King of Naples and the Duke of Urbino, Riario was hoping to unleash a deadly attack against the Duke of Ferrara, Ercole d'Este, who was a vicar of the Church and therefore subject to the pope's power. The cards of the Italian political game were about to be dramatically reshuffled once again.

On March 6, 1482, the Neapolitan envoy in Rome reported the

pope's reaction to the rumor that Federico would be switching his allegiance back to Sixtus and the Venetians and against the king. Sixtus replied: "This is a lie! the Duke of Urbino does not let himself be ruled by His Holiness. Rather, he wants to govern the Pope, the King and everybody else!" It was an unforgiving, and clearly heartfelt outburst. A few days later, the pope may have regretted it, since he reportedly was now "afraid not only of going to Santa Maria del Popolo," the church that he had rebuilt and where he usually heard Mass on Saturdays, "but even to walk in his own garden." The fear that the duke might mastermind a little "incident" for the pope was not so far-fetched anymore.

In Urbino, Gonzaga spy Contugi kept gathering confidential information. Federico had sent to Florence two mules heavily laden with the famously juicy Urbino figs, to be distributed to the people. In exchange, Lorenzo had dispatched a marvelous steed: Federico had no better horse in his stables, and he accepted it graciously. These gifts made the increasing tension between Urbino and Rome only more palpable. The enmity between Count Riario and Federico reached a high point. Riario was by now speaking overtly against the Duke of Urbino, claiming that Federico had tried to badmouth both him and Roberto Malatesta, lord of Rimini and the prospective captain of the Church. Girolamo, who in the meantime had also obtained the city of Forlì, provocatively teased the duke, remarking that the time had come for Italy to have captains equal or superior to him, so that the Church would no longer have to depend on his indecisive quibbling.

According to the papal historian Sigismondo de' Conti, Federico, who had been prudent on so many occasions, this time misjudged the situation he was caught in. In Rome, he had acquired a reputation for acting in his own self-interest and against the Holy Church. His veteran ambassador Piero Felici, who had previously been loved by both the pope and the count for his wit, his pleasant manners, and jovial personality, was now permanently expelled from their palaces. The very people who had collaborated to engineer the Pazzi plot were now mortal enemies. Hatred and greed had once brought them together, and now had split them apart.

THE FOX IN THE CAGE

ON MARCH 7, 1482, THE DUKE OF URBINO'S CONTRACT WITH the pope ran out. It was not renewed. Federico's career was nearing its end but his diplomatic bargaining talent was at its peak, and he did not shy away from any trick to convince his clients of their need for his services. Federico's marketing techniques included shouting to the foreign envoys he took around his ducal palace: "I have tried to make peace . . . now everybody screams 'war'! And so, let's go to war, in God's name!" Montefeltro was soon hired to defend the city of Ferrara against the Venetian and papal troops.

Lorenzo, along with the Duke of Milan and the King of Naples, offered him a golden deal. In times of peace, he was to receive 65,000 ducats; in times of war, his salary jumped to 119,166 ducats. Milan and Naples each paid him 25,000 at peace, and 45,833 at war. From Florence he was owed 15,000, and 27,500. For this whopping salary, the duke agreed to maintain 600 men-at-arms and 600 foot soldiers in wartime. (Notably, he had sent about 600 against Florence at the time of the Pazzi plot.) Federico operated with all the money and men he could possibly employ. He also relied on astrologers: the Florentine ambassador in Urbino had informed Lorenzo that the duke's departure from his town was set for April 23, because there was a good stellar conjuncture after the twentieth.

Federico first passed triumphantly through Florence to seal his fat *condotta*. The Florentine citizens organized a most lavish welcome for him. He arrived on a Sunday, almost exactly four years after the Pazzi conspiracy. He was hosted in the Tornabuoni palace, where he dined with a few wealthy Florentine citizens and Lorenzo. The next day, after a pious visit to the church of SS. Annunziata, Federico left the city. He slept one night in Lorenzo's magnificent villa in Cafaggiuolo, and then headed north.

Before reaching the military camp outside Ferrara, Federico decided to enter the city in order to confer with Duke Ercole d'Este, who had "the greatest fear" that the number of troops was too limited for the task of defending his city from the violent papal and Venetian attack. The Venetians had hired Roberto da Sanseverino as the commander-in-chief of their powerful army for a salary that was, for the first time, as big as that of the Duke of Urbino. The hot-tempered *condottiere* had finally made it—and he was eager to show that he could beat the grand old man. He sent Federico a fox in a cage, a none-too-subtle way of telling him that, despite all his cunning, he might end up entrapped. It was a cheap taunt, which provoked only a smile from the veteran.

But soon enough, the military challenge posed by the bloody siege started wearing on Federico, who wrote to Lorenzo on May 4, 1482: "The best remedy I can think of at this dangerous juncture is that your excellent Signoria should send the Duke of Ferrara as much infantry as possible . . . I care not to detain your Magnificence, feeling assured that once aware of the importance of this, your prudence will not delay the needful provisions." The Ferrarese were so desperate that Eleonora Aragon d'Este, Duchess of Ferrara, absurdly sent Federico a friar to preach to the enemy troops across the Po River. Federico's reply to the sermon was: "Why, Father, the Venetians are not possessed! Tell the Duchess it is money, artillery, and troops that we want to defeat them!"—not an exorcist.

In fact, the strategic situation was very serious. Federico managed to help out the besieged city of Ficarolo, a key bastion for the access to Ferrara. But Roberto da Sanseverino was a tough rival. Across the Po River, he had a road built in order to make a surprise attack on Ferrara. The road was more than five miles long but was constructed at break-neck speed, in two days and two nights, enabling Roberto to penetrate into the heart of the Ferrarese defenses. Federico managed to flood the area, sweeping away the road and cutting off Roberto's advance. But the fight continued. It dragged on throughout the hot summer. Federico's army was engulfed in damp marshes, which were now pullulating with another, and much deadlier, enemy: malaria.

SWAMPS OF FERRARA

SEPTEMBER 10, 1482

ON THE DAY HE DIED IN FERRARA, FEDERICO DA MONTEFELTRO, Duke of Urbino, was sixty years old. That same day in Rome, a few hours later, also saw the death of Roberto Malatesta, the new captain of the Church; he was only forty-five. His wife was one of Federico's daughters. Florentine diarist Luca Landucci commented sharply: "These two captains died just when they imagined they were at the height of their glory. What errors are made by the world! Men incur so many perils in order to slay and kill one another, and to obtain a short-lived fame on this earth they do not consider what it means to kill a man, and how soon they themselves will have to die and render an account of their lives."

By any Renaissance standard, Federico had enjoyed a remarkably glorious military career. But his death in the midst of the swamps, in that sticky, muggy summer, was far from glorious. His old but still strong muscles had turned painfully rigid and cold; his stomach was distended by malarial fevers. He had shivered and sweated his soul out. And he did not know that Roberto Malatesta, his fiery son-in-law, had been struck down by dysentery and exhaustion. Federico had died anguished about the fragile future of his ten-year-old son Guidobaldo—and about his own posthumous fame.

He could not know on what terms he would be remembered—for his military might or his humanistic talent, for the men he had slain or the books he had commissioned. To whom would he have to "render an account" of his life? If not to God, would it be to his vicar on earth, Pope Sixtus IV? Federico had served this irritable pontiff for nearly a decade. He had parted ways with Sixtus only in the last, decisive months of his life, but this rupture had cost him dearly.

Federico had not fully approved of this final war. He had embarked on it against his better judgment, and against the pope's own interest. He had been hired and lured into it by Lorenzo de' Medici, who would outlive him by ten years while gaining the superlative epithet of "Magnificent" for posterity; it was during that decade that Lorenzo would create for himself his lasting reputation as a patron of the arts. By 1482, Federico had certainly not accomplished any less than Lorenzo. He had built the wondrous Palace of Urbino, which hosted the greatest private library in existence at that time. Federico's aquiline profile was portrayed by the finest hand of the mid-1400s, Piero della Francesca, hiding the dark side of his personality. Yet the Light of Italy was now dimming sadly, while his clever rival was beginning to enjoy a cold vendetta: according to a later biographer, Lorenzo had sarcastically commented that "Federico had done a good thing to die in the enterprise of Ferrara because, if he had survived it, he would have overshadowed all of his own past luminous actions."

As he lay dying, Federico had asked to have his soul and body entrusted to the Franciscan friars. He was buried in the church of San Bernardino, just outside Urbino. His embalmed corpse would be visible for at least two centuries under the main altar; it resembled a wooden figure, fleshless and covered with white skin. It was dressed in an elegant robe of crimson and scarlet satin, with a sword by its side.

Finally, after so much war, he rested in peace.

PART III

The Sistine Chapel and Botticelli's Spring

The machinations and the covert ways

I knew them all, and was so skilled in them

My fame rang out to the ends of earth.

—DANTE, *Inferno*

11

OMINOUS ENDS

THE BOTTICELLI CODE

A KEY WITNESS TO THE EVENTS THAT UNFOLDED IN LATE-fifteenth-century Florence was Alessandro Filipepi, better known as Sandro Botticelli. Born in 1445, he studied painting under Fra Filippo Lippi and Antonio Pollaiuolo, and in the 1470s opened his own work-shop. He quickly became one of the most admired artists in Florence. On July 25, 1478, Botticelli was paid forty florins by the Signoria for having depicted the dead members of the Pazzi clan and all the traitors of the Republic on the walls of the Palazzo Vecchio in Florence. To eter-nalize their shame, Botticelli drew sketches of the corpses left dangling from the upper windows and reproduced them in life-size frescoes, so that anybody passing by the Piazza della Signoria could not miss the sin-ister sight.

Botticelli had worked for the Medici for years. After the Pazzi con-spiracy, he also executed the posthumous portrait of Giuliano that ap-pears on page 120. The intimate nature of that painting—made only for private consumption—bespeaks a close tie between the artist and the subject. But the public frescoes of the dead plotters were so glaringly re-alistic that the pope repeatedly demanded that they be destroyed: por-traying the hanging of clergymen (in this case, Archbishop of Pisa Francesco Salviati) was deemed a heretical act. In fact, one year before the papal absolution in the spring of 1481, the archbishop's image was carved out of the plotters' fresco (though the fresco remained in place until 1494, when the Medici were expelled from the city).

Only a few months after Sixtus IV's solemn pardon, Botticelli, along with Domenico Ghirlandaio and Cosimo Rosselli, two of the other most famous Florentine painters at the time, were summoned to Rome to decorate the interior walls of the Sistine Chapel, which the pope had started building in the Vatican in 1477. One can only speculate about the psychological hurdles that a sensitive artist like Botticelli would have had to face on such a mission. The very pope who had supported the bloody conspiracy in which his patron Giuliano had been killed, who had excommunicated his city for two long years and waged a devastating religious and military war against his people—this pope had now called him to Rome to paint the chapel that was his namesake and legacy.

Archival evidence to document the process by which the painters were selected for the prestigious job has never been found. It is possible that Lorenzo was involved in choosing Botticelli: perhaps this was simply a gesture of goodwill toward the pope. It is also possible, however, that Botticelli went to Rome on his own initiative, since the economic situation in Florence after the forceful peace was disastrous and even such renowned artists had trouble finding worthy commissions.

What is well documented is that Botticelli stayed in Rome for at least six months, from October 1481 to April 1482. During this period, he executed no less than three of the sixteen frescoes on the walls of the chapel. They were divided by theme into two symmetrical cycles: the Life of Moses on the south wall and the Life of Christ on the north wall. The original Latin *tituli,* or inscriptions, which were recoverd during the restorations of the late 1990s, bear constant reference to the Written Law (the Old Testament) in the Moses cycle and to the Evangelical Law (the Gospel) in the Christ cycle.

The selected biblical scenes are a combination of common episodes, like Moses and the Burning Bush or Moses on Mount Sinai, and much less known stories, for which the theological erudition of the pope was most likely an inspiration. The first extant fresco is the *Circumcision of the Son of Moses,* attributed to Perugino (to whom are also ascribed the elegant friezes around the pictures featuring golden oaks, the pope's della Rovere coat of arms). The second, *The Temptations of Moses,* is attributed to Botticelli, as is the fifth, *The Punishment of Korah,* one of the most gruesomely authoritarian episodes in Mosaic history. Some historians have thought the *Korah* fresco to be a reference to the heretical archbishop of Krain, Andreas Zamometic, whose appeal to a general council—secretly supported by Lorenzo—to depose the pope did in fact follow the completion of the cycles, in the summer of 1482. But by then, the Florentine painter was back home.

A more persuasive hypothesis is that the depiction of this ancient incident was a none-too-subtle reference to the recent violent war with Florence. Was it just a coincidence that the painter who had been most involved with the Medici family was chosen to depict such a controversial subject? The Sistine frescoes have been admired and studied for centuries but, surprisingly, hardly anyone has ever tried to look at them in the light of the contemporary and painful history that preceded their creation.

The background in *The Punishment of Korah* is occupied by an Arch of Constantine on which one reads the warning addressed to those who rebelled against divine authority: NEITHER DOTH ANY MAN TAKE THE HONOUR TO HIMSELF, BUT HE THAT IS CALLED BY GOD, AS AARON WAS.

The bearded profiles of Moses and Aaron, the brothers who governed the Jewish people in the political and the spiritual realms, correspond exactly to Sixtus IV's clean-shaven profile in the famous family portrait by Melozzo da Forlì described in chapter 4 and shown again on page 194. There is little doubt that the pope wanted to be portrayed as the biblical avenger of God's wrath against the rebels. The fate of Korah and his followers consumed by divine fire is depicted with expressive violence by Botticelli. And who might these rebels against supreme authority be? A hint is given by the Florentine pennant that flutters from the mast of the ship anchored in the background, next to the arch. It is a tiny detail, hardly visible from below, but from the painter's perspective, unmistakable.

The Latin title of the painting, *Conturbatio,* that is, *Revolution or*

 Detail from Punishment of Korah *showing the ship with a Florentine pennant.*

Commotion of the Bible, corresponds on the facing wall to the *Conturbatio* in the Gospel: the *Charge of the Keys to St. Peter,* literally the most charged of all the episodes because it is about the foundation of the Church itself.

The painter was Perugino, the only non-Florentine maestro and the uncontested leader of the Sistine enterprise: he painted the *Baptism of Christ* and the thematically most significant frescoes of the Christ cycle. Just in front of the *Punishment of Korah,* the *Charge* contains two arches modeled after the Arch of Constantine, commemorating Sixtus as the builder of the chapel. The inscription that runs from the one to the other boldly states, appropriately for a self-celebrating pope:

SOLOMON IS NO WISER THAN SIXTUS

As wise as he claimed to be, Sixtus refused to pay Botticelli for his work. The painter seems to have left Rome by April 1482, before the outbreak of the war of Ferrara could trap him in an unfriendly city. He later found himself forced to send a relative to lodge a request for compensation from the haughty and stingy pope.

LEFT PAGE: *Sandro Botticelli,* Punishment of Korah, *ca. 1482.*

LEFT: *Detail from Botticelli,* Punishment of Korah, *Moses and Aaron seen in profile.* RIGHT: *Detail from* Melozzo da Forlì, *Sixtus IV.*

GIULIANO'S REBIRTH

UPON HIS RETURN TO FLORENCE, BOTTICELLI HAD TO ATTEND
to an unfinished commission. It was a painting meant to celebrate a
wedding in the Medici family. The ceremony had been postponed from
May to July 19, 1482, probably to allow him time to finish the painting. The chosen day was a Friday, *venerdì* in Italian, so it was appropriate to celebrate Venus as the center of the painting. The goddess of Love
was to be depicted with a hint of melancholy for this painting celebrated
life after much death and destruction.

The *Primavera,* or *Allegory of Spring,* is arguably one of the most discussed works in the history of art. Its elusive nature has challenged
interpreters for centuries, to this day. Everything and the contrary of
everything has been said about the *Primavera,* and for each new interpretation, one must draw on elements of interpretation from other
scholars.

Two important botanical elements provide us with the key to the political context in which the painting should be read: the orange fruits
(*Citrus medica*) that hover atop the whole scene refer to the Medici family (whose coat of arms included golden balls), whereas the hellebore, the
toxic root of which was used to cure melancholy and madness (*pazzia*
in Italian), refers most poignantly (poisonously?) to the Pazzi family. The
hellebore is just under the feet of Venus, while the main allegorical figure dressed with flowers traditionally identified with Spring wears a wedding wreath made of the same hellebore and of myosotis, whose popular
name is forget-me-not.

The wedding the painting celebrated was bittersweet. As it happens,
just before the Pazzi conspiracy Giuliano de' Medici had been negotiat-

ing his marriage with Semiramide Appiani Aragona, the daughter of the lord of Piombino, a strategic sea bastion southwest of Florence. (In his confession Montesecco mentioned that some of the plotters had planned to capture and kill Giuliano while he was on his way to Piombino.) The new wedding contract between the woman promised to Giuliano just prior to his assassination and Lorenzo di Pierfrancesco de' Medici, Giuliano's cousin, was signed in August 1481, a few weeks before Botticelli's departure for Rome.

When the artist returned to Florence, his head filled with the imagery of the Sistine frescoes, a wicked idea might well have crossed his mind. The somewhat darker figure on the extreme right of the painting bears a striking resemblance to the head of one of the chief rebels in the *Korah* fresco. This figure has usually been identified with Zephirus, who breathes life into Venus as she arises afresh from the seawaters, in Botticelli's other famed picture *The Birth of Venus*. But the question arises of whether the repetition of this iconographic feature of a blowing face was a purely stylistic device, or whether it contributes more substantially to the allegorical import of the picture.

In a recent and most convincing reading of the *Primavera* two Italian scholars, working independently, recast the whole allegory in the light of an early Christian text, *De nuptiis Philologiae et Mercurii* (*Of the Marriage between Philology and Mercury*), by Martianus Capella, a Roman writer from Africa who composed it after the sack of Rome by the Vandals in AD 410. In this complex text, which suited the refined, erudite taste of the Medici patrons as well as the painter's, one finds each and every figure that appears in the painting: starting from left, Mercury (possibly a portrait of the groom, Lorenzo di Pierfrancesco de' Medici, later to become the best patron of Botticelli); the three Graces (typical Botticelli beauties, inspired by his own ravishing mistress, as were most of his other female figures); Venus, goddess of Love; and Spring, who is in fact Flora, the guardian of flowers. Next to her, Philology (possibly a

 LEFT PAGE: *Pietro Perugino*, Charge of the Keys to Saint Peter, *ca. 1482.*

portrait of the bride, Semiramide Appiani, although others identify her with the central figure of the three Graces) regurgitates flowers of wisdom instead of books.

In the light of Capella's text, the figure on the extreme right can be seen, not as Zephirus, but as an embodiment of Athanasia, or Immortality. If that was indeed Botticelli's thought, then the Sistine fresco, rather than depicting the deluge of the rebels, actually means the opposite: instead of succumbing under Moses's (that is, Sixtus's) wrath, the Florentine rebels are resisting the papal submission, to find immortality. On this subversive reading, the internal joke goes even further. In the *Primavera*, Immortality's protégée, the pregnant Flora, is both an allegory for Florentia (Florence), and for Fioretta. She is the city of Florence, prophetically pregnant with Hope and with Future. And she embodies the late Giuliano's last mistress, Fioretta Gorini, mother of Giulio de' Medici—with the myosotis and the hellebore around her neck—forgetting-not that the Pazzi brought the father of her child down. Meanwhile the goddess of Love is stepping onto the same poisonous Pazzi herb (now literally reduced to the ground). All of this, in the context of the wedding of another Medici heir, Lorenzo di Pierfrancesco de' Medici, with the woman who should have been betrothed to his assassinated relative. It is hard to imagine a more typically Florentine vendetta on the part of the ruling family. The subtle pleasure of knowing the esoteric meaning of the Sistine mise-en-scène and its connections to the Medici wedding picture must have been exhilarating.

THE SISTINE CHAPEL WALLS still retain many of their mysterious meanings. It is probably no coincidence that the Medici orange tree is placed on the side of Moses talking to God, whereas the della Rovere oak tree is depicted on the side of Moses killing at knifepoint an elegantly

 LEFT PAGE: *Sandro Botticelli,* La Primavera, *or* Allegory of Spring.

LEFT: *Detail of Korah's blow-ing face from* Punishment of Korah. RIGHT: *Detail of Zephirus/ Athanasia from* La Primavera.

dressed Egyptian and fleeing the scene. Is this yet another coded reference to the killer pope? Botticelli was well known for his sense of mischief and his twisted humor, and it is not impossible that he set out to play a practical joke on the pope himself.

Sixtus IV likely did not realize that Botticelli had subtly subverted the message he had been instructed to convey. One must wonder whether he could really appreciate the finesse of the Florentine painters. He tended to be more impressed with the flashy display of gold by the least talented of the Sistine team, Cosimo Rosselli. He had been so dazzled by Rosselli's use of the golden pigments that he ordered the other artists to follow his example in creating scintillating displays.

The Franciscan theologian had little education in the visual arts. His standard of taste was very low, and primitive, as one can gather from the cycle of frescoes in the Hospital of Santo Spirito, commissioned just a couple of years before the Sistine Chapel. But the subject matter was doctrinally daring—he fashioned himself as a pope-to-be, just coming out of the cradle.

Now the pope had awakened the Florentines' keen sense of competition. The Signoria put forth a project for an official response to the Sistine Chapel. On October 5, 1482, Perugino, Ghirlandaio, and Botticelli were commissioned to paint the Sala dei Gigli in the Palazzo Vecchio in Florence. On December 31, Perugino's commission was revoked and given to Filippino Lippi instead. There were rumors that Perugino was not getting along with the other Tuscan masters: this may be indirect proof of the ongoing Florentine feud.

Then, at some point in 1484, Lorenzo commissioned a series of frescoes from Botticelli, Ghirlandaio, Perugino, and Filippino Lippi for his villa of Spedaletto, near Volterra. The subjects of the frescoes, now lost, were rigorously pagan. Ghirlandaio painted Vulcan's factory. We do not know what Botticelli's subject was, but one might suspect that his frescoes carried out Lorenzo's program celebrating the Medici, this time in vengefully secular fashion. By the time they were completed, the pope had left this world.

THE MONTEFELTRO LEGACY

ACCORDING TO MANY CONTEMPORARY WITNESSES, POPE SIXTUS IV died of bitterness in August 1484, aged seventy, when he heard that the treaty of Bagnolo—which ended the war of Ferrara—had been signed: as someone who had thrived on wars, he could not stand the idea of a peace made without his consent. A contemporary eyewitness described his corpse as "black, deformed, with a swollen throat, looking like a devil in his sleep." Sixtus's solemn grave, now in St. Peter's Chapel, was posthumously surmounted by a spectacular bronze monument by Antonio Pollaiuolo, Botticelli's teacher.

Most of the people involved in the Pazzi conspiracy were not going to be honorably memorialized in history, and few of them died in their sleep. Count Riario, once deprived of the protection of his omnipotent uncle Sixtus IV, was assassinated in Forlì on April 14, 1488, almost exactly ten years after Giuliano's stabbing. Lorenzo did not claim any responsibility for the killing, but it later emerged that he had secretly incited the citizens of Forlì to get rid of Riario. The henchman Giustini also died a violent death: on November 13, 1487, he was challenged and killed by Paolo Vitelli da Castello, the son of an old enemy. Giustini's head was cut off and his clothes stolen: his corpse was left to rot on the ground, naked and headless, a sign of utmost disrespect.

Federico da Montefeltro was long since dead of malaria. But a heretofore unknown episode that took place in the duke's last months offers us an insight into the plotters' fate. On March 7, 1482, Urbino ambassador Felici had been expelled from the palaces of Sixtus and Count Girolamo Riario. Shamed and upset by the way he was treated in Rome, he informed his patron Federico of the humiliation he had suf-

Copy drawn from Pietro Perugino's Sistine altarpiece,
Assumption of the Virgin, *now destroyed.*

fered. Spy Contugi reported how the usually cold-blooded duke burst with rage upon reading the upsetting news:

> *Now, by God, we are plunged into the greatest enmity with Count Girolamo! The last straw was that the holy Pope built a very worthy hall in which he has had all the popes painted, and in the spot he re-served for himself he wanted to be portrayed with a huge* gonfalone *[the captain of the Church's flag] in his hand, and also with myself, the Duke of Urbino, portrayed as if I were receiving the* gonfalone *from his hand. The Count has ordered the master painters not to do it until fur-ther notice.*

Federico's "excited utterance" concerned the fate of that "very worthy hall" whose fame would never die—that is, the Sistine Chapel. In March 1482, the Christ and the Moses cycles on the walls as well as the por-traits of the martyred popes at the level of the windows were almost fin-ished, but the altar wall still was unadorned.

Pope Sixtus IV had planned for his commissioned portrait to figure at the heart of the new chapel, right on top of the altar. Federico might have been deluding himself about the possibility of ever being portrayed alongside the pontiff in the most sacred locus of the Roman Catholic Church: a military captain like him would hardly belong in that holy setting. It is possible that, in his rage, Federico was imagining things just to make the injustice he felt was perpetrated against him seem more un-fair. But we cannot rule out that the possibility was at least discussed. In the end Perugino painted an Assumption of the Virgin on the altar above the kneeling portrait of Sixtus IV; today it survives only in the form of a drawing.

If we are to believe Contugi's report, Count Riario, by dismissing the commission that would have eternalized Federico's figure in the holiest of papal places, had successfully hit the duke at his softest spot, at the heart of his supreme vanity. Federico was extremely attentive to his self-image, so much so that he had several portraits made in very studied poses. In one of the most famous of these he is sitting in a *studiolo*-like room, fully dressed in his armor covered with the Collar of the Ermine and the Order of the Garter, reading from a large manuscript.

But what is he reading in the picture? It is a hefty volume, only slightly leaning against the decorated shelf. Federico seems to hold it effortlessly, at arm's length. Given the solemnity of the occasion, this can hardly be a secular book. Giovanni Santi gives us an important clue, when he describes the way in which the Montefeltro Library was organized:

> . . . *Foremost on one hand*
> *The works of holy churchmen, all adorned*
> *And bound with wond'rous beauty.*

The bindings of Federico's books were so magnificent that the troops of Cesare Borgia, when looting the city of Urbino in 1502, stole all the richest ones, which were covered with gems and gold. And it is not surprising that among those, the "works of holy churchmen" would be particularly splendid. There is a very strong chance that Federico picked a specific volume out of his great collection and posed in front of the painter purposefully reading it. About a dozen volumes were in fact covered with a lavish red silk binding and silver clasps such as the one painstakingly depicted in the panel. Each one of these works is by a different Church Father. Among these manuscripts, only one matches the dimensions of the book. Federico is reading a work by St. Gregory the Great, also known as Pope Gregory I (590–604)—the fourth Church Father in the Latin patristic canon. The manuscript contains the *Moralia,* his celebrated commentary on the Book of Job. The *Moralia in Job* is a manual of Christian life, a book of moral and spiritual education which had a huge impact in the Middle Ages. Seen in the Renaissance as a militant pope and as an engaged intellectual, Gregory embodied a perfect combination of roles for which Federico would want to be remembered.

Federico is sitting on his elevated throne, intent on reading the book, possibly one written by a Christian pope about an Old Testament book, perhaps the most controversial and theologically challenging of them all: Job is the supreme example of the man enduring the trials of faith (*fede* in Italian, hence the many puns on Federico's name as the man "rich of faith" which are carved in the Urbino palace).

It is like a Renaissance perspectival game: in the background of the portrait of Gregory which hangs among the illustrious men in the Urbino *studiolo,* there is an elegant capital, on top of which sits an eagle holding a ducal emblem, the Montefeltro coat of arms. And the Order of the Garter is casually wrapped around the same column. Ultimately, the portrait is aimed at the creation of a self-image of the most refined, and most secretive, kind. The utterly realistic picture, deeply time bound, becomes a timeless icon of power.

THE MEDICI VENDETTA

LORENZO DE' MEDICI DID NOT BOTHER SITTING IN SUCH ELAB-orate poses. However, to put it in Machiavelli's words, Lorenzo "was loved by fortune and by God in the highest degree, because of which all his enterprises had a prosperous end and all of his enemies an unprosperous one." He acquired the posthumous title of "Magnificent" by becoming a great patron of the arts and the arbiter of political balance. In his own words, he set the example of virtue:

> *What the prince does the many also soon do*
> *for to their eyes the prince is ever in view.*

Lorenzo had learned the hard way how formidable a foe the Church could be if one confronted it directly. He set out to gradually bribe the new pope, Innocent VIII, into becoming a steady ally of the Medici. Under Innocent, Lorenzo's son Giovanni became a cardinal at age sev-

LEFT PAGE: *Justus of Ghent, or Pedro Berruguete,* Double Portrait of Federico da Montefeltro and his son Guidobaldo, *ca. 1475.*

GREGORIO INCAELVM RELATO

enteen. The letter that Lorenzo wrote to him in March 1492 can be considered his political testament, a mixture of prudent hypocrisy and will to retain power.

Lorenzo acknowledged his family's gratitude to divine Providence "for having conferred upon us in your person the greatest dignity we ever enjoyed. This debt has to be repaid by a pious, chaste and exemplary life . . . It gave me great satisfaction to learn that in the course of last year you had frequently, of your own accord, gone to communion and confession; nor do I conceive that there is any better way of obtaining the favor of Heaven . . . As you now are to live in Rome, that place of iniquity, the difficulty of conducting yourself by these admonitions will be increased . . . Listen to other cardinals rather than speak yourself . . . and never forget to favor your family and your native place . . . Farewell."

Lorenzo died a month later, in April 1492, of natural causes. Giovanni remembered his father's advice at the time of the conclave of 1513, from which he emerged as Pope Leo X. The Duchy of Urbino appeared soon enough on the agenda of the first ever Medici pontiff: for both dynastic and strategic reasons, it was one of the first targets of Florentine appetites. In 1516 the Magnificent's grandson Lorenzo the younger attacked Sixtus IV's grandson Francesco Maria della Rovere, who was also the son of Federico's daughter Giovanna da Montefeltro and had been ruling Urbino since 1508. Lorenzo the younger swiftly replaced him as the Duke of Urbino, and kept this title until his sudden death in 1519.

But the ultimate Medici vendetta was perpetrated silently, within the walls of the Sistine Chapel, fifty-five years after the Pazzi conspiracy. In 1533, the second Medici Pope, Clement VII, commissioned the fifty-eight-year-old Michelangelo to paint a *Last Judgment* on the Sistine altar wall, the same wall then occupied by Perugino's *Assumption of the Virgin.* Back in 1512, Michelangelo had decorated the Sistine ceiling for Pope

LEFT PAGE: *Justus of Ghent, or Pedro Berruguete,* Portrait of Gregory the Great in the Urbino *studiolo, ca. 1475. The Montefeltro eagle sits on the top of the capital, and the Order of the Garter is wrapped around it.*

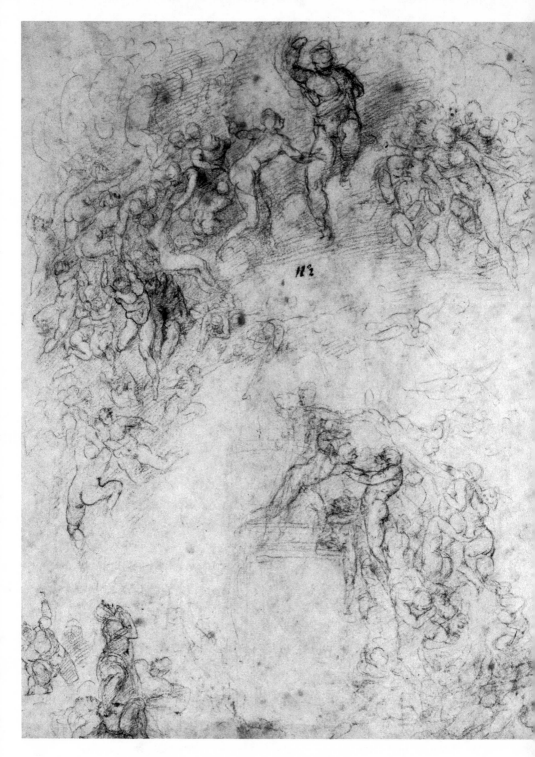

Michelangelo Buonarroti, sketch of the Last Judgment *on the Sistine Chapel altar wall, 1534.*

Julius II, Sixtus IV's nephew, who had made sure that his uncle's portrait was left untouched. The master painter knew better than anybody else that the altar wall was the most sacred spot in the chapel. In a preparatory drawing executed in early 1534, before he moved to Rome to start work on the apocalyptic fresco, Michelangelo left blank an arched spot corresponding to the space occupied by Perugino's *Assumption*. Next to the towering figure of Christ, depicted as judge of all souls, he sketched a kneeling Madonna, visually echoing the figure of Sixtus IV praying on his knees to the ascending Virgin Mary that appeared in Perugino's work. He even decorated the top of the altarpiece with some dynamic figures, contrasting with the static style of his predecessor. Apparently, this early project was rejected by the Medici pope.

When Michelangelo arrived in Rome, in September 1534, just a few days before Clement VII died, he learned that the altar wall—with Perugino's fresco—had been completely erased. No artist would have dared remove an altarpiece commissioned by the very pontiff who had built the chapel. Only another pope would have been able to order its destruction. And that is exactly what Clement VII did, as one of his last acts in this world.

Since that time, no one has paid attention to the simple fact that Clement VII—Giulio de' Medici—was the posthumous son of Giuliano de' Medici, the famous victim of the Pazzi plot instigated by Sixtus IV. The Medici pope had killed the image of his father's murderer. Considered in this new light, the *Last Judgment* becomes a double-edged way of sending a late pope to hell. This is just one of the reasons why the fame of the heroes and antiheroes of this story rings out "to the ends of earth."

Afterword

Not in my wildest dreams did I imagine that coming to the United States would lead me to solve one of Italy's oldest and bloodiest mysteries. When I arrived at Yale in 1995 to begin work toward my PhD, I decided to enroll in a paleography class in order to learn how to read ancient handwriting. When I met the professor, Vincent Ilardi, a distinguished historian of the Sforzas, he immediately suggested that I write a biography of my ancestor Cicco Simonetta, the longtime chancellor of the ruling Milanese family. But how could I do research on this obscure character and remote period while so far away from the original sources?

This question was soon, and amazingly, answered. Professor Ilardi had in fact built a huge microfilm collection of diplomatic documents of the Sforza period (1450–1500), which bears Ilardi's name. It comprises about two thousand reels and about two million documents, all stored in the subbasement of Sterling Memorial Library. This extensive collection of dispatches allowed me to enter into the daily life of my ancestor, one of the major but overlooked political figures of the Italian Renaissance.

In 1998, while investigating the political relationship between Cicco Simonetta and Federico da Montefeltro, Duke of Urbino, after the assassination of Duke Galeazzo Maria Sforza in 1476, I came across some enigmatic letters written by Federico in the aftermath of the 1478 Pazzi conspiracy. Reading these letters piqued my interest, and I soon began to look into the intriguing possibility of Federico's personal and active involvement in the infamous attempt to kill the two Medici brothers.

In a biography of the duke written by Walter Tommasoli in 1978, I noticed a reference to a private archive in Urbino where some ducal family letters of the late 1400s had been preserved. For about three years I tried to gain access to the archive, which holds the Ubaldini family papers and a few documents from the Montefeltro family, to which they were related. The curator kept telling me that these documents did not exist. Finally, in June 2001, when that curator was no longer in charge, I was granted permission to visit the archive. There I found a well-preserved batch of letters from the years 1478–1480. Some were addressed to Ottaviano Ubaldini, Federico da Montefeltro's half brother, but one (the longest of them all) was an original dispatch sent by the duke himself to his ambassadors in Rome. The date, February 14, 1478, made me think that this could be the smoking gun I was looking for, but the letter was heavily ciphered and I had no way of knowing its contents. I received permission from Countess Luisa Ubaldini to copy the document, and I brought the copy back with me to the United States.

I decided to use Cicco Simonetta's *Rules for Extracting Ciphered Letters Without a Sample,* his tract about the art of code-breaking. I did not know before I went to the United States that this existed, that it was originally part of Cicco's *Diaries,* or that the four pages on which it was written had been stolen from Milan and brought to Paris under Napoleon. I retrieved the autograph of the *Rules* in the Ilardi Collection and, as I describe in chapter 5, by following Cicco's tips I was able to start the process of decoding. After a few weeks of hard work I finally managed to crack the code. It was a truly exciting breakthrough, which confirmed all of the indirect evidence I had been collecting and proved Federico da Montefeltro's devious involvement in the Pazzi conspiracy.

I continued to assemble many other documents and finally in 2003 I published my findings in an article in *Archivio Storico Italiano* (the oldest academic journal in Italy, founded in 1888). To my surprise, there were no immediate reactions among scholars. But to my even greater astonishment, the media did respond. In early 2004 the Russian *Pravda,* then the Italian *La Repubblica*—with a full-page article by New York correspondent Alberto Flores d'Arcais—and later many other international newspapers reported the discovery. In February 2005, the History Channel released a documentary on a simplified version of the decoding story.

I decided to write this book in order to tell my own, fuller version of the Pazzi conspiracy. Two recent books, *April Blood: Florence and the Plot Against the Medici* (2004) by Lauro Martines and *Medici Money: Banking, Metaphysics, and Art in Fifteenth-Century Florence* (2005) by Tim Parks, deal with some of the same historical characters, but these authors have very different approaches and focuses from mine: the first gathers what is already known about the plot, from the perspective of the Pazzi family, but does not look at it through the lens of new evidence; the second retells the tale of the rise and fall of the Medici wealth. My intention has been to fill in the blanks of the picture, adding new archival discoveries and new interpretations. I have tried to reconstruct as accurately as I could the behind-the-scenes historical truth about two consecutive plots in Italian Renaissance history. I have also hypothesized a connection between the Sistine Chapel and the Pazzi conspiracy that has never before been explored.

It had always struck me as odd that Sandro Botticelli, the quintessential Florentine artist, had been summoned to Rome by Pope Sixtus IV, the most violent foe of the Medici at the time. Botticelli was a client of the Medici who had posthumously portrayed Giuliano de' Medici and also painted the hanging corpses of the Pazzi plotters on the walls of the Palazzo Vecchio. How could he have accepted the job of decorating the papal chapel without even thinking of his beloved patrons? The last chapter of this book is an attempt to answer that question.

Not everyone will agree with every detail of my interpretation of Botticelli's works. As a literary scholar and historian, I try to keep my eyes at once on texts and images, and on their original context. If this endless exercise in critical thinking has failed somewhere, my consolation is that it will be improved by the next discovery.

Acknowledgments

I would like, first of all, to thank Vincent Ilardi, who encouraged me from the start to study the world of diplomacy, and Giuseppe Mazzotta—my advisor at Yale and beyond—who inspired me to enter the intricate interplay of Renaissance power and literature. I wish to acknowledge friends, students, and colleagues who at different times have offered their input to improve the shape and content of this book: Anne Atik, Catherine Bindman, Alba Branca, Bill Connell, Jonathan Kagan, Kristin Kamm, Claudia La Malfa, Laura Malinverni, Tom Mayer, Pietro Moretti, Turi Munthe, Pia Pera, Ileene Smith, Will Stenhouse, and last but not least Karin Weber, whose support never faltered. Special thanks to Sarah Flynn for her professional editing contribution.

For their generous and timely help in getting some of the pictures I am grateful to Fabrizio Fenucci, Werner Hanak, Natalie Lettner, Elisabetta Panceri, and Ute Kagan Wartenberg.

My wonderful agent, Elizabeth Sheinkman, has worked with tireless and gracious effectiveness to find a good home for this book. I am also indebted to Felicity Blunt, her affable assistant at Curtis Brown in London.

My editor at Doubleday was Kristine Puopolo. Her quick reaction to the manuscript secured its publication, while her thoughtful corrections and suggestions improved tremendously its style.

Finally, I wish to thank my wife, Noga Arikha, the toughest editor and the sweetest companion, who has lovingly and actively accompanied every stage of the writing of this book.

The book is dedicated to my mother, Nella, who gave birth to me in a hospital in Pavia, only a few yards away from the castle where Cicco Simonetta was imprisoned at the end of his long life.

Sources

A Note on Sources

I have consulted most of the documents in the original, but I read many of the diplomatic dispatches in the *Ilardi Microfilm Collection of Renaissance Diplomatic Documents (ca. 1450–1500)* at Yale (http://www.library.yale.edu/Ilardi/il-toc.htm).

ABBREVIATIONS

ARCHIVES AND LIBRARIES

ASFi	Archivio di Stato di Firenze
ASMa	Archivio Gonzaga, Archivio di Stato di Mantova
ASMi	Archivio Sforzesco, Archivio di Stato di Milano
BAV	Biblioteca Apostolica Vaticana, Vatican City
BE	Biblioteca Estense, Modena
Bein.	Beinecke Library, New Haven
BL	British Library, London
BNCF	Biblioteca Nazionale Centrale, Florence
BNP	Bibliothèque Nationale, Paris
MAP	Archivio Mediceo avanti Principato, ASFi
Marc.	Biblioteca Nazionale Marciana, Venice
PE	Potenze Estere, ASMi
PML	Pierpont Morgan Library, New York
Triv.	Biblioteca Trivulziana, Milan
Ubaldini	Ubaldini Family Private Archive, Urbino

MANUSCRIPT
PRIMARY SOURCES

Giovanni di Carlo-Giovanni di Carlo, *Libri de temporibus suis* (BAV, Vat. lat. 5878).

Montano *Confession*-Cola Montano (ASFi, Carte Strozziane, III Serie, n. 379); translated into Italian by Lorenzi, *Studio storico*, pp. 47–88.

Montesecco *Confession*-Gian Battista Montesecco, exists in various manuscript copies; published in Roscoe, *Life of Lorenzo*, and Capponi, *Storia*.

PRINTED PRIMARY SOURCES
(MOST QUOTED)

Acta-Acta in Consilio Secreto in Castello Portae Jovis Mediolani, A. R. Natale ed. Milan. 3 vols. 1963–69.

Baldi-Bernardino Baldi, *Vita e Fatti di Federigo di Montefeltro Duca di Urbino*. 3 vols. Rome, 1824.

Carteggio-Carteggio degli oratori mantovani alla corte sforzesca (1450–1500), coord. and dir. F. Leverotti. 16 vols. Milan, 2001.

Corio-Bernardino Corio, *Storia di Milano*. Turin, 1978.

Corrispondenza-Corrispondenza dell'ambasciatore Giovanni Lanfredini, I (13 aprile 1484–9 maggio 1485) E. Scarton ed. Salerno, 2005.

Dennistoun-James Dennistoun, *Memoirs of the Dukes of Urbino, illustrating the arms, arts, and literature of Italy, from 1440 to 1630*. 3 vols. London, 1851.

Diari-Diari di Cicco Simonetta, A. R. Natale ed. Milan, 1962.

Federico di Montefeltro-Federico di Montefeltro. Lo stato. Le arti. La cultura, G. Cerboni Baiardi, G. Chittolini, P. Floriani eds. 3 vols. (I–III). Rome, 1986.

Ficino-*The Letters of Marsilio Ficino*. 7 vols. London, 1994.

Landucci-Luca Landucci, *A Florentine Diary from 1450 to 1516 by Luca Landucci*. London–New York, 1927.

Lettere-Lorenzo de' Medici, *Lettere*, R. Fubini ed., I (1460–1474); II (1474–1478); N. Rubinstein ed., III (1478–1479); IV (1470–1480); M. Mallett ed., V (1480–1481); VI (1481–1482); VII (1482–1484). Florence, 1977–.

Lettere di Stato-Federico da Montefeltro, *Lettere di Stato e d'arte (1470–1480)*, P. Alatri ed. Rome, 1949.

Machiavelli, *Discourses*-Niccolò Machiavelli, *Discourses on Livy,* trans. and ed. J. Conaway and P. Bondanella. Oxford–New York, 1997 (*indicating chapters*).

Machiavelli, *Florentine Histories*-Niccolò Machiavelli. *Florentine Histories: A New Translation* by L. F. Banfield and H. C. Mansfield, Jr. Princeton, 1988 (*chapters indicated*).

Machiavelli, *Prince-The Prince* by Niccolò Machiavelli *with Related Documents.* Trans., ed., and intro. W. J. Connell. Boston–New York, 2005 (*chapters indicated*).

Morgante e Lettere-Luigi Pulci, *Morgante e Lettere,* D. De Robertis ed. Florence, 1984.

Paltroni-Pierantonio Paltroni, *Commentarii della vita et gesti dell'illustrissimo Federico Duca d'Urbino,* W. Tommasoli ed. Urbino, 1966.

Parenti-Piero Parenti, *Storia fiorentina 1476–78—1492–96,* A. Matucci ed. Florence, 1994.

Poliziano, *Congiura*-Angelo Poliziano, *Della congiura dei Pazzi (Coniurationis commentarium),* S. Perosa ed. Padova, 1958.

Santi-Giovanni Santi, *La vita e le gesta di Federico di Montefeltro duca d'Urbino,* L. Michelini Tocci ed. Vatican City, 1985.

Strozzi, *Ricordo*-Filippo Strozzi, *Ricordo,* in Capponi, *Storia della repubblica fiorentina.* Vol. II, pp. 520–23. Florence, 1875.

Valori-Niccolò Valori (to be ascribed to his son Filippo), *Vita di Lorenzo de' Medici,* E. Niccolini ed. Vicenza, 1991.

Vespasiano-Vespasiano da Bisticci, *Commentario de la vita del signore Federico duca d'Urbino,* in *Vite,* A. Greco ed. Florence, 1970. Pp. 355–416.

Notes

Renaissance Italy: For a general introduction to Italian city-states, one can still profitably read the classic Burckhardt, *The Civilization.*

"While I was still mere flesh and bones": Dante, *Inferno,* XXVII, 73–78.

"since it is necessary for a prince": Machiavelli, *The Prince,* chapter 17.

PART I: WINTER 1476–SPRING 1478

1. MILAN IS FOR MURDER

In the first half of the fifteenth century: On the Visconti wars with Florence, see the classic Baron, *The Crisis.*

When the condottiere *Francesco Sforza suddenly:* See Ilardi, "The Italian League."

"The soul of Duke Giovanni": Giovanni Maria Visconti, Duke of Milan, was murdered in 1412.

"And such is the fate of cruel man": See Antonio Cornazzano's *Del modo di regere et di regnare* (PML M. 731).

He tried on a decorative breastplate: Many details of the narrative in this chapter come from Bernardino Corio's *History of Milan,* first published in 1503 (pp. 1398–1410); Machiavelli, *Florentine Histories,* drew his dramatic rewriting from it; the other major eyewitness account is the letter by Orfeo da Ricavo to Sforza Bettini, Milan, January 1, 1477 (ASFi, Carte Strozziane I, filza XXXXV, cc. 96–97), published in Casanova, "L'uccisione"; see Belotti, *Il dramma;* see also Ilardi, *The Assassination.*

he had had an instinto: Corio, pp. 1398ff.

"All the ink in Tuscany": Galeazzo Maria Sforza to Francesco Sforza, Florence, April 17, 1459 (Simonetta, *Rinascimento,* p. 118). On Galeazzo, Lubkin, *A Renaissance Court,* is very informative. For the 1471 visit: Wright, *A Portrait,* and also her *The Pollaiuolo Brothers.*

the penitential season of Lent: Machiavelli, *Florentine Histories,* VII, 28.

In his portrait of a dandified Galeazzo: See Strehlke, "Li magistri," p. 14.

he begged Galeazzo not to walk: Casanova, "L'uccisione," p. 304.

He embraced and kissed the boys: The touching detail of Galeazzo's goodbye to his sons comes from Machiavelli, *Florentine Histories,* VII, 34. I suspect that Machiavelli heard the story directly from Hermes Sforza, who visited Florence in 1503, when Machiavelli was secretary of the Republic.

The façade of the "blessed church": Casanova, "L'uccisione," p. 304.

"Sic transit gloria mundi!": Santi, p. 463.

"Make room!": Ibid.

"I am dead": Casanova, *"L'uccisione,"* p. 305; see also other sources, like Parenti, 3.

The Mantuan ambassador Zaccaria Saggi: See Saggi's many letters in *Carteggio;* in particular on Galeazzo's murder, Zaccaria Saggi to Ludovico Gonzaga, Milan, December 26, 1476 (in Belotti, *Il dramma,* pp. 186–87). But D'Adda, *"La morte di Galeazzo,"* p. 287, quotes another eyewitness report according to which "Zaccaria fled in fear."

Cicco was a "very good shield": Zaccaria Saggi to Ludovico Gonzaga, Cremona, August 21, 1471 *(Carteggio,* VIII, p. 550). On Cicco, see Simonetta, *Rinascimento,* pp. 127ff.

Cicco replied that "these were rotten things to do . . .": Cicco Simonetta to Gerardo Cerruti, Milan, February 13, 1473 (ASMi PE Romagna 178; cf. Simonetta, *Rinascimento,* p. 123).

Girolamo Olgiati was "very literate and erudite": Casanova, *"L'uccisione,"* p. 306.

"What a thousand armed phalanxes could not do . . .": Corio, p. 1407; cf. D'Adda, *"La morte di Galeazzo,"* p. 286–87. On Olgiati and Lampugnani, cf. Belotti, *Il dramma.* On Sallust's influence, see P. J. Osmond, *Catiline and Catilinarism in the Italian Renaissance* (unpublished essay; I wish to thank the author for sharing it with me).

"Pull yourself together, Girolamo!": Corio, p. 1408.

Apparently, Lampugnani's wife had also fallen prey: The allegation about Galeazzo's rape deserves a closer analysis. In a letter dated June 14, 1468, Lampugnani had duly informed Cicco Simonetta that his wife was not following him to Genoa, where he had been posted from Milan on a diplomatic mission. But having heard that the Milanese envoys had left without him, Lampugnani asked Cicco to give him the chance to "clear his innocence," in case he had unwillingly disappointed the duke for some mysterious reason. It is possible that, under the circumstances, Cicco would cover up his lord's nasty plans to sleep with his subject's wife, but one has to acknowledge that Lampugnani might have been slightly paranoid about the supposed abuse. This allegation was wholly based on circumstantial evidence. (Interestingly, the verb *sforzare* in Italian also means "to rape").

"Everything was done," added Orfeo da Ricavo: Casanova, *"L'uccisione,"* p. 307.

"be favorable to our enterprise . . ." Machiavelli, *Florentine Histories,* VII, 34; see also Frazier, *Possible Lives,* p. 151.

as did some well-timed tax cuts: See Belotti, *Il dramma,* p. 154, Cicco's letter of January 8, 1477, to fix a fair price of grains.

directing a desperate appeal to the pope: On Bona's appeal, see Breisach, *Caterina Sforza,* p. 26; see Bona of Savoy to Celso Maffei, Milan, early January 1477 (BNP It. 1592, 95–96; see also the theological debate, BNP It. 1592, 97).

among them was Lucia Marliani: On her alleged role in Galeazzo's burial, see Vaglienti, "Anatomia"; see also the thrilling historical novel by Laura Malinverni, *Una storia del Quattrocento.*

must have had a "secret virtue": Machiavelli, *Florentine Histories,* VIII, 18; Simonetta, *Rinascimento,* p. 161.

which gave full governing powers to the council: Bona of Savoy to the Secret Senate, Milan, December 30, 1476 (ASMi 932; *Lettere,* II, pp. 249–50); see Fubini, *Osservazioni e documenti;* see also Simonetta, *Rinascimento,* p. 157–58. On Gian Giacomo Simonetta, see ibid., pp. 135–36.

Galeazzo's first cousin Roberto da Sanseverino: See Simonetta, *Rinascimento,* pp. 197ff., with bibliography.

had actually moved into Galeazzo's private apartments: Zaccaria Saggi to Ludovico Gonzaga, Milan, January 31, 1477 (ASMa b. 1626).

2. OVERLY CAUTIOUS

He hired Florentine architect Antonio Averlino: On his work for the Sforza castle, see Welch, *Art and Authority.*

What's more, these two brilliant brains shared: Pelling, *The Curse,* argues that the Bein. Ms. 408 was in fact created by Filarete with the help of Cicco's cryptographic techniques.

Cicco had selected the best agents: For a series of biographies of the Sforza ambassadors and a collection of Cicco's ciphers, see Cerioni, *La diplomazia,* and Cicco's *Diari.*

instituted the first resident ambassadors: Ilardi, "The First Permanent Embassy."

obtain what he wanted "the military way": Acta, January 6, 1477.

could do so only "as private courtiers": Sforza Maria Sforza to Federico Gonzaga, Naples, January 12, 1479 (ASMa b. 1608).

was "more shadow than fact": Ibid.

In early February, the three accomplices hired a man named Ettore Vimercati: For his trial, see Fubini, *Osservazioni e documenti,* pp. 77ff.; cf. Magenta, *Visconti e Sforza,* II, pp. 390–92; on the Simonetta family rules, see Simonetta, *Rinascimento,* p. 130; cf. Pecchiai, *"Il cuoco di Cicco Simonetta."*

He would have succeeded, "had Cicco not been alerted": Ercole d'Este a Nicolò Bendidio, Florence, February 9, 1477 *(Lettere,* II, p. 296).

thanking Lorenzo and Giuliano de' Medici for their heartfelt condolences: Lorenzo and Giuliano de' Medici to Bona of Savoy, Florence, December 29, 1476.

recalling their "old friendship": Bona of Savoy to Lorenzo de' Medici, Milan, January 6, 1477 *(Lettere,* II, pp. 247–50).

In January 1477 Cicco had also sent as gifts: Lorenzo de' Medici to Bona of Savoy, Florence, January 18, 1477 *(Lettere,* II, p. 262). The coded meaning of the gift is my own interpretation.

his best falcon-trainer, a man named Pilato: Galeazzo Maria Sforza to Lorenzo de' Medici, Milan, July 11, 1476 (MAP XLVII 253; *Lettere,* II, pp. 239–40). On the rise of the Medici family, see Rubinstein, *The Government;* Parks, *Medici Money.*

"Quant'è bella giovinezza": In Lorenzo's collected poems; see Parks, *Medici Money,* p. 239.

"the content of the republic's letters ...": Lorenzo de' Medici to Tommaso Soderini and Luigi Guicciardini, Florence, February 17, 1477 *(Lettere,* II, pp. 280–89; cf. 290–93, in which he writes a separate postscript to be shown, at the ambassadors' discretion, only to Cicco.)

Cicco had first met Lorenzo: For Lorenzo's trip to Lombardy in 1465, see *Lettere,* I, pp. 14–16. On the Visconti-Sforza Library, see D'Adda, *Indagini storiche.*

"As long as I live and whatever becomes ...": Lorenzo to Bianca Maria and Galeazzo Maria Sforza Dukes of Milan, Florence, June 9, 1466. *Lettere,* I, pp. 21–22.

"clean": Lorenzo de' Medici to Andrea Petrini (his agent in Milan), Florence, February 17, 1477, *Lettere,* II, p. 296, referring to the plot against Cicco by Vimercati).

Federico da Montefeltro's condotta, or hiring contract: Lettere, II, p. 292.

"This is a very little thing, very easy . . . ": Federico da Montefeltro to Lorenzo de' Medici, Fossombrone, January 25, 1477 (MAP XLVII 396); another letter of the same content was written from Gubbio, May 24, 1477 (MAP XLV 283).

"Today, peace in Italy is dead.": Corio, p. 1410.

"We urge you to do all you can . . .": The Signoria of Florence to Sixtus IV, to Ferrante of Aragon, to the Republic of Venice, and to Federico da Montefeltro, Florence, December 29, 1476, in Casanova, *"L'uccisione,"* pp. 311–13.

after the "untimely and most atrocious"; the assassination had killed his pensiero bello: Santi, pp. 469–70. Santi also digressed in his versified biography about the dangers of living like a tyrant. If a private citizen (like Lorenzo) wants to administer the republic and become important, he will inevitably begin to degenerate and spread trouble around him, which results either in death or exile. Torments, woes, and pains multiply themselves, Santi continued. The tyrant lives to die a violent death, surrounded by a "sea of doubts," "slave of a thousands thieves," and "criminals." It is better to enjoy one's riches in hiding, avoiding the "dangerous style" of rule. Indeed "cruel fate" and "bitter death" had hit Galeazzo, who had feared neither the powerful and strong (like Federico), nor the poor and powerless. The Duke of Milan, so confident in his wealth and might, lording over a state of which all Italy was in awe, now lay dead in the ground, killed by a lowly servant (Santi, pp. 466–69).

"I will write to Nomio": Lorenzo de' Medici to Gentile de' Becchi, Florence, February 1, 1477 *(Lettere,* II, pp. 272–76).

It was under Gonzaga's scrutiny that finally, on February 24: Published in Rosmini, *Dell'istoria di Milano,* IV, pp. 158–62.

He knew one man: On his relationship with Sanseverino, see Simonetta, *Rinascimento,* pp. 197ff. Pulci had inserted a cameo of Sanseverino in his poem celebrating the 1469 Florentine joust that Lorenzo had predictably won. For all the letters by Luigi Pulci to Lorenzo de' Medici, from 1473 to early 1477, see *Morgante e Lettere,* pp. 983ff.

"Despite the fact that he is an insipid . . .": Angelo Della Stufa to Galeazzo Sforza, Florence, April 19, 1476 (ASMi PE Firenze 291).

"I heard about the duke's death . . .": Luigi Pulci to Lorenzo de' Medici, January 3, 1477 *(Morgante e Lettere,* p. 1000).

Cicco did not approve of "the hellish picture": The Dukes of Milan to Filippo Sacramoro, Milan, March 19, 1477 (ASMi PE Firenze 292).

Once a powerful maritime republic, over the last decades Genoa: See Federico da Montefeltro to the Dukes of Milan, Urbino, April 17, 1477 (ASMi PE Marca 149; the letter is published with no date in *Lettere di Stato,* pp. 57–58).

He targeted one captain, Donato del Conte: For his capture, see Zaccaria Saggi to Ludovico Gonzaga, Milan, May 26, 1477 (ASMa b. 1627).

"I was bored with the Council's meetings . . .": Roberto da Sanseverino to the Marquis of Monferrato, Asti, May 28, 1477 (Rosmini, *Dell'istoria di Milano,* IV, p. 164).

"some stratagem that goes against any good": Lorenzo de' Medici to Roberto da Sanseverino, Florence, May 29, 1477 (ASMi PE Firenze 292; *Lettere,* II, pp. 258–61).

"human things are subject to change . . . ": Lorenzo de' Medici to Filippo Sacramoro in Milan, Florence, June 5, 1477 *(Lettere,* II, pp. 367–71).

"Ma la fortuna attenta sta nascosa": The quote is from Pulci's *Morgante,* Cantare 1.12.1–2.

"I am sorry for anyone's misfortune . . .": Federico Montefeltro to the Dukes of Milan, Gubbio, June 3, 1477 (ASMi PE Umbria 141).

"select few who govern and they suffer . . .": Tommaso Soderini to Lorenzo de' Medici, Milan, June 30, 1477 (MAP XXXII 113; cf. Fubini, *Italia quattrocentesca,* p. 112).

3. NOTHING UNSAID

Federico da Montefeltro was born: For the biographies of Federico, see Scrivano, *Biografie;* and, in chronological order, Paltroni, Santi, Vespasiano da Bisticci, Baldi, Dennistoun, Tommasoli, Roeck. See also Bonvini Mazzanti, *Battista Sforza.*

The Gubbio studiolo *mirrored Federico's:* See Raggio, *The Gubbio Studiolo.*

That morning, preparing for dictation, Federico undoubtedly summoned: The duke's secretary was Federico Galli who, according to De' Rossi's biography, went on to live until he was 106 years old; more important from our standpoint, the biographer emphasized the fact that "the Duke always wanted to see his letters and subscribe them personally" *(Vita,* p. 84).

The duke's letter to Cicco Simonetta: Federico da Montefeltro to Matteo [Benedetti] in Milan, Urbino, July 2, 1477 (ASFi, Urbino, Classe I, Div. G., filza CIV, n. 12; *italics mine*). This letter was published in Fubini, *Federico da Montefeltro,* pp. 451–58. This seminal essay was the first to outline Montefeltro's role in the buildup of the Pazzi conspiracy; its Appendix contains other key documents.

Fortunately for Federico, Cicco Simonetta had warned: Cf. Corio, disputed by Baldi.

had no knowledge of the plot: For Federico's role in the murder of his stepbrothers, see Scatena, *Oddantonio.*

as a result of a mischievous move by his opponent: Guidangelo de' Ranieri. For the incident in the mock-joust, see Santi, pp. 152–55. Perhaps he is the same mentioned in Santi, pp. 129–30, as a brave soldier.

One of the victims was a Jewish merchant named Menahem ben Aharon: For his Hebrew library, see Delio Proverbio's essay in the Morgan exhibition catalogue *Federico da Montefeltro and His Library.*

The condottiere *was welcomed triumphantly:* See Sacramoro da Rimini to Galeazzo Maria Sforza, Florence, June 26, 1472 (ASMi PE Firenze 283) on the Florentine citizenship and other gifts, including the intention of giving him Luigi Scarampo's house. According to Vespasiano da Bisticci he was given the villa in Rusciano which belonged to Luca Pitti, the failed anti-Medici plotter of 1466.

He was granted Florentine citizenship and was promised: See Francesco Prendilacqua to Ludovico Gonzaga, Urbino, April 2, 1473 (ASMa b. 845; quoted in Paltroni, p. 275) on the reception of the helmet, produced by Antonio Pollaiuolo.

Disputationes Camaldulenses: A critical edition of Cristoforo Landino's work with a facing English translation is being edited by Jill Kraye.

Landino avoided any reference to the sack of Volterra: For Federico's role in it, see at least Paltroni, pp. 267–76, and Santi, pp. 390–407.

make a "clone" out of wax: Corio, p. 1369.

a little treatise on code-writing, De furtivis litteris: See Valentini, "Uno scritto ignorato."

4. THE INVISIBLE HANDS

"all the people who understand . . .": Baccio Ugolini to Lorenzo's secretary Niccolò Michelozzi, Rome, January 16, 1477 (BNCF, Ginori Conti, 29, 18).

"if it wouldn't create a scandal . . .": Lorenzo de' Medici to Baccio Ugolini, Florence, February 1, 1477 *(Lettere,* II, p. 269). Lorenzo's visit to Sixtus in 1471, *Ricordi.* For basic background on Sixtus IV and the della Rovere family: *Un pontificato;* Lombardi, "Sisto IV"; see also Clark, *Melozzo da Forlì.*

"incredible goodness and true love": Pietro Riario to Lorenzo de' Medici, Rome, August 14, 1472 (MAP XLVI 184; quoted in *Lettere,* I, p. 392). On Pietro Riario, see Santi, pp. 425–28; partially translated by Dennistoun, I, pp. 195–96.

Federico da Montefeltro, for his part: Sacramoro da Rimini to Galeazzo Maria Sforza, Rome, November 9, 1473 (ASMi PE Roma 73). On Imola see Breisach, *Caterina Sforza.* See Cicco's *Diari* for Caterina's wedding ceremony in Milan (January 14, 1473).

"candle of the Virgin Mary": Federico da Montefeltro to Lorenzo de' Medici, Naples, July 29, 1474 (MAP LXI 155). This letter is commented by Lorenzo's secretary Niccolò Michelozzi writing to Gentile Becchi, Florence, August 8, 1474 (BNCF, Ginori Conti, 29, 67); in several letters of the following days Michelozzi reports about the suspicious activities of Federico, who might be acting like "an evil malicious traitor." For the Roman ceremony, see Baldi, III, pp. 234–35 and the important addenda P-Q-R, pp. 278–81; see Dennistoun, I, pp. 209–11.

"awaited like a Messiah": Gian Pietro Arrivabene to Federico Gonzaga, Rome, August 13 and 21 and October 1, 1474 (ASMa b. 845) for Federico's Collar of the Ermine and his attention to fashionable clothing. On Federico in Città di Castello, see Santi, pp. 440–42 (p. 444 quote of the "deadly hatred").

"she-cat who licks you in front . . .": See Tommasoli, *Vita,* pp. 159–60; Santi, p. 446, pp. 449–50; on Piero Felici's last mission in Florence, see Filippo Sacramoro to Galeazzo Maria Sforza, Florence, October 10, 1474 (ASMi PE Firenze 288).

Later the same month, in Urbino: Santi, pp. 453–57 (translated by Dennistoun, who also collected many other documents about the king of England in his Appendix VII: I, pp. 424–32).

It should have come as a warning sign that: On the jousting horse, Federico da Montefeltro to Lorenzo de' Medici, Urbino, December 30, 1474 (MAP XXX 1079; *Lettere* II, 123).

"small in body but great in spirit": Parenti: 12:17. On Francesco Pazzi, see Poliziano, *Congiura,* pp. 12–16, and Santi, p. 493.

This was Francesco Salviati: See Poliziano, *Congiura,* pp. 10–12.

"would mind his own business . . .": Francesco Nori to Lorenzo de' Medici, Rome, January 19, 1475 (MAP LXI 98; *partially ciphered*).

"they would join their hands to God . . .": Federico da Montefeltro about Lorenzo de' Medici, as reported by Francesco Maletta to Galeazzo Maria Sforza, Naples, July 13, 1475 (ASMi PE Napoli 227; *Lettere,* II, p. 117).

"all my troubles derive from the same source . . .": Lorenzo de' Medici to Galeazzo Maria Sforza, Florence, September 7, 1475 *(Lettere,* II, pp. 121–27); quoted in Parks, *Medici Money,* p. 205: "Puffed up by his Majesty . . ."—cutting the reference to the Duke of Urbino.

"If the fish is not worthy of you . . .": Francesco Salviati to Lorenzo de' Medici, Pisa, June 20, 1476 (MAP XXXIII 479).

The following account of the events: Montesecco *Confession,* released May 4, 1478, printed on August 4 by the Florentines (note that other historians, including Martines, *April Blood,* have used this key document, but this is the first "chronological" reconstruction of the sequence of reported events).

"Such proceedings of justice are limited . . . ": Francesco Salviati to Nicolò Baldovini, Rome, July 11, 1477 (BL Add. 24.213, 40; *italics mine*).

"enter into evil"; "a gutsy pope": Machiavelli, *The Prince,* respectively chapters 17 and 11.

"Men cannot govern states . . . ": Machiavelli, *Florentine Histories,* VII. 6. This maxim was attributed to Cosimo de' Medici by various Florentine contemporary writers.

"Magnificent Lorenzo": Girolamo Riario to Lorenzo de' Medici, Rome, September 1, 1477 (BNP It. 2033, 36).

"Your Lordships of Milan . . . ": Sacramoro da Rimini to the Dukes of Milan, Rome, September 14 and 16, 1477 (ASMi PE Roma 84).

"secret expenses": Tommasoli, *Vita,* p. 274.

"any deliberation or enterprise . . . ": Lorenzo de' Medici in consultation with the Florentine officials to Francesco Salviati, Florence, September 18, 1477 (*Lettere,* II, p. 416).

"very hard job at hand . . . ": Federico da Montefeltro to the astrologer Antonuccio da Gubbio, published in *Lettere di Stato,* p. 113, is translated and commented by Dennistoun, I, p. 233, but referred to a later siege (Castel Sansavino or Poggio Imperiale).

Ugolini had some understanding: Baccio Ugolini to Lorenzo de' Medici, Rome, October 6 and 25, 1477 (MAP XXVI 189 and 388; *partially ciphered*); in the hardly legible ciphered part of the P.S., he wrote that the pope spoke "to *Mantua,*" that is, to Cardinal Francesco Gonzaga, Rodolfo's brother.

5. ELIMINATE THEM!

"more a city in itself than a palazzo": Baldassarre Castiglione's *Book of the Courtier* (I, 2); the Urbino palace was built by Luciano Laurana and Francesco di Giorgio.

He also hired humanists: Santi, p. 423; for the *studiolo* and the library, see *Federico da Montefeltro and His Library.*

In early October 1477 Federico summoned: For Federico's troops movements, Iacopo Ammannati to Lorenzo de' Medici, Siena, October 9, 1477 (MAP XXXIV 206, in Ammannati's *Lettere,* p. 2158).

It is unclear whether this was: Santi, pp. 489ff.; See also Tommasoli, *Vita,* p. 275.

bad humors: See Santi, p. 491; for the surgical details see Petrus Paulus Pegnis to the Dukes of Milan, Urbino, January 31, 1478 (ASMi PE Marca 149). On the humors, see Noga Arikha, *Passions and Tempers. A History of the Humours,* New York, 2007.

In November Count Riario dispatched his favorite henchman: See my entry in the *Dizionario Biografico degli Italiani*; *Lettere,* II, p. 456, also for *Felici . . . had been summoned to the Curia.* See letter by Federico da Montefeltro to Piero Felici, of February 11, 1478, quoted in *Lettere,* II, p. 463, reply to the ciphered letter to the Duke of Urbino by his Roman ambassadors, Rome, February 6, 1478 (in Fubini, *Federico da Montefeltro,* pp. 462–72). See also Federico da Montefeltro to Piero Felici, Urbino, February 7, 1478 (PML, MA 4338), in which he thanks him for communicating to him the support of the Duchess of Milan (Cicco) to his "honor," that is, his *condotta*.

The words in Federico's coded letter: Federico da Montefeltro to Piero Felici and Agostino Staccoli, Urbino, February 14, 1478 (Ubaldini; *almost completely ciphered*. I discovered it in summer 2001, and published it in 2003; see also Afterword).

Cicco's Rules: Regule and extrahendum litteras zifratas, sine exemplo attributed to Cicco Simonetta, pages cut from his *Diari,* Pavia, July 4, 1474 (BNP It. 1595, 441r).

Fortunately, these same symbols happened: Vat. lat. 998 (BAV). I discovered it in summer 2004; I thank Nick Pelling for his tip.

Shortly after Guidobaldo had received the gift: Clark, *Melozzo da Forlì,* thought that Guidobaldo's portrait was by Melozzo, but recent reattribution ascribed it to Bartolomeo della Gatta (Simonetta, *Federico da Montefeltro*).

"Piero. I received your letter . . .": Ottaviano Ubaldini to Piero Felici, Urbino, February 15, 1478 (Ubaldini).

Raffaele Riario was Girolamo's nephew: He was made cardinal on December 10, 1477. According to Filippo Sacramoro he arrived on March 5, 1478, at the Pazzi villa; see the letter by Raffaele Riario written in Montughi on March 30, 1478 (MAP XXXVI 392): this means that he stayed around Florence for at least a month before the conspiracy struck (see Fubini, *Federico da Montefeltro,* p. 432).

the officially pro-Medici philosopher Marsilio Ficino gave Jacopo Bracciolini: See Simonetta, *Rinascimento,* pp. 181ff.; on Ficino's involvement in the plot, Fubini, *Quattrocento fiorentino,* pp. 235–301 (*Ficino e i Medici all'avvento di Lorenzo il Magnifico* and *Ancora su Ficino e i Medici*).

"Knowing Sir Jacopo, son of Poggio": See the two letters on behalf of Jacopo Bracciolini written by Girolamo Riario to Lorenzo de' Medici, Rome, January 15, 1478 (MAP XXXIV 49 and 275).

On March 27, a secret meeting: See the official letter of King Ferrante of Naples, Sarno, April 1, 1478, referring to the March 27 meeting, in Fubini, *Federico da Montefeltro,* pp. 467–68.

Giustini rushed all the way back to Urbino: Matteo Contugi to Federico Gonzaga, Urbino, April 1, 1478 (ASMa b. 846).

one of his favorite weapon-makers: Ibid.

"the Duke of Urbino and some others . . .": Giovanni Lanfredini to Lorenzo de' Medici, Venice, January 3, 1478 (*Lettere,* II, p. 468); see Leonardo Botta to the Dukes of Milan, Venice, January 18, 1478 (ASMi PE Venezia 363; see Ilardi, *The Assassination,* p. 100).

"Watch yourself!": Filippo Sacramoro to the Dukes of Milan, Florence, September 13, 1477 (ASMi PE Firenze 293; *Lettere,* II, p. 413).

"The words, the countenance, the most recent acts . . .": Sacramoro da Rimini to Cicco Simonetta, Rome, April 2 and 24, 1478 (ASMi PE Roma 85).

The high point of Cicco's government: See Simonetta, *Rinascimento,* p. 158; Frazier, *Possible Lives,* p. 156.

PART II: SPRING 1478-SUMMER 1482

6. FLORENCE IS FOR FEAR

There are a few published Renaissance reports: Sources for this chapter are multiple: Montesecco's *Confession;* Poliziano, *Congiura;* Strozzi, *Ricordo;* Landucci 15–19; Parenti, *Storia fiorentina,* pp. 12–20; Conti, *Storie,* pp. 22ff. (talks about the "devil as the sower of war," as pointed out by Chambers, *Popes, Cardinals and War,* p. 75); Machiavelli, *Florentine Histories,* VIII, 1–9.

starsi alla dimesticha: Parenti 14:81; *anghio:* Parenti 15:84.

stomacans: Giovanni di Carlo, 136r.

"Watch out, O brother: by wanting . . .": Giovanni di Carlo, 136v and Machiavelli *Florentine Histories,* VIII, 2.

"a cargo of Indian spices and Greek books . . .": Edward Gibbon as quoted by John Hale, *England and the Italian Renaissance,* p. 83. Description of the Medici Palace and quote from Virgil *(Aeneid.* II, pp. 248–49): Giovanni di Carlo, 140v–141r.

"thing truly worthy of memory": Machiavelli, *Florentine Histories,* VIII, 6.

Somebody else spread the rumor that a number of unidentified crossbowmen: Parenti 17:166.

"Take this, traitor!": Parenti 18:182. Machiavelli, *Discourses,* III, 6, argues that Francesco Pazzi shouted, giving Lorenzo the chance to save himself from the attack.

helped by a young man from a wealthy family: Giovanni di Carlo, 142r; it was a member of the Cavalcanti family.

with their hearts in their throats: Strozzi, *Ricordo,* 521.

he had to visit his ailing mother: Parenti 17:152.

They had set themselves up: Poliziano, *Congiura,* p. 38; Machiavelli, *Florentine Histories,* VIII, 7; cf. VII, 26 for another plot narrating the courage of Cesare Petrucci (see also Simonetta, *Rinascimento,* p. 187).

According to Giovanni di Carlo's History: Giovanni di Carlo, 140r.

"naive soul": Giovanni di Carlo, 140v; Machiavelli, *Florentine Histories,* VIII, 6; also Parenti, 18:205–10, speculates on the "occult cause" that prevented Montesecco from acting against Lorenzo.

The immediate, chaotic aftermath of the conspiracy was vividly described: Filippo Sacramoro to Cicco Simonetta, Florence, April 27 and 28, 1478 (ASMi PE Firenze 294); see Cicco's *Diari,* pp. 237–39.

"ferocity of his soul": Giovanni di Carlo, 143v; various details about the "payback," passim.

"in the name of the Holy Spirit to be pronounced cardinal": Filippo Sacramoro, April 27 (*quoted above*).

Somebody did claim from li indicij de li panni: Filippo Sacramoro, April 27, (*quoted above*).

Jacopo's daughter was deprived: Giovanni di Carlo, 144v.

the first portrait was transformed into one . . . : See Wright, *The Pollaiuolo Brothers,* p. 136.

On the last day of April, the funeral of Giuliano de' Medici: Landucci, p. 17 ("Ascension Day").

A commemorative bronze medal that he had cast: See Barocchi and Caglioti, *Eredità del Magnifico,* pp. 62ff.

In the middle of the courtyard he could see: Ibid.

7. EXTREME MEASURES

"The political régime which was founded . . .": See Rubinstein, *The Government of Florence.*

"Nonetheless, things having happened in the way . . .": Federico da Montefeltro to Lorenzo de' Medici, Urbino, May 1, 1478 (MAP XLV 284, published in Viti, *Lettere familiari,* pp. 484–85 with the wrong date of May 11).

The Milanese envoy in Florence: Filippo Sacramoro to Cicco Simonetta, Florence, April 27 [2 letters] and 28, 1478 (*quoted above*); May 3, 1478; and Cicco Simonetta to Filippo Sacramoro, Milan, April 30, 1478 (ASMi PE Firenze 294).

An anonymous Florentine poem: See Flamini, "Versi in morte," pp. 321 and 330–34 (partially translated in Martines, *April Blood,* p. 184).

"From this situation in Florence . . .": Federico da Montefeltro to Cicco Simonetta, Urbino, May 8, 1478 (ASMi PE Marca 149).

Federico's secretary sent to Cicco's son: [Federico Galli] to Gian Giacomo Simonetta, Urbino, May 13, 1478 (ASMi PE Marca 149). I discovered these two key documents in spring 1998 and began my quest.

"most excellent": Machiavelli, *Florentine Histories,* VIII, 18; *The Prince,* chapter 22 (see Simonetta, *Rinascimento,* p. 127).

Without naming names, Cicco then alluded: The Dukes of Milan to Lorenzo de' Medici, Milan, May 9, 1478 (ASMi PE Firenze 294; autograph corrections by Cicco Simonetta).

"word by word": Filippo Sacramoro to the Dukes of Milan, Florence, May 12, 1478 (ASMi PE Firenze 294).

Lorenzo's reply of May 12 to Cicco: Lorenzo de' Medici to the Dukes of Milan, Florence, May 12, 1478 (*Lettere,* III, pp. 21–23).

Then he spoke in his nasal voice: Giovanni di Carlo, 148v–153v, for Lorenzo's oration and the response to it; Machiavelli, *Florentine Histories,* VIII, 10–11. See Rubinstein, "Lorenzo de' Medici," p. 86 (quoting ASFi, Consulte e pratiche, 60, ff. 159r–160r).

army of lawyers: See De Benedictis, *Una guerra d'Italia,* pp. 37–40, on the legal battle between Lorenzo and Sixtus IV.

Florentine Synodus: See the autograph in ASFi, Miscell. Repubblicana, n. 264; BE for the only extant incunable; *Dissension* (Bein.); Montefeltro Bible, Urb. lat. 2 (BAV); see *La Bibbia di Federico;* exhibition catalogue *Federico da Montefeltro and His Library.*

And Arezzo was the town: Giovanni Lanfredini to the Dieci di Balia, Foggia, September 28, 1485 (*Corrispondenza,* p. 320: it is interesting that the seasoned Florentine ambassador recalled this detail seven years later, while denouncing "the ambition of the priests").

"You say to me that I should become . . .": Gentile Becchi to Federico Galli [Cafaggiolo], November 4, 1478 (in Fubini, *Federico da Montefeltro,* pp. 469–70).

On June 21 Federico thanked Lorenzo: Federico da Montefeltro to Lorenzo de' Medici, Urbino, June 21, 1478 (MAP XXXVI 824, in Viti, *Lettere familiari,* pp. 485–86).

saddle-chair: See Giovanni Angelo Talenti and Filippo Sacramoro to the Dukes of Milan, Florence, June 25, 1478 (ASMi PE Firenze 295); Sforza Bettini to Lorenzo de' Medici, Camucia, June 28, 1478 (MAP XXXIV 171).

"nasty war": Santi, pp. 504ff.

After their three-hour-long secret meeting: Matteo Contugi to Federico Gonzaga, Urbino, June

17, 1478 (ASMa b. 846). Contugi was the resident spy in Urbino on behalf of the Gonzaga, Marquis of Mantua, competitor of the Montefeltro.

They were probably wrapped into cheese shapes: Matteo Contugi to Federico Gonzaga, Urbino, June 17, 1478 (*quoted above*); for other gifts to Federico transported with the same ingenious technique, see Lorenzo da Rieti to Ludovico Gonzaga, Milan, February 25, 1478 (ASMa b. 1626); see also the poem on Cicco's demise by a Baldassarre da Bologna in Marc., misc. 1945, 48 (see Simonetta, *Rinascimento,* p. 163).

unum velle et unum nolle: Cicco Simonetta to Lorenzo de' Medici, Milan, July 3, 1478 (MAP XLV 188).

When Lorenzo received this letter: Landucci, p. 20.

Feast of San Giovanni: Landucci, p. 20.

8 . LIVES AT STAKE

In his dialogue The Art of War *as much as in his* Florentine Histories: Machiavelli, *The Art of War.*

The battles of the Pazzi war: Conti, *Storie,* pp. 41ff.; Baldi, III, pp. 246–57; Santi, pp. 505ff.

He boasted in a letter to Matthias Corvinus, king of Hungary: Quoted from Dennistoun, I, pp. 236–37 (Italian names in Allegretti, *Diarii Senesi,* in *Rerum Italicarum Scriptores,* XXIII, pp. 784ff.). The first year of war is evoked in the boasting letter by Federico da Montefeltro to King Matthias Corvinus of Hungary, Dennistoun, I, pp. 234–35 (*Lettere di Stato,* pp. 51–52).

On July 25, an angry and anxious Pope Sixtus IV: Sixtus IV to Federico da Montefeltro, Rome, July 25, 1478 (MAP LXXXIX 247; Acton, *Pazzi Conspiracy,* p. 104). Dennistoun, I, p. 230n, comments that the letter is "curious rather from the eccentricity of its illiterate style, in which barbarous Latin forms a strange medley with uncultivated Italian."

"Naked and on their knees": Santi, pp. 516–17.

A Florentine official who was trying to resist: Episode of the 1478 siege of Castellina from the *Book of the Courtier* (II, 52).

Cain: Matteo Contugi to Federico Gonzaga, Ferrara, October 16, 1478 (ASMa b. 1229).

Florentine Castle of Sansavino: Santi, pp. 521–56.

"more than a thousand horses": Ibid., p. 544.

"Sometimes a captain needs to be . . .": Ibid., p. 554.

In early August 1478, for example, he helped Genoa: See Cicco's *Diari,* pp. 252ff.; Gallo, *Commentarius,* pp. 67ff.; Zaccaria Saggi to Federico Gonzaga, Milan, August 9, 1478 (ASMa b. 1626, in Carteggio XI, pp. 100ff.).

In this most tragic moment of his career: Cicco Simonetta to Lorenzo de' Medici, Milan, December 29, 1478 (MAP LXXXVIII 281); for Cicco's library, Simonetta, *Rinascimento,* pp. 131ff.

"scarier than that of the Turks": Gian Giacomo Simonetta to Lorenzo, Milan, January 9 and 22, 1479 (MAP XXXIV 274–75 and 433).

it came too late: The draft for peace of May–June 1479 in *Lettere,* IV, pp. 355–57; already in the draft of July 1479 (ibid., pp. 359–61) the explicit clause about maintaining Cicco's "status and good condition" was suppressed.

"dictator of your letters": Ferrante of Aragon to the Dukes of Milan, Naples, August 15, 1478, in Zimolo, "Le relazioni"; see Simonetta, *Rinascimento,* p. 219.

"worm coming from the earth": Ferrante of Aragon to the Dukes of Milan, Naples, January 12, 1479 (in Magenta, *Visconti e Sforza,* II, p. 399).

"because of his unbelievable fatness": Corio, p. 1422. Zaccaria Saggi to Federico Gonzaga, Milan, September 7, 1479 (ASMa b. 1626, in *Carteggio* XI, pp. 433ff.). Most of the information in this section is from his dispatches.

vivere allegramente: Zaccaria Saggi to Federico Gonzaga, Milan, September 28, 1479.

"Madonna, in little time I will lose my head...": Corio, p. 1423; Machiavelli, *Florentine Histories,* VIII, 18 (on Tassino, see Simonetta, *Rinascimento,* pp. 161ff.).

When Lorenzo received the news about Cicco's imprisonment: Lorenzo de' Medici to Girolamo Morelli, Florence, September 11 and 18, 1479 *(Lettere,* IV, pp. 190 and 200ff.).

While the Simonetta brothers were rotting: On Giovanni Simonetta's work being read to Ludovico Sforza, see Zaccaria Saggi to Marsilio Andreasi, Milan, September 29, 1479 (ASMa b. 1626).

"We will sack all those palaces...": Gian Francesco Mauruzzi da Tolentino to Girolamo Riario, Milan, October 13, 14 and 18, 1479 (MAP LXXXIX 300, 185 and 350; *partially ciphered*).

Orlando: That is, Roland, the famous paladin of Charles Magne. See *Morgante e Lettere.*

"Willingly, O Lord, would I go along...": Baldi, III, pp. 254–56

"stratagem used by Federico against the Medici": De' Rossi, *Vita,* p. 74.

Evidence of Federico's shifting plans comes from: See his *Confession* in Lorenzi, *Studio storico,* pp. 56, 76–77.

9. TRAVELING SOUTH

"throw myself into the arms...": Lorenzo de' Medici to Girolamo Morelli, Florence, September 25, 1479 *(Lettere,* IV, p. 215); for the trip to Naples, see De Angelis, *Lorenzo a Napoli.*

Early in 1479 a spy in Urbino: Matteo Contugi to Federico Gonzaga, Urbino, February 5, 1479 (ASMa b. 846).

Giovanni di Carlo recorded it: Giovanni di Carlo, 171r for Niccolò Giugni's fictional speech mocking Lorenzo.

At the beginning of the Pazzi war: Santi, p. 517.

Federico thoughtfully added that: And other quotes from ibid., pp. 615–16.

"dear and much loved Lorenzo": Alfonso of Aragon to Lorenzo de' Medici, Pisa, December 4, 1479 (MAP XLV 224).

"following the given order": Lorenzo de' Medici to Alfonso of Aragon and to Federico da Montefeltro, Florence, December 6, 1479 *(Lettere,* IV, pp. 249–52).

"Most Illustrious Lords. Given that...": Lorenzo de' Medici to the Signoria of Florence, San Miniato, December 7, 1479 *(Lettere,* IV, pp. 265–70).

There were some historical precedents: Episodes of 1435 (capture and release of Alfonso V of Aragon) and 1465 (capture and death of Iacopo Piccinino) in Machiavelli, *Florentine Histories,* V, 5; VII, 8; VIII, 19.

The "immortal" Francesco Sforza: he died on March 8, 1466.

"old ahead of time": Piero de' Medici to Lorenzo de' Medici, Florence, March 15, 1466 (MAP XX 142; see Luigi Pulci to Lorenzo de' Medici, Florence, March 12, 1466, PML, MA 1390 Auto. Misc. Ital.)

"the greatness of his enemies . . . ": Machiavelli, *Florentine Histories,* VIII, 19.

In his later confession, the scheming Cola Montano: See Montano *Confession,* p. 62, and Valori's biography of Lorenzo for the details of the stay in Naples.

Ippolita Sforza, Princess of Calabria: See Simonetta, *Rinascimento,* pp. 211ff.; see also the document-based historical novel by Laura Malinverni, *Il ramo di biancospino.*

A prophecy of King Alfonso to King Ferrante: Letters, 5, pp. 23–30. On Giustini, Lorenzo's departure from Naples, and Michelozzi's mediation, *Lettere,* IV, pp. 321–40: Lorenzo de' Medici to Niccolò Michelozzi, Florence, March 16, 1480, thanking the Duke of Urbino on his behalf if he will not insist on including his trip to Rome among the peace conditions. See Francesco Gaddi to Lorenzo, Rome, March 18, 1480 (MAP XXXVII 26) for the pro-Medicean rejoicing.

Giovanni di Carlo gave a firsthand account: Giovanni di Carlo, 173v, on Lorenzo's return to Florence and on the peace conditions; 174v on the creation of the College of the Seventy as a "true tyranny of the powerful."

"a wife and a mother full of concern and anxiety": Elisabetta Visconti to Lorenzo de' Medici, Milan, January 19, 1480 (MAP LI 4).

"dangerous dangers": See chapter 3, above, for Federico's warnings about Lorenzo.

The Urbino poet Giovanni Santi: Santi, p. 618.

In May 1480 the spy Contugi: Matteo Contugi to Federico Gonzaga, Urbino, May 18 and 22, 1480 (ASMa b. 846). The anonymous policymaker is called "our friend."

"I have been jailed, robbed and disgraced undeservedly . . .": See *Diarium Parmense, Rerum Italicarum Scriptores,* XXII, p. 323.

So the trial began: Cicco's trial records are published in Rosmini, *Dell'istoria di Milano,* IV, 190–215 (see Simonetta, *Rinascimento,* p. 162).

10. RESTING IN PEACE

the poet Bonino Mombrizio: See Frazier, *Possible Lives.*

"I was faithful to the Prince . . .": Corio, 1429.

"forgetful both of honor and maternal duty": Ibid., p. 1430.

"Which kind of patriotism are you invoking? . . .": Giovanni di Carlo, 183v–187v, for Sixtus IV's lengthy response to the Florentine ambassadors; the official letter of absolution in Carusi, "L'istrumento," p. 290.

"Moreover, to strengthen his position . . .": Matteo Contugi to Federico Gonzaga, Urbino, November 28, 1481 (ASMa b. 846; see *Lettere,* VI, p. 74).

"You can be most certain that . . . ": Federico da Montefeltro to Lorenzo de' Medici, Fossombrone, November 29, 1481 (MAP XLV 285).

Contugi, however, would not be: Matteo Contugi to Federico Gonzaga, Urbino, December 13, 1481 (ASMa b. 846); Dante, *Inferno,* XXXI, pp. 55–57.

"This is a lie! the Duke of Urbino . . .": Sacramoro da Rimini to the Duke of Milan, Rome, March 6, 1482 (ASMi PE Roma 91).

"but even to walk in his own garden": Anello Arcamone to the King of Naples and the Duke of Milan, Rome, March 12, 1482 (ASMi PE Roma 91).

Urbino figs: Matteo Contugi to Federico Gonzaga, Urbino, between February 18–March 9, 1482 (ASMa b. 846); see *Lettere,* VI, p. 274. Contugi also on Federico's "marketing" and the details of his *condotta* (see *Lettere,* VI, p. 339).

According to the papal historian Sigismondo de' Conti: Conti, *Storie,* pp. 120–21ff. on the War of Ferrara. On Federico's plans and concerns about astrology, see many letters for the context: Guidantonio Vespucci to Lorenzo, Rome, March 9, 1482 (MAP XXXVIII 109); Pier Filippo Pandolfini to Lorenzo, Urbino, March 31, 1482 (MAP LI 103); Pier Filippo Pandolfini to Lorenzo, Urbino, April 12, 1482 (MAP LI 117, 161r).

Montefeltro was soon hired to defend the city of Ferrara: See also *Lettere,* VI, pp. 265–341; Dennistoun, I, pp. 247–56; Santi, pp. 644ff. (p. 662 on Federico's visit to Florence and meeting with Lorenzo); Baldi, III, pp. 262–66.

needful provisions: Federico da Montefeltro to Lorenzo de' Medici, Revere, May 4, 1482 (MAP XXXVIII 444; translated in Dennistoun, I, pp. 251–52). See Chambers, "Visit": perhaps we can identify the "Pietro miniador" as Guidaleri, who came from Mantua in May 1482 to bring a map of the river Oglio and of the surrounding castles, which was commissioned by Federico for his war operations in defense of Ferrara (see *Federico da Montefeltro and His Library,* cat. 2).

Federico's reply to the sermon was: Dennistoun, I, pp. 253–54, from Marin Sanudo's *Diaries.*

"These two captains died just when . . .": Landucci, p. 36; for Federico's death, Baldi, III, pp. 267–72 and 283; Santi, pp. 740–43; Conti, *Storie,* p. 145, also on Roberto Malatesta's burial.

Light of Italy: The epithet used by Baldassarre Castiglione in the opening of his *Book of the Courtier* (I, 2); *"Federico had done a good thing . . .":* De' Rossi, *Vita,* pp. 76–77.

It was dressed in an elegant robe: Baldi, III, p. 271; Dennistoun, I, p. 271.

PART III: THE SISTINE CHAPEL AND BOTTICELLI'S *SPRING*

11. OMINOUS ENDS

In fact, one year before the papal absolutions: Bredekamp, *The Medici,* esp. pp. 293–95. On p. 294: In April 1480 the Florentine authorities informed Rome that they had complied with this request: "We have had the picture of the Archbishop of Pisa eradicated and have removed every element that could in any way demean the standing of the archbishop" ("Habbiamo facto levare la pittura dell'Archivescovo di Pisa, e tolto ogni cagione che potessi in qualche modo dedecorare il grado Archiepiscopale"). The quote is from Uccelli, *Il Palazzo del Podestà,* p. 173.

Archival evidence to document the process: See my entry on "Work Begins on the Sistine Chapel (1477–1482)," with bibliography. Ettlinger, *The Sistine Chapel,* is the most extensive study of the topic to date; it gives a theological more than historical interpretation of the whole cycle. Monfasani, *A Description,* publishes and summarizes a very important document, the description of the decorated chapel by Andrea Trapeziuntius, dated May 1482. Goffen, *Friar Sixtus IV,* proposed theological reading of the cycle in "Franciscan terms," based on the newly discovered *Tituli,* the original Latin inscriptions of the frescoes. Shearman, *La storia della cappella Sistina,* provides an overview after the Vatican restorations. New evidence in Nesselrath, ed., *Gli affreschi dei Quattrocentisti nella Cappella Sistina.*

heretical archbishop of Krein, Andreas Zamometic: Ettlinger mentions the Zamometic hypothesis. But Lorenzo had not yet sent his agent Baccio Ugolini to Basel, from where he reported about the attempted anti-pope council: see letters by Baccio Ugolini to Lorenzo de' Medici, Basel, September 20 and 30, and October 25, 1482 (MAP XXXVIII 490, 493, and 519; cf. *Lettere,* VII, p. 116; a copy with autograph variants of the letter of September 30 is in BNCF, Ginori Conti, 29, 97, where there is also another letter by Baccio Ugolini to the Dieci di Balia, Basel, October 2, 1482).

lodge a request for compensation: On Botticelli's missed payments, see Covi, "Botticelli and Sixtus IV."

The Primavera, *or* Allegory *of* Spring: Secondary literature on the *Spring* is very wide-ranging. I drew from selected sources: Levi D'Ancona, *Botticelli's Primavera* (but not from her less than persuasive *Due quadri del Botticelli*); most important, La Malfa, "Firenze e l'allegoria," and Villa, "Per una lettura della *Primavera,*" both came to the convincing conclusion that Martianus Capella's tract is the main structural inspiration for the *Spring.*

well known for his sense of mischief: On Botticelli's wicked humor, see Giorgio Vasari's *Vita:* "Sandro Botticelli was a very good-humoured man and much given to playing jokes on his pupils and friends."

Count Riario, once deprived of the protection: On Gerolamo Riario's assassination, see Pellegrini, *Congiure di Romagna.*

Spy Contugi reported how: Matteo Contugi to Federico Gonzaga, Urbino, between February 18 and March 9, 1482 (ASMa b. 846), in Simonetta, *Federico da Montefeltro architetto,* pp. 97–98.

But what is he reading in the picture? On the *Double Portrait* see *Federico da Montefeltro and His Library,"* cat. 1.

"Foremost on one hand . . .": Santi, p. 420 (translated by Dennistoun, I, p. 56).

"was loved by fortune and by God . . .": Machiavelli, *Florentine Histories,* VIII, 36.

"What the prince does the many also soon do . . .": The quotation, also in Machiavelli, *Discourses,* III, 29, comes from Lorenzo de' Medici's *Rappresentazione di San Giovanni e Paolo.*

Lorenzo acknowledged his family's gratitude: Lorenzo de' Medici to Giovanni de' Medici, Florence, March 1492, in Capponi, *Storia,* pp. 528–30.

Considered in this new light, the Last Judgment: See Hall, *Michelangelo's Last Judgment.*

Other Sources

Acton, H. *The Pazzi Conspiracy: The Plot against the Medici.* London, 1979.

Ammannati Piccolomini, I. *Lettere (1444–1479).* P. Cherubini ed. 3 vols. Rome, 1997.

Barocchi, P., and Francesco Caglioti eds. *Eredità del Magnifico,* Museo Nazionale del Bargello. Florence, 1992.

Baron, H., *The Crisis of the Early Italian Renaissance. Civic Humanism and Republican Liberty in an Age of Classicism and Tyranny.* Princeton, 1966.

Belotti, B. *Il dramma di Girolamo Olgiati.* Milan, 1929.

Bonvini Mazzanti, M. *Battista Sforza Montefeltro. Una "principessa" nel Rinascimento italiano.* Urbino, 1993.

Bredekamp, H. *The Medici, Sixtus IV and Savonarola: Conflicting Strands in Botticelli's Life and Work,* in *Sandro Botticelli. The Drawings for Dante's* Divine Comedy. London, 2000. Pp. 292–97.

Breisach, E. *Caterina Sforza. A Renaissance Virago.* Chicago, 1967.

Burckhardt, J. *The Civilization of the Renaissance in Italy.* New York, 1954.

Capponi, G. *Storia della repubblica fiorentina.* 2 vols. Florence, 1875.

Carusi, E. "L'istrumento di assoluzione dei Fiorentini dalle censure di Sisto IV." *Archivio Muratoriano* 16 (1915): pp. 286–92.

Casanova, E. "L'uccisione di Galeazzo Maria Sforza e alcuni documenti fiorentini." *Archivio storico lombardo,* ser. 3, 12 (1899): pp. 299–332.

Cerioni, L. *La diplomazia sforzesca nella seconda metà del Quattrocento e i suoi cifrari segreti.* 2 vols. Rome, 1970.

———. "La politica italiana di Luigi XI e la missione di Filippo di Commines (giugno–settembre 1478)." *Archivio storico lombardo* (1950): pp. 58–143.

Chambers, D. S. *Popes, Cardinals and War: The Military Church in Renaissance and Early Modern Europe.* London–New York, 2006.

———. "The Visit to Mantua of Federico da Montefeltro in 1482." *Civiltà mantovana* XXVIII (1993): pp. 5–15.

Clark, N. *Melozzo da Forlì. Pictor Papalis.* London, 1990.

Conti, S. de'. *Le storie de' suoi tempi, dal 1475 al 1510.* Rome, 1883.

Covi, D. "Botticelli and Sixtus IV." *Burlington Magazine* 111 (October–December 1969), pp. 616–17.

D'Adda, G. *Indagini storiche, artistiche e bibliografiche sulla Libreria visconteo-sforzesca del Castello di Pavia.* Milan, 1875.

———. "La morte di Galeazzo Maria Sforza." *Archivio storico lombardo* (1875): pp. 284–94.

De Angelis, L. "Lorenzo a Napoli: progetti di pace e conflitti politici dopo la congiura dei Pazzi." *Archivio storico italiano* CL (1992): pp. 385–421.

De Benedictis, A. *Una guerra d'Italia, una resistenza di popolo. Bologna 1506.* Bologna, 2004.

De' Rossi, G. *Vita di Federico di Montefeltro.* V. Bramanti ed. Florence, 1995.

Ettlinger, L. D. *The Sistine Chapel before Michelangelo. Religious Imagery and Papal Primacy.* Oxford, 1965.

Flamini, F. "Versi in morte di Giuliano de' Medici, 1478." *Propugnatore* (1889): pp. 315–34.

Frazier, A. *Possible Lives: Authors and Saints in Renaissance Italy.* New York, 2005.

Fubini, R. *Federico da Montefeltro e la congiura dei Pazzi: politica e propaganda alla luce di nuovi documenti.* In *Federico di Montefeltro.* Vol. I. Pp. 355–470.

———. *Italia quattrocentesca: politica e diplomazia nell'età di Lorenzo il Magnifico.* Milan, 1994.

———. "*Osservazioni e documenti sulla crisi del ducato di Milano nel 1477, e sulla riforma del Consiglio Segreto ducale di Bona Sforza.*" In *Essays Presented to Myron P. Gilmore.* Vol. I. Florence, 1977. Pp. 47–103.

———. *Quattrocento fiorentino: politica, diplomazia, cultura.* Pisa, 1996.

Gallo, A. *Commentarii de rebus Genuensium et de navigatione Columbi.* In *Rerum Italicarum Scriptores²,* XXIII, 1. E. Pandiani ed. Città di Castello, 1910–11.

Goffen, R. "Friar Sixtus IV and The Sistine Chapel." *Renaissance Quarterly* 39 (1986): pp. 218–62.

Hale, J. R. *England and the Italian Renaissance. The Growth of Interest in Its History and Art.* Intro. N. Penny. London, 1996.

Hall, M. B. (ed.). *Michelangelo's* Last Judgment. Cambridge (UK), 2005.

Ilardi, V. "The Assassination of Galeazzo Maria Sforza and the Reaction of Italian Diplomacy." In *Studies in Italian Renaissance Diplomatic History.* London, 1986.

———. "The First Permanent Embassy Outside Italy: The Milanese Embassy at the French Court, 1464–1483." In *Politics, Religion and Diplomacy in Early Modern Europe. Essays in Honor of De Lamar Jensen.* Kirksville, MO, 1994. Pp. 1–18.

———. "The Italian League, Francesco Sforza, and Charles VII (1454–1461)." In *Studies in the Renaissance.* Vol. 6 (1959): pp. 129–66.

La Malfa, C. "Firenze e l'allegoria dell'eloquenza: una nuova interpretazione della *Primavera* di Botticelli." *Storia dell'arte* 97 (September–December) 1999: pp. 249–93.

Levi D'Ancona, M. *Botticelli's Primavera: A botanical interpretation including astrology, alchemy and the Medici.* Florence, 1983.

———. *Due quadri del Botticelli eseguiti per nascite in Casa Medici: nuova intepretazione della Primavera e della Nascita di Venere.* Florence, 1992.

Lombardi, G. "Sisto IV." In *Enciclopedia dei Papi* II. Rome, 2000. Pp. 701–17.

Lorenzi, G. *Cola Montano. Studio storico.* Milan, 1875.

Lubkin, G. *A Renaissance Court. Milan under Galeazzo Maria Sforza.* Berkeley, 1994.

Magenta, C. *I Visconti e gli Sforza nel Castello di Pavia e le loro attinenze con la Certosa e la storia cittadina.* 2 vols. Milan, 1883.

Malinverni, L. *Il ramo di biancospino. Storie di donne del Quattrocento.* Rome, 2006.

———. *Una storia del Quattrocento. Misteri, ambizioni e conflitti nel Ducato di Milano. L'amore tra Lucia Marliani e Galeazzo Maria Sforza.* Florence, 2000.

Martines, L. *April Blood. Florence and the Plot against the Medici.* Oxford, 2003.

Miglio, M., et al., eds. *Un pontificato ed una città: Sisto IV (1471–1484).* Rome, 1986.

Monfasani, J. "A description of the Sistine Chapel under Pope Sixtus IV." *Artibus and Historiae* VII (1983): pp. 9–16.

Nesselrath, A., ed. *Gli affreschi dei Quattrocentisti nella Cappella Sistina. Restauri Recenti dei Musei Vaticani.* Vatican City, 2004.

Parks, T. *Medici Money: Banking, Metaphysics, and Art in Fifteenth-Century Florence*. New York–London, 2005.

Pecchiai, P. "Il cuoco di Cicco Simonetta." *Archivio storico lombardo* (1923): pp. 502–13.

Pellegrini, M. *Congiure di Romagna. Lorenzo de' Medici e il duplice tirannicidio a Forlì e a Faenza nel 1488*. Florence, 1999.

Pelling, N. *The Curse of the Voynich. The Secret History of the World's Most Mysterious Manuscript*. Surbiton, 2006.

Piazzoni, A. M., ed. *La Bibbia di Federico da Montefeltro. Commentario al codice*. 2 vols. Modena, 2005.

Poliziano, A. *The stanze of Angelo Poliziano*. Trans. D. Quint. Amherst, 1979.

Raggio, O. *The Gubbio Studiolo and Its Conservation*. Metropolitan Museum of Art, New York, 1999.

Roeck B. *Mörder, Maler und Mäzene: Piero della Francescas "Geisselung": eine kunsthistorische Kriminalgeschichte*. Munich, 2006.

Roeck, B. and A. Tönnesmann. *Nase Italiens: Federico da Montefeltro, Herzog von Urbino*. Berlin, 2005.

Roscoe, W. *Life of Lorenzo de' Medici, called the Magnificent*. Philadelphia, 1803.

Rosmini, C. *Dell'istoria di Milano*. 4 vols. Milan, 1820.

———. *Dell'istoria intorno alle militari imprese e alla vita di Gian-Jacopo Trivulzio detto il Magno*. 2 vols. Milan, 1815.

Rubinstein, N. *The Government of Florence Under the Medici (1434–1494)*. Oxford, 1997.

———. "Lorenzo de' Medici. The Formation of his Statecraft." *Proceedings of the British Academy* 63 (1977): pp. 71–94.

Scatena, G. *Oddantonio da Montefeltro I Duca di Urbino*. Rome, 1989.

Scrivano R. Le biografie di Federico, in *Federico di Montefeltro*. Vol. III. Pp. 373–92.

Shearman, J. La storia della cappella Sistina, in *Michelangelo e la Sistina*. Rome, 1990. Pp. 19–28.

Simonetta, M. *Federico da Montefeltro architetto della Congiura dei Pazzi e del Palazzo di Urbino, Atti del Convegno Internazionale di Studi "Francesco di Giorgio alla Corte di Federico da Montefeltro."* Florence, 2004. Pp. 81–101.

———. "Federico da Montefeltro contro Firenze. Retroscena inediti della congiura dei Pazzi." *Archivio storico italiano* CLXI (2003): pp. 261–84.

———. "Giustini, Lorenzo." In *Dizionario biografico degli Italiani*. Vol. 57. Rome, 2001. Pp. 203–8.

———. *Rinascimento segreto: il mondo del Segretario da Petrarca a Machiavelli*. Milan, 2004.

———. "Work Begins on the Sistine Chapel (1477–1482)." In *Great Events from History, 1454–1600*. Pasadena, 2005. Pp. 104–6.

———, ed. *Carteggio degli oratori mantovani alla corte sforzesca (1450–1500)*. Vol. XI (1478–1479). Rome, 2001.

———, ed. *Federico da Montefeltro and His Library*. Pref. J. J. G. Alexander. Morgan Library and Museum, New York (exhibition catalogue), June 8–September 30, 2007. Milan, 2007.

Soranzo, G., in *Rerum gestarum Francisci Sfortiae Mediolanensis Ducis Commentarii, Rerum Italicarum Scriptores* 2 XXI, 2. G. Simonetta ed. Bologna, 1932–59.

Strehlke, C. B. " 'Li magistri con li discepoli': Thinking about art in Lombardy." In *Quattro pezzi lombardi (per Maria Teresa Biraghi)*. Brescia, 1998.

Tommasoli, W. *La vita di Federico da Montefeltro (1422–82).* Urbino, 1978.

Uccelli, G. B. *Il Palazzo del Podestà.* Florence, 1865.

Vaglienti, F. M. "Anatomia di una congiura. Sulle tracce dell'assassinio del duca Galeazzo Maria Sforza tra storia e scienza." In *Rendiconti dell'Istituto Lombardo Accademia di scienze e lettere* CXXXVI/2 (2002).

Valentini, R. "Uno scritto ignorato del duca Federico." *Urbinum* (1914): pp. 11–14.

Villa, C. "Per una lettura della *Primavera.* Mercurio *retrogrado* e la Retorica nella bottega di Botticelli." *Strumenti critici* 86, XIII (1998): pp. 1–28.

Viti, P. "Lettere familiari di Federico da Montefeltro ai Medici." In *Federico di Montefeltro.* Vol. I. Pp. 471–86.

Welch, E. S. *Art and Authority in Renaissance Milan.* London–New Haven, 1995.

———. "Sight, Sound and Ceremony in the Chapel of Galeazzo Maria Sforza." *Early Music History* 12 (1993): pp. 151–90.

Wright, A. "A Portrait of the Visit of Galeazzo Maria Sforza to Florence in 1471." In *Lorenzo the Magnificent, Culture and Politics.* M. Mallett and N. Mann eds. London, 1996. Pp. 65–90.

———. *The Pollaiuolo Brothers: The Arts of Florence and Rome.* New Haven, 2004.

Zimolo, G. C. "Le relazioni fra Milano e Napoli e la politica italiana in due lettere del 1478." *Archivo storico lombardo* (1937): pp. 403–34.

Illustration Credits

Cover image: Detail from *Portrait of Federico da Montefeltro* by Piero della Francesca, Uffizi Museum, Florence: Scala / Art Resource, NY

p. ii: Map of Florence in Poggio Bracciolini, *Florentine History*, from the Montefeltro Library: Copyright Biblioteca Apostolica Vaticana, Vatican City

p. viii: Map of Italy in Francesco Berlinghieri's *Geography*, 1482, from the Montefeltro Library: Copyright Biblioteca Apostolica Vaticana, Vatican City

p. 6: Opening page of Dante's *Inferno*, ca. 1478, from the Montefeltro Library: Copyright Biblioteca Apostolica Vaticana, Vatican City

p. 14: Piero Pollaiuolo, *Portrait of Galeazzo Maria Sforza:* Uffizi Museum, Florence, Scala / Art Resource, NY

p. 25: Portrait of Cicco Simonetta holding chancellery papers, ca. 1475: Copyright Bibliothèque Nationale de France, Paris

p. 31: *Lorenzo de' Medici,* Florentine 15th or 16th century, probably after a model by A. Verrocchio and O. Benintendi: Samuel H. Kress Collection, Image © 2007 Board of Trustees, National Gallery of Art, Washington

p. 43: *Studiolo from the Ducal Palace in Gubbio:* Courtesy The Metropolitan Museum of Art, Rogers Fund, 1939 (59.153). Image © The Metropolitan Museum of Art

p. 44: Portraits of Ferrante of Aragon and of Federico da Montefeltro, from the Montefeltro Library: Copyright Biblioteca Apostolica Vaticana, Vatican City

p. 49: A Hebrew manuscript, from the Montefeltro Library: Copyright Biblioteca Apostolica Vaticana, Vatican City

p. 50: Federico da Montefeltro holding a copy of Cristorofo Landino's *Disputationes Camaldulenses*, from the Montefeltro Library: Copyright Biblioteca Apostolica Vaticana, Vatican City

p. 52: Ermine and Ostrich, from the Montefeltro Library: Copyright Biblioteca Apostolica Vaticana, Vatican City

p. 60: *Pope Sixtus IV appointing Bartolomeo Sacchi, called Platina, the Prefect of the Vatican Library* by Melozzo da Forlì: Vatican Museums, Vatican City, Scala / Art Resource, NY

p. 65: The Order of the Garter, from the Montefeltro Library: Copyright Biblioteca Apostolica Vaticana, Vatican City

pp. 82–83: Details from the Urbino *studiolo:* Courtesy Galleria Nazionale delle Marche, Urbino

p. 87: Portrait of Pope Sixtus IV: Copyright Biblioteca Apostolica Vaticana, Vatican City

pp. 89–91: Coded letter and details: Courtesy Ubaldini Archive, Urbino; Montefeltro Codebook, from the Montefeltro Library: Copyright Biblioteca Apostolica Vaticana, Vatican City

p. 95: Bartolomeo della Gatta, *Portrait of Guidobaldo da Montefeltro:* Copyright Galleria Colonna, Rome

p. 99: Equestrian portrait of Federico da Montefeltro in Poggio Bracciolini, *Florentine History*, from the Montefeltro Library: Copyright Biblioteca Apostolica Vaticana, Vatican City

p. 107: Map of Florence in Poggio Bracciolini, *Florentine History*, from the Montefeltro Library: Copyright Biblioteca Apostolica Vaticana, Vatican City

p. 118: *Giuliano de' Medici* by Andrea Verrocchio: Andrew W. Mellon Collection, Image © 2007 Board of Trustees, National Gallery of Art, Washington

p. 120: *Giuliano de' Medici* by Sandro Botticelli: Samuel H. Kress Collection, Image © 2007 Board Trustees, National Gallery of Art, Washington

p. 121: The Pazzi Medal: Courtesy The Kagan Collection, New York

p. 138: Opening page of the Montefeltro Bible, from the Montefeltro Library: Copyright Biblioteca Apostolica Vaticana, Vatican City

p. 143: War machine, in Roberto Valturio's volume, *De Re Militari*, from the Montefeltro Library: Copyright Biblioteca Apostolica Vaticana, Vatican City

p. 158: *Strozzi panel:* St. Martino Museum, Naples, Scala / Art Resource, NY

p. 161: *Sketch of hanged man* by Leonardo da Vinci, Musée Bonnat, Bayonne, Scala / Art Resource, NY

p. 164: *Bust of Ferdinand II of Aragon* by Guido Mazzoni: Capodimonte Museum, Naples, Scala / Art Resource, NY

p. 166: *Bust of a Lady* by Francesco Laurana: Copyright The Frick Collection, New York

p. 192–194, 200: *Punishment of Korah, Dathan, and Abiron* by Sandro Botticelli: Sistine Chapel, Vatican City, Scala / Art Resource, NY

p. 194: Detail of *Pope Sixtus IV appointing Bartolomeo Sacchi, called Platina, the Prefect of the Vatican Library* by Melozzo da Forli: Scala / Art Resource, NY

p. 196: *Delivering the Keys of the Kingdom to Saint Peter, 1481–1483* by Pietro Perugino: Sistine Chapel, Vatican City, Scala / Art Resource, NY

p. 198: *Primavera (Spring)*, post-restoration, by Sandro Botticelli: Uffizi Museum, Florence, Scala / Art Resource, NY

p. 200: *Punishment of Korah* (detail); *La Primavera* (detail) by Sandro Botticelli: Scala / Art Resources, NY

p. 203: Copy drawn from Pietro Perugino's Sistine altarpiece, *Assumption of the Virgin*: Copyright Albertina Museum, Vienna

p. 206: Justus of Ghent, or Pedro Berruguete, *Double Portrait of Federico da Montefeltro and his son Guidobaldo*, ca. 1475: Courtesy Galleria Nazionale delle Marche, Urbino

p. 208: *Portrait of Gregory the Great in the Urbino studiolo* by Justus of Ghent, or Pedro Berruguete: Courtesy Galleria Nazionale delle Marche, Urbino

p. 210: *Study for the Last Judgment* by Michelangelo Buonarroti: Casa Buonarroti, Florence, Scala / Art Resource, NY

Index

Note: Page numbers in *italics* refer to illustrations and captions. Because people of the Renaissance era often had no true surname, many people referred to in this book are indexed under their first name, following the conventions of the Library of Congress.

About the Author

Marcello Simonetta was born in 1968 in Pavia, near Milan, and raised in Rome. He studied literature and history of ideas at the University of Rome La Sapienza, from which he received a B.A. in 1993. In the mid-nineties he worked as a documentary filmmaker. He then accepted a fellowship at Yale University, where he spent six years. He initially worked on twentieth-century Italian literature, but after discovering Yale's rich collections of Renaissance archives, began to focus on the intricate connections between politics and humanism in late fifteenth-century Italy. In 2001 he was awarded a PhD in Italian literature and history and went on teaching this subject as an assistant professor at Wesleyan University. In 2004 he published *Rinascimento Segreto: Il mondo del Segretario da Petrarca a Machiavelli,* a revised version of his dissertation.

The story of Simonetta's code-cracking discovery about the Pazzi conspiracy attracted the attention of the international media and was featured in a documentary first aired by the History Channel in 2005.

In 2007, he curated an exhibition on Federico da Montefeltro and His Library at the New Morgan Library and Museum, in New York City.